INTERNSHIPS:
PERSPECTIVES ON
EXPERIENTIAL LEARNING

INTERNSHIPS

PERSPECTIVES on EXPERIENTIAL LEARNING

A Guide to Internship Management for
Educators and Professionals

Edited by Andrew Ciofalo
Associate Professor of Writing and Media
Coordinator of the Media Program
Loyola College in Maryland

KRIEGER PUBLISHING COMPANY
MALABAR, FLORIDA
1992

Original Edition 1992

Printed and Published by
KRIEGER PUBLISHING COMPANY
KRIEGER DRIVE
MALABAR, FLORIDA 32950

FROM A DECLARATION OF PRINCIPLES JOINTLY ADOPTED BY
A COMMITTEE OF THE AMERICAN BAR ASSOCIATION AND A
COMMITTEE OF PUBLISHERS:

This publication is designed to provide accurate and authoritative information in
regard to the subject matter covered. It is sold with the understanding that the
publisher is not engaged in rendering legal, accounting, or other professional service. If legal advice or other expert assistance is required, the services of a competent
professional person should be sought.

Library of Congress Cataloging-in-Publication Data
Internships : perspectives on experiential learning : a guide to
  internship management for educators and professionals / Andrew
  Ciofalo, editor. — Original ed.
      p.   cm.
  Includes bibliographical references.
  ISBN 0-89464-581-1 (alk. paper)
  1. Mass media—Study and teaching (Internship) 2. Business
education (Internship) 3. Experiential learning. I. Ciofalo,
Andrew, 1935–
P91.3.I57   1992
302.23'071'1—dc20   91-26331
                                                                              CIP

10 9 8 7 6 5 4 3 2

DEDICATION

To Judy, my favorite experiential teacher.

CONTENTS

IV. RUNNING INTERNSHIP PROGRAMS

V. INTERNSHIP CASES

ACKNOWLEDGMENTS

"Perspectives on Learning in Internships," *The Journal of Experiential Learning*, Fall 1983. Reprinted with permission of David Thornton Moore.

"Integrating the Traditions of Experiential Learning in Internship Education," *The Journal of Experiential Learning*, Fall 1983. Reprinted with permission.

"The Vague Aches of Interns," *College English*, November 1983. Copyright 1983 by the National Council of Teachers of English. Reprinted with permission.

"Effects of College Internships on Individual Participants," *Journal of Applied Psychology*, August 1988. Copyright 1988 by the American Psychological Association. Reprinted by permission of the APA and M. Susan Taylor.

"Update: Broadcast Intern Programs and Practices," *Journalism Educator*, Summer 1988. Reprinted with permission of Milan D. Meeske.

"Internship Practices in Public Relations," *Public Relations Review*, Summer 1980. Reprinted with permission.

"Practica and Internships for Technical Writing Students," *Technical Writing Teacher* (1983, volume 10, number 2,3:89–60). Reprinted with permission.

"Accounting Internships and Subsequent Academic Performance: An Empirical Study," *The Accounting Review* (vol. LXII, No. 4, October 1987). Reprinted with permission.

"Six Internship Models," *Journalism Educator*, Spring 1983. Reprinted with permission of Bruce Garrison.

"Suggestions for Implementing or Improving an Internship Program," *Communication Education* (vol. 33, January 1984, pp. 53–61). Reprinted with permission of the Speech Communication Association (SCA) and Jarice Hanson.

"A Perspective on Internship Grading Problems and a Solution," *Journalism Educator*, Spring 1988. Reprinted with permission of author.

"Internship Programs—Bridging the Gap." Reprinted from *Management World*, September 1980, with permission from AMS, Trevose, PA 19047. Copyright 1980 AMS.

"Post-Internship Seminar Can Solve Academic Credit, Grading Problems," *Journalism Educator*, April 1981. Reprinted with permission of Bruce Garrison.

I. INTRODUCTION

1
WHAT EVERY PROFESSOR AND WORK-SITE SUPERVISOR SHOULD KNOW ABOUT INTERNSHIPS

Andrew Ciofalo

AN INTRODUCTION

Internships and experiential learning are held in low regard by college faculties. Likewise, professionals consider much of the theory taught in the pre-professional disciplines to be irrelevant. However, if learning is viewed as an inductive process, then an easy transition can be seen from internship to theory, from the specific to the general, from the concrete to the abstract. Experiential and classroom learning are part of a single continuum, and various forms of experiential learning have existed in the classroom for years. Faculty and professionals should put aside their differences as a matter of degree and not substance. They should develop a unified epistemology relating practice to theory, positioning themselves at opposite poles on the same knowledge axis.

Internships are an addictive mode of experiential learning that academic purists would rather do without but cannot resist. Faculties in mass communications have been tending toward the generic communications curriculum that would eliminate professional skills courses and those internships that spring from them. However, the more the curriculum is generalized the greater the need for internships and other forms of experiential learning to demonstrate technical proficiency of graduates. Thus it would seem that whether an academic program is pre-professional or theory based, it cannot shake loose of the internship impulse. The educational-industrial complex seems to demand that form of experiential learning almost as a pre-condition for employment and as a cost-effective personnel and training policy. Both businesses and media enterprises hire a high percentage of students out of their intern cadre. The remaining interns are always at the top of the employable list. Everyone else goes on to graduate school, which isn't all that bad.

When the various Humanities departments begin to include in their recruitment packages lists of the kinds of jobs that, for example, classics or English majors typically get, then the extent to which higher education has been corrupted and co-opted is evident. Yet, who are we to challenge the shift in societal values and the historical context of change that have continually repositioned the role of the university, and education in general, since the Middle Ages? Is the pursuit of knowledge for the sake of knowledge an elitist carryover? Is careerism a debasing democratization (the grimy residue of the Industrial Revolution and the resultant technocracy)? And what do these questions have to do with internships anyway?

Everything.

If the main business of the university were to prepare students for jobs, then a symbiotic relationship between academe and industry would make economic sense. The fact is that despite the pre-professional programs there remains an intellectual distance between the teachers and the doers. The university creates the "software" that extracts the theory from the "database" of practice; and universities give credits for critical/analytical activities (thinking) and not for the entry of raw data (application). However, professors mistakenly think that theory is the precursor of practice, when in reality it is derivative. Not only does this notion lurk subliminally behind the generic curriculum—one devoid of any hint of professionalism—but it also caters to the bias against experiential learning. The result is that credits are given reluctantly for internships, and students doing internships are often saddled with irrelevant academic trappings in order to get credit.

Faculty need to be disabused of the belief that internships are merely opportunities for the practical application of knowledge gained in the classroom. And the professionals need to acknowledge that theory holds up a mirror to practice (with all its formulas, instincts, skills and creativity). Depoliticizing the gap between the theoreticians and the professionals (even intramurally) clears the way for fresh insights into the value of experiential education as a conveyor of primary knowledge. In fact, a strong argument could be made that internships should precede theory courses, a configuration more consonant with the inductive approach to learning typical of scientific inquiry and literary criticism.

The following educational schema probably would be more compatible with an inductively-based strategy: practical course, internship, theory course (in that order). And in some instances the internship could come first. It may ruffle a few egos, but non-communications majors have been known to master the press release or the news story form in the first few weeks of an internship without the benefit of a theory or practical course. Similarly, an accounting intern could assimilate a few basic activities that would make him functional in low level accounting practices. Becoming a professional journalist or accountant requires intellectual advancement beyond the formula to a full grasp of the theoretical underpinnings.

Such a radical epistemology is not likely to dislodge preconceived notions despite the fact that it makes perfectly good cognitive sense. It is tantamount to a call for curricular reform and rejection of the voguish generic curriculum to expect a shifting of priorities that would install experiential learning into an appropriate educational niche.

The fact is that experiential learning is not new to business or mass communications education. Masscom uses it in media labs, simulated reporting assignments, dummy advertising campaigns and public relations campaigns and various classroom activities, such as creating a magazine as is done every semester in the graduate program at The Medill School of Journalism at Northwestern University. Business students often take on real-life projects as an outreach of classroom education and utilize case studies, gaming and simulations in association with theory courses. While faculty are reluctant to admit that experiential learning has any primary value outside the classroom, professionals are equally reluctant to assign relevancy to the theory preached in the schools.

A graphic depiction of the relationship between practical courses, theory courses and internships might look something like this:

	Experiential(%)	Theoretical(%)
INTERNSHIP COURSE	70	30
PRACTICAL COURSE	50	50
THEORY COURSE	20	80

Of course, this is a hypothetical breakdown, but it illustrates the intermingling of the various modes of learning regardless of the type of course. Faculty may wish to assess their courses individually to determine the exact percentages for each course. And professionals should do likewise in order to define just how much theory is being imparted in an experiential learning situation. Both might be surprised at the results.

This analysis hints that the dichotomy between experiential learning and classroom learning is an illusion. Questions about the value of experiential learning assume the subordination of that form to classroom learning, and hence the subordination of practice to theory. The resultant answers then dwell on the differences between the forms. By changing our assumptions, we can frame questions that would elicit answers stressing the *similarities* between experiential and classroom learning.

Hopefully, that process can begin with this collection of articles by faculty and professionals in both the business and masscom disciplines. The teachers and the doers need to probe intellectually the substance and methodology behind their respective learning situations and together build a new pedagogy and epistemology that would unite all forms of learning.

The division between the two camps is clearly evident in this collection of articles from scholarly and professional or trade journals. Note that the authors referenced by David Thornton Moore and Jon Wagner are never referred to by the academics writing in either the masscom or business scholarly journals. That is because those two come out of a different academic tradition and orientation. Scholars in education, psychology and social science have written extensively on theories of learning (including experiential), but few of their ideas have crossed over to influence the faculties involved in the pre-professional disciplines.

This collection is by no means complete, nor was it intended to be. It is meant to be a brief journey through some of the key ideas and conceptions that are representative of those extant in the field. More importantly, it will serve the purpose of acquainting disparate disciplines, as well as practitioners and professors, with varying viewpoints so that they can begin to reprocess the given knowledge and pedagogy. A synthesis of these ideas could mean a consistent approach to the incorporation of experiential learning in all disciplines and a supporting cognitive theory. A good start would be for those interested in this quest to begin following the paper trail through the footnotes of the various academic articles. The field begs for a complete bibliography, and the masscom and business disciplines need to replicate the research done in the social sciences as well as develop their own primary research. We should find out why the social sciences (including education) are so comfortable with requiring and giving credits for internships, while masscom has been agonizing inconclusively since 1971 over how to incorporate internships into the masscom educational scheme.

The foregoing concerns are addressed primarily in the first chapter, a collection of five articles under the heading, "Learning from Experience." From this lofty cerebral starting point the collection bores into more concrete and specific discussions of internships and ends with some interesting and suggestive cases in the final section of case examples from the college point of view and from industry's.

Unlike most guides, this brief book does not provide an easy how-to approach to setting up internships. Instead it gives a non-monolithic overview of varying philosophies and techniques and a major suggestion that internship programs and internships work better when the perspectives of educators and professionals on experiential learning converge. The field would benefit from a consistent philosophy of experiential learning, endorsed by the appropriate academic and professional associations and codified by some form of accreditation. Educators and professionals can best accomplish this end through serious application of a synthesis of the ideas herein presented. Such an inductively fueled grass roots process has the best chance of percolating to the top in the form of a unifying theory.

II. LEARNING FROM EXPERIENCE

2
PERSPECTIVES ON LEARNING
IN INTERNSHIPS

David Thornton Moore

Internships are often viewed as secondary learning experiences in which academic theory is tested in the field. However, there are definite parallels between the learning that occurs in the classroom and in the internship, both in the mental processing required to assimilate new information and in the hierarchical structures of the delivery system. However, whereas most academic knowledge is presented by the teacher as fixed and immutable, experiential knowledge is often derived through the analytical and synthesizing efforts of the learner.

Talking about learning in internships is harder than many people think. In years of research and reading about students who work in a real-world setting for educational credit, I have heard participants—both students and teachers—make claims like these: "I have learned a lot about people"; "I learned how to be more confident"; and, "I learned all about city government." Pressed to elaborate on these statements, many of my respondents began to stutter: "Well, you know, like how to get along with different people, you know?" These disappointingly vague answers do not necessarily indicate that, in fact, the students learned nothing of substance in their field experiences (although, regretfully, that may be the case). Rather, this inarticulateness points, I suggest, to the lack of a clear and productive vocabulary for describing what one has learned by working.

Many practitioners and writers in the field of experiential education implicitly assume or explicitly claim that activity in non-classroom settings leads to two basic forms of learning: personal growth, or development in such "affective" areas as self-concept, attitudes about school and work, social interaction skills, and practice or retention of academic and practical skills. For the purposes of this paper, I will set aside the question of personal or effective growth in classroom and internship environments. Instead, let us focus here on the intellectual, cognitive, mental domain of learning.

Some of the classic theoretical treatments of experiential learning contribute to the common assumption that "academic" learning happens in classrooms and is at best "tested" or refined through engagement with non-school, experiential activities (Coleman, 1977; Kolb, 1976). This apparent belief that classroom learning and field learning are clearly dichotomous, that they may be complementary but exceedingly different experiences, worries me. Obviously, in some respects they are very different at times: in purpose, in social organization, in skills required, in outcomes. But several years of firsthand research in internship sites (Moore, 1981, 1982) convinces me that the lines between the two formats are not so clear cut as some people suggest. In fact, the two often overlap.

There are two important dimensions of comparison in the relationship between academic learning and field learning. The first concerns the kinds of mental work one is expected to perform in either setting. The second involves the forms of social relations in which one engages while participating in a particular learning environment.

"MENTAL WORK" IN INTERNSHIPS

To some extent, the first dimension is about "subject matter," or the substantive knowledge the intern encounters and uses in the process of working in class or placement. That substance may be about local government, or business principles, or computational skills, or the structure of a complex organization. Any of those "subjects" may be handled either in a classroom or in a workplace. What concerns me more than substance, however, is process: What is the student expected or able to do with it? How does the student engage and use the facts, skills, principles, values, procedures or worldviews that make up the social stock of knowledge in the environment? There are several ways of talking about the mental work that a person does in a classroom or placement setting. Bloom (1956) proposes a taxonomy of educational objectives for school in which he outlines six progressively complex forms of intellectual performance:

- Knowledge (remembering, by recognition or recall, of ideas, material or phenomena)
- Comprehension (understanding the literal message in a communication)
- Application (correct and appropriate use of knowledge)
- Analysis (breaking knowledge down into component parts and detecting relations among them)
- Synthesis (putting together elements to form a whole)
- Evaluation (making judgments about the value, for some purpose, of ideas, solutions, materials, etc.)

This framework for categorizing levels of knowledge-use has been used extensively in the development and study of school curricula. In similar ways, it could be used to understand the forms of thinking performed by interns in work or other non-classroom environments. I have no particular stake in the Bloom taxonomy; there are other schemes that help one to analyze mental operations (cf. Piaget in Wadsworth, 1971; Bruner, 1973; Luria, 1976). The point here is not so much to propose a specific theory as to raise the questions: Is the knowledge presented to the learner as fixed, masterable, indisputable? What operations is the learner expected, enabled, forbidden to do with the knowledge? Can the student-intern add to the knowledge, reorganize it, transform it, even reject it?

Typically, knowledge in schools is defined in advance, presented as certain, displayed intact on cue (cf. Mehan, 1979). Especially at the lower grades, but even into college, students ingest facts and ideas, store them whole, and present them back to the teacher. The knowledge acquired in this way may get more and more complex, but it remains fixed and external to the student. In some instances, of course, a student may be encouraged to invent knowledge, or at least to transform it.

Knowledge-use in internship settings appears to vary somewhat more than that in classroom, according to our observations in thirty-five different workplaces where students participated in an experiential learning program. In many sites, interns are presented "facts" as immutable, unchallengeable, once-and-for all.

Item: A student placed in a curriculum development firm was asked to calculate the "readability levels" of some new texts. She was shown the formula for determining the grade-level of a passage, and then set about figuring it for a set of entries. Her supervisor presented the formula as fixed, necessary (if slightly silly); the student was **not** permitted to invent a different method.

In other situations, students undertook complex tasks which demanded considerable flexibility and creativity of intellect.

Item: An intern in a city council-member's office decided, after running into problems locating information, to reorganize the legislative files. He set up a system for receiving, categorizing, storing and retrieving information about the substance and progress of various bills passing through the Council. To complete the job, he had to understand not only filing techniques, but also the important dimensions of legislation, the kinds of things people would need to know about bills.

In our extensive observations of student-interns, we also discovered that the "reflection" component of thought, so often claimed by experiential educators to be missing from the "real world," in fact appears more frequently than we expected. While it is true that people working in a business or other organization do not often stop to discuss the abstract, generalized implications of their work, or to apply explicit theories to their practices, we nonetheless found a number of instances in which workers did formulate general principles, did articulate working theories, did consider alternative approaches to complex problems. Theorists such as Coleman and Kolb both seem to have a picture in mind of an intern diving into a practical arena with no preconceptions about the field, with no hypotheses about the way things will work; they suggest that the new worker uses a "trial and error" strategy. To some small extent, that may be true. But to a larger extent, we find that the student-worker approaches each new problem with some working framework, some set of hunches or principles or guidelines that shape her strategy. Those approaches may emerge from the student's own thought processes and experiences, or may be presented in advance of the work by other members of the organization. The fact is that most productive organizations cannot afford too many mistakes, and so will structure the task environment for the intern clearly enough to avoid costly errors. That means that the student, in first encountering the task problem (in the phase we called "establishing"), has to get some more or less general information about the nature of the job, the kinds of skills and knowledge one needs to perform it, and the criteria by which performance will be judged. In many cases, that "establishing" included rather extensive discussion of the theoretical or conceptual underpinnings of the work.

> *Item*: In a hospital speech clinic, before the student ever had a chance to work directly with children, she first heard about the kinds of speech defects the clinic handled, about their possible causes and treatments, about diagnosis, about the kinds of materials used in different cases; then she observed systematically as the professional speech therapists worked with several kids, and discussed the cases and the treatments afterward.

Even when the "establishing" phase of the work did not explicitly cover theories or general strategies, the "processing" phase often did. By processing, we meant those activities through which the student received monitoring and feedback on her performance on a task, and opportunities for reconstructing the problem and designing a new approach. Feedback of one form or another was very common in the worksites. The "reflection" type of processing was seen less frequently, but definitely occurred.

Item: A student-intern working as a reporter for a small community newspaper received a general assignment from his editor, to do a piece on graffiti artists in the neighborhood. She gave him broad instructions about how to locate his subjects and how to interview them; but she left the construction of a first draft up to him. When he presented his rough copy to her, the editor sat down with him and reviewed it carefully, asking questions about specific points but also making more general comments about the way one puts together a feature article.

The common wisdom about knowledge-use in internships, as I argued above, is that practical experience may be good for practice of academic learning, may be effective in the process of knowledge retention, but that it is not good for academic, intellectual, complex learning, for the acquisition and manipulation of difficult and respectable theories and concepts. Hundreds of hours of observation in thirty-five internship sites convinces us that the common wisdom cannot be held universally true. We watched students acquire and use some very complicated and scholarly knowledge: about the institutional relations among segments of the municipal bureaucracy; about the etiology and treatment of speech disorders; about the principles of consumer protection law. But more than that, we saw students perform very advanced forms of mental work, kinds of thinking we rarely witness in school classes: the interpretation of a tangled situation involving tenants and landlords, and the construction (synthesis) of a strategy for seeking relief for the tenants; the evaluation of manuscripts submitted to a writer's agent; the ad hoc production of systematic and coherent answers to children's questions in a history museum. To be sure, we also observed people doing some terribly mundane thinking: answering phones and taking messages; performing a specific procedure for separating blood in a hospital lab; even walking dogs. The point is not that internships always encourage higher forms of learning—just that they can, given the right circumstances.

Experiential educators should not succumb to the academic myth that systematic, rigorous, complex mental work occurs only in classrooms; or that practical experience is good only for practice and retention. Rather, they should pay close attention to the kinds of mental operations interns will be encouraged and expected to perform in the course of doing their work. Thinking in the real world may indeed supplement and reinforce school-based learning; but it can also do far more to develop valid and important learning in its own right.

SOCIAL RELATIONSHIPS IN INTERNSHIPS

The second dimension of comparison between academic and experiential settings centers on the kinds of social relations in which one engages while participating in a particular environment. For educational purposes, those relations have two kinds of significance. First, the forms of personal growth a person undergoes in the course of a given experience is integrally connected to the ways she engages in interactions with others. Through our observations, we came to realize that claims about "building self-esteem" and "developing a sense of responsibility" in experiential learning programs make sense only if the real-world interactions move the person in those directions. We saw students engaged in work that could hardly build self-esteem, for example: walking dogs or cleaning cages in an animal shelter; typing reams of envelopes to mail out brochures in a museum; filing. In other situations, however, we saw students interact with supervisors and co-workers in highly responsible, rewarding ways: taking charge of a tour of elementary school students in a history museum; helping a senior citizen ward off eviction by a greedy landlord; teaching a child with a stammer how to enunciate certain new sounds. In each of these cases, the critical fact was that the intern was performing a task that demanded responsible behavior, other people counted on the student to come through as expected; and they often let her know that the job had been important to them. In classrooms, students rarely have the opportunity to be truly responsible—not just punctual or obedient, but to have others actually count on them for something meaningful.

The second significance of social relations in learning environments concerns the extent to which people can participate in the definition, creation, use and transformation of knowledge. This questions touches on the sociology of knowledge: Who gets to know what? and Who decides that? The issue combines role theory with learning theory. In some situations, knowledge is distributed among roles in a fixed and hierarchical way: The people, at the top know more and control the knowledge-access of those below them. In other situations, social relations are more level, more collegial, and all participants have roughly equal access to the various kinds of facts, skills and ideas in use.

Traditional school classrooms generally manifest the fixed and hierarchical form of social relations and knowledge distribution. The teacher possesses the important knowledge, and decides when and how to transmit it to the students; for their part, the students have the role obligation of taking in the requisite knowledge and displaying it on command. One indication of this kind of social relation in classrooms is that teachers ask questions to which they already know the answers (cf. Mehan, 1979). Their only purpose can be to check and control the behavior and learning of the students. In fact, Mehan argues that much of the learning students do in classrooms has to do with social relations: They have to learn how to "behave" in the various contexts that make up the school days. Of course, that kind of learning and performance is important in any social context.

Internships, as contrasted with classrooms, represent a wider range of social relations. Frequently, workplaces look very much like classes in certain respects: The boss knows, tells the worker, and the worker does as told.

Item: At County Hospital, a student working in the blood lab was shown how to operate the centrifuge to separate blood for testing. He repeated that mandated procedure again and again, recorded the results in the appropriate form in a notebook, and forwarded that information to the necessary places. He did not improvise, experiment or transform the knowledge he was given.

In some situations, the knowledge used by the intern was tremendously complex and subtle, and highly responsible in its application— but the student was still given little latitude in the definition and use of knowledge.

Item: In a municipal consumer protection agency, a student worked on the complaint phones, taking calls from consumers and helping them solve their problems. The job required broad knowledge of consumer laws and agency procedures, a sensitivity to the caller, and an ability to interpret specific situations in the light of labyrinthine regulations. Still, the supervisor of the phone room claimed that there were rather definite and immutable procedures to be followed, and that the student could not be allowed to invent new approaches or advance new interpretations.

On the other hand, some interns came to occupy a full and virtually equal position in the work environment, to participate completely in the definition and use of knowledge. In these more "democratic" or "collegial" settings knowledge was regarded as more flexible, more situational, more expansive than in the other places. People analyzed practical and theoretical problems together, and collaborated in finding the information and methods best suited for their solution. Experience and knowledge always counted for something, of course, but newcomers could contribute as well as veterans.

> *Item*: The student who worked as a tour guide in a history museum spent a good deal of time being gradually inducted into that role; she progressed from passive observer to helper to performer of limited segments to a complete guide. In the process, she also improvised new styles for handling certain kinds of situations, certain questions and behaviors from the students she led; she was encouraged to add her own understanding to the construction of the tour guide role.

> *Item*: Students working in the office of a progressive member of the City Council were treated as competent (if beginning) members of the staff, and were helped to take on more and more responsibility for their own work. They were shown how to find and use information, not given answers. Moreover, they were prompted to treat constituents the same way: to help callers mobilize their own resources to solve their problems, rather than to solve the callers' problems for them.

There is a strong connection between the dimensions of mental work and social relations, and it lies in the kinds of thinking (and, by extension, learning) that people are expected and enabled to do in the course of performing certain activities. In their most simplified forms, the two dimensions can be described in polar terms. The types of mental work or knowledge-engagement done in either classrooms or internship sites can be regarded as falling somewhere between these two extremes:

1. rote/algorithmic: knowledge is fixed and certain, and is used according to a mandated procedure;
2. creative/transformative: knowledge is fluid and situational, amenable to addition or change; higher operations are required;

Similarly, the types of social relations found in classrooms and work sites may be described as combinations of the following opposites;

3. hierarchical/controlled: the distribution of knowledge is static and top-down, and the higher-ups determine what the others will know;

4. collegial/participatory: knowledge is widely distributed across roles, and all members can participate in its creation and use.

No single context falls clearly into one extreme or the other. There is always some room for inventiveness; there is always some control. These dimensions, however, may be useful conceptual tools for the practitioner who is trying to think systematically about the nature of a learning environment, whether a classroom, a work site, a family home or a playground. The concepts pull us away from oversimplified, rigid claims about the kinds of learning that can occur in different types of environments. They can help experiential educators relieve themselves of the burdensome assumption that out-of-school learning is somehow inferior or subordinate to academic learning.

People operating in the "real world" do not work totally without theory or principle, without systematic bodies of knowledge and skill, without complex mental processes. First-hand experience in those work roles can—if it is properly set up, monitored and enhanced—spark forms of learning that are fully as developed, sound and rigorous as anything encountered in classrooms. That is not to say, once again, that all work experience is educational in these terms. Nor is it even to say that creative knowledge-engagement and collegial social relations are always "better" than rote and hierarchical. Clearly, there are times when knowledge is in fact certain and fixed, and when top-down control is perfectly functional and appropriate. My point, rather, has been to propose that both practitioners and researchers in experiential education consider these dimensions—that ways we use knowledge, and the ways we relate to others—in locating, developing, monitoring and supplementing non-school learning experiences.

REFERENCES

Bloom, Benjamin, ed., 1956, *Taxonomy of Educational Objectives: Handbook I: The Cognitive Domain*. New York: Longman.

Bruner, Jerome S. (Jeremy M. Anglin, ed.), 1973, *Beyond the Information Given*. New York: W. W. Norton.

Coleman, James S., 1977, Differences between experiential and classroom learning. In Morris T. Keeton, ed., *Experiential Learning*. San Francisco: Jossey-Bass.

Kolb, David, 1976, *Learning Style Inventory*. Boston: McBer and Co.

Luria, A. R., 1976, *Cognitive Development: Its Cultural and Social Foundations*. Cambridge, MA: Harvard University Press.

Mehan, Hugh, 1979, *Learning Lessons*. Cambridge, MA: Harvard University Press.

Moore, David Thornton, 1981, Discovering the pedagogy of experience. *Har-*

vard Educational Review 50:2 (May 1981), pp. 287–300. 1982, Students at work: Identifying learning in internship settings. *Occasional Paper #5*, Washington, DC: NSIEE.

Wadsworth, Barry J., 1971, *Piaget's Theory of Cognitive Development*. New York: David McKay.

3

INTEGRATING THE TRADITIONS OF EXPERIENTIAL LEARNING IN INTERNSHIP EDUCATION

Jon Wagner

There are three related models of experiential learning: group process, games/simulation, and internships/field studies. The first two are utilized extensively in the traditional classroom setting for courses in the social sciences and the sciences [as well as business, writing, communications, ed.]. However, the internship, with a broader curricular application, diverges from the other two in that it stresses the cognitive impact of the environment (work setting) itself. A pedagogical history of the now defunct Field Studies Program at the University of California (Berkeley) shows how all three models can be integrated into one program combining several disciplines.

Theories about experiential education have been proposed since antiquity and vigorously debated since the emergence of higher education in the Middle Ages (Chickering, 1977; Houle, 1976). In the last few decades, however, the more general tradition of learning from experience had found practical expression in three different models of formal instruction: group process, simulation-games, and field experience. The growing popularity of experiential education in secondary schools, colleges and universities (Keeton and Tate, 1978; Hamilton, 1980) raises a number of important questions about these models: What differences exist between them? In what circumstances can each model contribute most effectively to educational enterprises? And, what possibilities exist for integrating them in practice?

While these questions can be addressed theoretically, I would like to consider them here in terms of educational practice. To do so, I will examine the process by which all three traditions of experiential education were effectively integrated within a particular educational experiment: the Field Studies Program at the University of California, Berkeley. Before describing that process—and its implications for more general issues of educational reform—let me outline each of these three traditions in more detail.

THREE MODELS

Experiential learning generated through "group process" builds upon the interpersonal interaction of individuals in a group setting. These interactions can be examined as analogs of interpersonal relations which exist in the world beyond the group, or as representations of individual predispositions.

As an educational vehicle, "group process" has been refined through the development of T-groups, sensitivity training sessions, leadership workshops, group psychotherapy and the like (Milman and Goldman, 1974; Borman and Lieberman, 1976). In developing "group work" as an instructional vehicle, practitioners drew upon a history of social research into the dynamics of group behavior, particularly as it is manifest in the workplace.

The institutional applications of group process work are presently so varied as to almost defy unifying classification (Cooper, 1973), though several attempts have been made to do so in recent years (Klein, 1978, Lennung, 1978). As a tradition of experiential learning, however, group process activities remain an approach subscribed to by an identifiable constituency of supporters and professional practitioners (Cooper and Alderfer, 1978).

Simulation-games represent a second model of experimental learning which has developed greatly in the last few decades. This approach has been used in learning programs related to physical education, military training, city planning, theater performances, social studies, international affairs, architecture, industrial engineering, psychology, economics, and business management, as well as other more specialized areas too numerous to mention (Shubik, 1960; Guetzkow, 1962; Zuckerman and Horn, 1970).

As vehicles of experiential education, simulation-games rely on "gaming" activities to engage students in distinctive patterns of action and interaction (Coleman, 1968). The patterns are structured to develop skills and understanding which can be transferred beyond the immediate context of the game and to simulate important external realities.

A third model of experiential education emphasizes the integration of academic inquiry with off-campus student experience in work, travel, volunteer service, or some other non-academic endeavor. Students may participate, for example, in cross-cultural exchanges, outdoor or wilderness trials, or community service activities, all of which are organized and recognized as an integral part of their undergraduate education (Chickering, 1977). In other cases, students combine ongoing work experience or internships with academic study in related areas (Duley and Gordon, 1977). In some institutions, provisions are also available for crediting—through a process analogous to "advanced placement" the learning which students have gained through direct experience before they even enroll, a format which has proved to be particularly valuable to older, returning students (Meyer, 1975; Moon and Hawes, 1980).

All three models refer explicitly to a common body of theory about experiential learning. As Keeton and Tate have described it,

> Experiential learning refers to learning in which the learner is directly in touch with the realities being studied. It is contrasted with learning in which the learner only reads about, hears about, talks about, or writes about these realities, but never comes into contact with them as part of the learning process. (1978:1)

Chickering (1976:63) offers a parallel definition in which experiential learning "means that learning that occurs when changes in judgment, feelings, knowledge or skills result for a particular person from living through an event or events."

Given this broad conception, theoretical aspects of one model of experiential learning can certainly be applied to the other two. And they are. Citations to a few general formulations—such as those provided by Agryis and Schon (1974); Kolb and Fry (1975); and Coleman (1976)—appear with great frequency in the literature associated with each of the three different models. In addition, practitioners in each of the three traditions all state that they are working within the experiential context of learning which John Dewey identified, described and promoted during the early part of this century. In theory, then, there are grounds for a great deal of agreement and integration.

In practice, however, there are grounds as well for disagreement and disintegration. For example, all three models emphasize the educational value of analyzing direct experience, but they occupy different positions along the social environmental continuum which runs between the classroom and the world beyond. The group process model underlines what individuals can learn by examining closely interaction process within the instructional setting itself. Simulation-games make explicit but symbolic connections between exercises in an instructional setting and real problems of the world. The off-campus model calls attention to the educational value of participation in non-academic settings themselves.

The three models also draw implicitly upon different traditions of scholarship and research. Practice in group process is associated most closely with theory and research in social psychology, and the sociology of small group interaction, both of which are cast within a "clinical context" (Janowitz, 1978). The simulation and gaming approach, in contrast, is seen more in terms of "experimental" science, whether it be in psychology, physics or biology (Dawson, 1962; Meier, 1961). Off-campus approaches to experiential education are commonly practiced in anthropology, sociology, botany and zoology (Chickering, 1977). While each model of experiential education can call upon a rich tradition of scholarship, distinctions between such traditions are still very much alive."Clinicians," "experimenters," and "field workers," are not known for working closely together.

In practice, these implicit distinctions between the three models have usually overshadowed their theoretical commonalities. As a result, professional and institutional segregation of the activities they inspire is the rule, rather than the exception. Instruction in physical education, the natural sciences, art, or architecture, for example, may rely heavily on laboratory simulations, studios and the like, and yet ignore the interpersonal group process in which students are engaged, as well as related opportunities for field experience. Group process workshops, on the other hand, are rarely designed to build upon student reports of the off-campus situations in which they are involved on a continuing basis. And, the educational agendas for programs emphasizing off-campus experience all too frequently ignore the lessons to be learned from examining group process and the conceptual and technical understanding which can be enhanced through directed simulations and games.

What are the costs of this specialization and segregation in the design of experiential education programs? Are there techniques and concepts in one of the three models which could be productively examined or used by those working in other two? Could these different traditions be integrated in practice within a particular program? And, if so, how would it look?

OFF-CAMPUS EXPERIENCE

The Field Studies Program at the University of California, Berkeley, was an interdisciplinary academic unit for administering and developing field-based and experiential instruction (Heskins, 1977). Founded in 1971, the program underwent a number of important changes in ten years during which it operated on the campus. While these did not fundamentally alter its administration as a program of "experiential learning," they brought into the program elements of each of the three models described above.

The program began as a clearinghouse through which students

interested in community work were matched with community organizations and agencies which needed volunteers. Another of its "clearinghouse" functions was to refer students to campus faculty members with whom they might pursue related projects of independent study for academic credit. In both respects, the program's design was elaborated within a climate of reaction to the traditional lecture-discussion format of instruction which Coleman (1976) has identified as "information assimilation," and which dominated—and still dominates—the campus.

In its first year of operation, the Field Studies Program directed over 600 students to off-campus placements, as well as sponsored a series of voluntary discussion sessions in which they could review with their peers the nature of their field experience. Fourteen work-study students were hired to coordinate both seminars and field placements. The program was administered by a full-time director and supervised by the chair of an Academic Senate committee established to encourage instructional improvements on the campus. The program was funded by that same committee and a small, extramural grant.

At the end of the first year, however, changes were made in the program's design and operation which turned it from a clearinghouse into a unit of academic instruction. First, a Faculty Governing Board was established by the Chancellor to oversee the program and to provide formal connections with the academic affairs of the university. Second, the voluntary discussion sections previously run by work-study students were transformed into required academic seminars, each of which focused on a particular topic (e.g., alternative schools, child care, community mental heath, consumer protection, women, criminal justice, media, labor, and public advocacy). And third, while the program continued to employ eight work-study students to assist in the coordination of seminar and field placements, six other individuals were hired as "teaching associates" to actually conduct the seminars under the supervision of sponsoring faculty members. In recruiting for these associate teaching positions, the program administrators and the Faculty Board looked for graduate students and Ph.D.'s who also had a background of professional experience as lawyers, child care administrators, social workers, city planners, psychotherapists, etc.

Taken together, these developments increased the deliberation with which the program addressed both the campus and the field. The Faculty Governing Board took an active interest in ensuring that students were academically challenged by their off-campus experience, and not just "sent out into the field to do as they wished." At the same time, the teaching associates brought questions from both their academic disciplines and professional fields to the students enrolled in their seminars. The reaction to traditional instruction which had initially inspired the program was tempered by the academic environment in which it had to survive, and yet provisions were made to preserve an educationally productive tension between off-campus experience and campus-based instruction (Hursh and Borzak, 1979).

Up until its recent demise—a result of budget cuts to the university and campus-wide re-organization—the program continued to offer a dozen or so courses, each of which combined an academic seminar with student participation in related field internships. Seminars enrolled from fifteen to twenty students and met once a week for three hours. Students worked in their internships—which were arranged for them by seminar instructors—for another ten to twelve hours each week. In its last few years, courses focused on the media, child development, public advocacy, international economics, business and labor history, publishing, criminal justice, urban animal behavior, art, fiction writing, and environmental aesthetics.

In conducting these courses, Field Studies teachers worked from two quite different kinds of "texts". One of these was a set of assigned readings which were organized according to a week-by-week thematic syllabus, much like readings for more traditional academic courses. Other "texts," however, were provided by the students themselves through written and oral reports of their field experience. While the academic content and focus of the course was determined by the instructor, the manner in which that content was examined owed a great deal to the students' observations of the field settings in which they were engaged. Both written evaluations by students and a series of outside evaluations (Lunsford, 1973; Pilisuk, 1976; Scriven, 1978; and Goodman, 1982) confirmed the fact that the process worked and that the program was effective in challenging students to integrate field experience with academic inquiry.

To understand this effectiveness, however, it is important to note that the Field Studies Program was more than "field-based." Initially designed around opportunities for field internships, the program quickly incorporated two other features which were essential to the educational effectiveness it achieved in working with student, off-campus experience.

GROUP PROCESS

The first of these changes had to do with the conduct of seminar discussions. From the start these had emphasized student participation and initiative, for two reasons: leadership for establishing the program in the first place came largely from students, and the first seminars were organized and conducted by work-study students themselves. Within the first few years, however, responsibility for conducting the seminars was transferred from work/study students to "teaching associates" and leadership passed from students to Program Administrators and the Faculty Governing Board.

Field Studies courses continued to encourage students to become self-conscious about learning from their own experience and that of their peers. This approach was refined and elaborated with models such as group psychotherapy, Quaker meetings and the women's movement providing ideas for incorporating a broad range of individual experience into group formats without losing sight of a collective focus. Incorporation of elements from each of these models into the Field Studies Program occurred as a result of personnel appointments. For example, the director was a professionally trained social worker experienced in group process in a variety of settings. She hired a number of instructors who had been trained as psychotherapists and community mental health workers. Similarly, several instructors in the program had become skilled in feminist group practice and these individuals provided other teachers with examples from their own specialized experience as to tactics for encouraging successful discussion. Group process skills were disseminated throughout the staff during the program's continuing series of in-service workshops on teaching/learning strategies.

How did group process skills contribute to the program's effectiveness in field-based instruction? First, seminar discussion tactics were borrowed from group process work to help students articulate and analyze their field experience. A "check-in" period, for example, during which each student would report briefly on internship developments which had taken place during the past week, became a common feature of courses offered through the Program. "Check-in" reports could be relatively straightforward for individual students, and yet challenging and stimulating to the group as a whole. A student interning in a corporate public relations office, for example, might simply comment that her "host" organization was currently responding to a local labor strike. Another student in the class, however, might be interning in a union involved directly or indirectly with the strike. Still a third student might be working for a local newspaper which was covering the strike. What might appear as a matter-of-fact to each of these students, could become much more problematical in the context of reports from the other two. By providing a safe context in which to make such reports, the instructor could broaden student concerns beyond those of their individual field internships. By underlining differences between these individual reports, the instructor could further challenge the group into original intellectual work.

"Check-in" reports were also used to examine personal and professional interests related to the course. In the "Public Advocacy" seminar, for example, a student commented during "check-in" on his growing reservations about the effectiveness of public interest law and his future in that area. As other students questioned him about this matter, however, it became clear that his concern was more with the lack of financial rewards for public interest law in comparison with corporate law. "They just don't make as much money as they should," he said. Several other students questioned how much importance should be granted to money in making a career choice, but the initial speaker critiqued their comments in response: "Look, you're just like me. You took this course because you wanted to be a lawyer in the first place. We're all interested in money."

At this point the instructor intervened in what had moved from a "check-in" process to a group discussion, and asked the class several questions about the social and economic organization of legal work. How are lawyers in different branches of law paid for their services? Why are they paid in different ways? Has this always been the case? What exceptions can be identified to the generalizations we would like to make about these matters? And what are the consequences of these different patterns of remuneration for how the law is practiced? She concluded her series of questions by asking them if they knew the salaries paid to different people in the legal offices in which they served as interns, and the source of funds which supported the offices themselves. To the group's surprise—but not to hers—no one actually knew. Once this had been established, she asked them to take that upon themselves as a research assignment for the coming week. As a result of the group process and her intervention, a student's personal concerns about his economic future had become the starting point for examining the economic structure of legal work, a project to which the students would be contributing data from the field settings in which they served as interns.

At issue in integrating field work with group process was a question about the domain of student experience which could be appropriately examined within the context of a Field Studies course (Borzak and Hursh, 1977). Should students be asked to limit their comments about the field to "observations" which might be externally verifiable, or should they be encouraged to comment about the broader phenomena of their "experience" in the field? Should the comments of their peers be treated simply as "data" about the field, or should they be challenged by reference to the personal and professional ambitions which students brought to the field, the course, and the seminar itself?

The program remained committed to the broader context of educating its students—asking about an individual's "experience" as well as her or his "observations"—but it drew upon group process traditions to preserve the focus and structure of the seminars themselves. "Check-in" sessions led to challenges and further discussion. Individual reports and testimony were compared with each other within the collective context of the seminar. "Feed-back" and evaluation sessions were conducted at the end of each seminar, not only to summarize content, but also to comment on the manner in which it had emerged during the session itself. Instructors moved back and forth in their efforts to facilitate effective group process, calling upon the class at one moment to respect what each individual had to say, then encouraging the class as a whole to critically examine these reports in the light of course content and assigned readings.

The broad domain of student experience embraced by the group process of Field Studies seminars also carried over into personal exchanges between students and program instructors. The assignment of a "journal," for example, was used not only to challenge students to articulate their field experience, but also as a vehicle for communication between the student and teachers. While it was common in journal reviewing to direct students to readings related to the issues of their field work, these exchanges were also seen as occasions for raising questions about personal and professional development. In response to a student's description of difficulties encountered with discipline in a child care center, for example, an instructor might write something like the following:

> You seem to be having some difficulties with the exercise of your authority in the field. That's perfectly understandable, considering the place where you are working, but why don't we talk about what you can learn from these difficulties and how you can move beyond them. Perhaps you'd like to focus your term paper on this issue.

Exchanges similar to this might occur in the seminar itself, or between an instructor and a few students within a tutorial session arranged to clarify term papers. It is important to note, however, that attention directed to student "experience" in the field and in the seminar was not offered as therapy. An effective therapeutic strategy would have to grant priority to personal development and attend to whatever issues a student was confronted with at the time. In Field Studies courses, on the other hand, the experiential domain was broadened primarily around the issues of the course itself. If a student was ill, or had a death in the family, or was having a problem adjusting to dormitory life, that was the student's own "personal" problem. If, on the other hand, the student was troubled by matters directly related to the focus of the course—e.g. poor leadership in field settings, difficulties encountered in dealing with clients or supervisors, or the inability of an organization to do what it intends to do—these were taken as appropriate topics for classroom discussion. Students enrolled in the courses were thus confronted by a dual challenge: to develop personal familiarity with their field setting, and to question the assumptions of that understanding through group discussion with their peers.

INSTRUCTIONAL SIMULATIONS

In its last years of operation, the Field Studies Program drew upon yet a third tradition of experiential learning to improve the effectiveness of its course offerings. As with group process, elements of the simulation and gaming model were not taken in whole, but rather borrowed piecemeal in response to the instructional demands of a particular course.

The incorporation of simulations and gaming exercises into the more general Field Studies instructional mix was made explicit in 1976 in a search for an "academic coordinator" to assist the program director. The individual selected on the basis of this search was given responsibility for conducting the program's in-service workshops. Given his background and interests, these at first focused on the use of instructional simulations and gaming exercises in field-based education.

In one such workshop, for example, the academic coordinator scheduled a presentation from a professor of architecture who had developed a number of classroom simulations for his undergraduate studio course (Lifchez, 1979). Even though the Field Studies Program offered no architecture courses of its own, Field Studies teachers discussed the manner in which similar simulations could enhance instruction in their own courses.

In bringing this third tradition of experiential education into its own instructional activities, however, the program made good use of a valuable resource already on hand: the professional work with which many of its teachers were engaged as a complement to their part-time appointments in the program. The instructor for the media and writing courses, for example, was a practicing professional journalist; the instructor for the course on public advocacy, a lawyer; and the instructor for the courses in child development, a child therapist.

This professional experience provided program instructors with a rich background for developing field-related instructional simulations. In the media course, for example, instead of asking students to prepare a proposal for their final paper, the instructor required that they write an actual "query letter," such as that used by a professional journalist in submitting proposals to commercial publications.

In the public advocacy course, students were introduced to legal interviewing skills through an in-class simulation. Similarly, in the child development course, students were asked to make recommendations regarding prepared scenarios of "problem children," much as they would have to if they were to administer a child care center in the field.

These interactive simulations helped the program integrate field experience with critical inquiry in three important respects. First, they helped students develop an appreciation of social phenomena as "rule governed" behavior. As such they illuminated the larger social world as a phenomenon itself, as something to be examined rather than a given (Mills, 1959; Berger and Luckmann, 1967). Second, the in-class simulations helped students try out a variety of unfamiliar roles which they encounter in their field work, some of which they might actually have to take on themselves within their internships. In this latter regard, simulations provided a context intermediate between normal classroom discussions and the "real" situations of student involvement in the field (Argyris and Schon, 1974). And third, they gave in-class experience some of the potency usually reserved for experience in the field. Given the variety of field placements with which students in a particular class were involved, in-class simulation and gaming exercises performed an important integrative function. They had the power to bring a group of quite different students close together for a short period of time in performance of a common, course-related task.

A "mock court" exercise in the public advocacy class was a particularly effective example of this kind of simulation, and in their course evaluations, thirteen of fifteen students enrolled stressed the importance of this exercise in giving them a sense of the class as a whole.

PRINCIPLES AND PRACTICE

This history of the program's pedagogy is necessarily abbreviated and suggestive. There are areas in which the three models of experiential education were interdependent, confounded or superimposed. It is also impossible to identify all the contributions which each made to the overall instructional effort of the program. And, it should be noted, instructors in the program did not self-consciously identify with any of the three models of experiential education outlined above. That is, they made use of instructional elements without participating as "members" of the traditions they represent. In their own minds they were Field Studies Program teachers, not "experiential educators."

If other programs seek the same kind of integrated approach to experiential education which characterized the Field Studies Program, these practical, institutional resources must be kept clearly in mind. Simply placing students in the field and in classrooms, for example, may not provide the kind of "experiential learning" that we would like to associate with experiential education (Ehrensaft and Wagner, 1981). In much the same way, asking seminar instructors to pay attention to group dynamics and simulations may have little effect unless the teachers have previous training in those areas or are willing and in a position to learn about them directly from their peers. A career in which an individual has managed to integrate both academic inquiry and field experience provides a model within the teacher's own experience for the kind of integrated inquiry in which students are to be thoughtfully instructed. And finally, a peer culture which supports individual teachers as well as collective inquiry about teaching effectiveness represents a program resource of inestimable value. Without practical resources such as these, agreement about the theory of experiential learning may be of little consequence in ensuring that a program's instructional goals are actually achieved.

Another way of summarizing these observations is to underline the fact that whatever else it might be, the campus is also a workplace. Field Studies teachers were successful at providing integrated experiential education to Berkeley students because of their individual talents and the resources that they were given or invented for themselves. But that they even tried was tied closely to the fact that every day, and, in many ways, it was their job to do just that.

REFERENCES

Agryis, Chris and Schon, Donald, *Theory in Practice: Increasing Professional Effectiveness*, Jossey-Bass, San Francisco, 1974. Berger, Peter and Luckmann, Thomas, *The Social Construction of Reality*, Doubleday, New York, 1967.

Borman, Leonard D. and Lieberman, Morton, eds., "Special Issue," *Journal of Applied Behavioral Science*, vol. 12, pp. 261–463, July 1976.

Borzak, Lenore and Hursh, Barbara, "Integrating the Liberal Arts and Preprofessionalism Through Field Experience: A Process Analysis," *Alternative Higher Education*, no. 2, pp. 3–16, 1977.

Chickering, Arthur W., "Developmental Change as a Major Outcome," in *Experiential Learning*, ed. Morris Keeton, pp. 62–107, Jossey-Bass, San Francisco, 1976.

Chickering, Arthur W., *Experience and Learning: An Introduction to Experiential Learning*, Change Magazine Press, New Rochelle, N.Y., 1977.

Coleman, James S., "Academic Games and Learning," *Proceedings of the 1967 Institutional Conference on Testing Problems*, ETS, Princeton, NJ, 1968.

Coleman, James S., "Differences Between Experiential and Classroom Learning," in *Experiential Learning*, ed. Morris Keeton, Jossey-Bass, San Francisco, 1976.

Cooper, Carl L., *Group Training for Individual and Organizational Development*, S. Warger, Basel, 1973.

Cooper, Carl L. and Alderfer, Clayton, *Advances in Experiential Social Processes*, John Wiley and Sons, Ltd, New York, NY, 1978.

Dawson, Richard E., "Simulation in the Social Sciences," in *Simulation in Social Sciences: Readings*, ed. Harold Guetzkow, Prentice-Hall, Englewood Cliffs, NJ, 1962.

Duley, John and Gordon, Shiela, *College-Sponsored Experiential Learning—A CAEL Handbook*, Educational Testing Service, Princeton, NJ, 1977.

Enrensaft, Diane and Wagner, Jon, *Integrating Theory and Practice in Experiential Learning*, TIES/Field Studies, University of California, Mimeographed, Berkeley.

Goodman, Oscar, "Cultural Understanding and Field-Based Learning," *External Evaluation of the Cultural Literacy Project*, Field Studies Program, University of California, Mimeographed, Berkeley, 1982.

Guetzkow, Harold ed., *Simulation in Social Science: Readings*, Prentice-Hall, Englewood Cliffs, NJ, 1962.

Hamilton, Stephen, "Experiential Learning Programs for Youth," *American Journal of Education*, vol. 88, no. 2, pp. 179–215, February 1980.

Heskin, Alan D., "The Field Study Program," *Alternative Higher Education*, vol. 2, pp. 119–33, 1977.

Houle, Cyril O., "Deep Traditions of Experiential Learning," in *Experiential Learning*, ed. Morris Keeton, pp. 19–33, San Francisco, 1976.

Hursh, Barbara and Borzak, Lenore, "Toward Cognitive Development Through Field Studies", *Journal of Higher Education*, vol. 50, no. 1, 1979.

Keeton, Morris and Tate, Pamela, "The Boom in Experiential Learning," in *New Directions for Experiential Learning: Learning by Experience—What, Why, How*, ed Morris Keeton and Pamela Tate, pp. 1–8, Jossey-Bass, San Francisco, 1978.

Klein, Edward B., "An Overview of Recent Tavistock Work in the United States," *Advances in Experiential Learning Social Processes*, ed. Carl L. Cooper and Clayton Alderfer, pp. 181–202, John Wiley and Sons, Ltd, New York, NY, 1978.

Kolb, David A. and Frye, R., "Toward an Applied Theory of Experiential Learning," in *Theories of Group Processes*, ed. Cary Cooper, John Wiley and Sons, New York, 1975.

Lennung, Sven-Ake, "A Classification of Experiential Social Processes: A European Perspective," in *Advances in Experiential Social Process*, ed. Cary L. Cooper and Clayton Alderfer, pp. 29–38, John Wiley and Sons, New York, Ny, 1978. Lifchez, Raymond, "Seeing Through Photographs: Projections and Simulation," in *Images of Information*, ed. Jon Wagner, pp. 217–232, SAGE, Beverly Hills, CA, 1979.

Lunsford, Terry F., *Evaluating Field Studies at Berkeley*, TIES/Field Studies, University of California, Mimeographed, Berkeley, 1973.

Mills, C. W., *The Sociological Imagination*, Oxford University Press, New York, 1959.

Pilisuk, Marc, *Campus-Community Education: An Evaluation of the UC Berkeley Undergraduate Field Studies Program*, TIES/Field Studies, University of California, Mimeographed, Berkeley, 1976.

Scriven, Michael, "Report to the Vice Chancellor, Ira M. Heyman," 1978.

Shubik, Martin, "Bibliography on Simulation, Gaming, Artificial Intelligence and Allied Topics," *Journal of the American Statistical Association*, vol. 55, pp. 736–751, 1960.

Wagner, Jon, "Field Study as a State of Mind," in *Field Study: A Sourcebook for Experiential Learning*, ed. Lenore Borzak, pp. 18–49, SAGE, Beverly Hills, CA, 1981.

Zuckerman, D. and Horn, R., *Guide to Simulation Gaming for Education and Training*, Information Resources, Lexington, Mass., 1970.

4
FACULTY vs. PRACTITIONER: A PEDAGOGICAL TUG OF WAR OVER INTERNSHIPS

Andrew Ciofalo

Uncertain of the cognitive parity from one internship to the next, faculties are becoming more reluctant to certify internships for credit without some campus-based collateral requirements. The popularity among students of internship courses is apparently unrelated to the knowledge imparted and rests on spurious grounds which rightfully concern faculty, as borne out in a study of Loyola College (Maryland) interns over a four year span. [Also see Robert Kendall's article in Section III, ed.] The research and literature suggest that the quality of the internship is directly related to the structure of the on-site program and the dedication of the on-site supervisor. Credit can be freely extended for internships if supervisors meet the minimum standards for adjunct faculty status and the internship courses are supported by syllabi and other traditional academic accouterments.

The academic legitimacy of internships in masscom and business curricula is an issue that won't go away easily. There is no doubt that both students and communications enterprises benefit from internships.[1] But the assessment of the benefits devolving upon students is left to a faculty that is usually unfamiliar with the pedagogy of experiential learning. The result is that credit is uneasily extended for activities that seem unrelated to the objectives expected of traditional classroom-based learning.

Giving ill-considered academic status to internship courses in mass communication programs increases the vulnerability of the communications discipline to outside criticism. Bruce Garrison, writing in *Journalism Educator* in 1981, commented that according to faculty critics "the overall academic program becomes diluted" when internships are given full status as academic courses, thus "endangering the quality of the curriculum."[2]

John De Mott, writing about summer internships at a time before internships had migrated massively into the main academic year, argued that "since . . . the average school or department of journalism is seldom in a position to oversee [internship] activity satisfactorily, there is a natural reluctance to grant academic credit."[3]

Faculties are rightfully concerned about transferring the control and responsibility for evaluating student performance to an off-campus practitioner who is not academically certified. De Mott, citing Hugh Cowdin's report on *Academic Credit for Internships* (Roundtable #80, American Society of Journalism School Administrators, 1978) illustrates how the appropriate role of the supervising practitioner in internships is at the center of a schism between teachers of theory and skill courses.

> While conceding that internship supervision can differ in quality from newspaper to newspaper, Prof. David B. Whittaker of Western Kentucky University believes that "it is pompous nonsense to argue that newspaper editors . . . are not qualified to teach people how to write and edit. If they are good editors, chances are they are . . . good teachers."
>
> "Today's editors are not itinerant, uneducated printers. Most have bachelor's degrees, and more than a few have master's.
>
> "On the other hand, I know a lot of faculty members who have little or no professional experience, and I think they are the ones whose credentials are suspect if they are teaching . . . the so-called skills courses.
>
> "In my judgement, it is not a question of whether the . . . editor is qualified to teach, but rather a question of will he take the time."[4]

The same concerns about teaching ability apply to public relations practitioners and account or creative personnel in advertising. But until these concerns are addressed, the regular faculty will continue to bind interning students to campus-based supervision through such legitimizing ploys as internship classes, research papers and diaries. All of these collateral activities have been tried with mixed results by the Media Program at Loyola College in Maryland, where close to 80% of the 170 communication majors (1987) in the Writing and Media Department are in the advertising or public relations concentration.

The Loyola media faculty and the college administration, through a Committee on Student Internships, completed a study in the Spring 1987 semester of the structure of internship education. Faculties from disparate disciplines were unable to identify or agree on a pedagogical structure for internship courses. Instead, the committee attempted to simply contain the problem by permitting only one internship course to be counted toward graduation. (The Media Program had already decertified internships as applicable to the communications major.)

The frustration of the committee surfaced in its summation, opting for an administrative cure for a pedagogical ill.[5]

> The committee unanimously feels that internships are, and are going to continue to be, an important addition to the educational experience of many students. However, the committee feels that while there have been many excellent and educational internships, the informal structure under which they have been allowed to develop has also resulted in some abuses by students, employers, and faculty, and that it is now time to replace this system with a more formal structure.

By also recommending that the College Placement Office serve as the administrative center for campus-wide internship activity, the committee effectively distanced the faculty from the internship supervisory role. To cool down the boiling internship pot, the committee further recommended that students be made responsible for an additional burden of pre-internship paperwork and circuitous registration procedures.[6] Incidentally, the "Rutgers Model" also eliminates the student dilettante by imposing heavy record-keeping and procedural responsibilities on students before and during the internship.[7]

Garrison, reporting on an approach embraced initially by Marquette University in 1981, echoes the continuing concern that the "student's scholarly development and intellectual growth" is not fostered outside the context of a "complete theory course" (i.e., classroom-based course) but also worries that "without instructional attention and guidance [supporting projects] are often reduced to diaries and other far less-than-analytical activities. . . . "[8]

The inability to cut the internship's umbilical tie to the classroom persists despite the fact that most practitioners, who have always been responsible for on-the-job training, are more qualified to teach practical courses, either on or off the campus, than many theoreticians and researchers. There is no record in the masscom literature of there having been a careful examination of the difference between the learning that occurs in the class and in the field. Is there simply a difference in the pedagogical delivery system or are there significant epistemological factors at work? The reason this question has been left unexamined is that there has been a rather uncritical acceptance of the idea that all learning happens in the classroom and is tested through internships in the field.[9]

This assumption is frequently challenged by media students themselves. Sam G. Riley writing in *Journalism Educator* cited one such student who described her newsroom internship experience as follows: "I feel I've learned more about journalism than just how to handle quotes."[10] Riley comments about the internship experience, "Not only do interns begin to understand the dynamics of interacting with interviewees, officials, and the general public, but they experience human interaction of a different kind in the newsroom itself."[11] In a 1987 survey of Loyola College in Maryland interns over the past four years, almost 64% said that they learned more from an internship than any classroom experience.[12] Thus there are strong indications that a different kind of learning, more than just applied theory, occurs in internships.

Despite the apparently grim assessment of classroom teaching implied by the Loyola respondents, other answers on the survey revealed that students were actually differentiating between the kinds of learning derived from internships and classes. That's why these same students overwhelmingly agreed (77%) that "no student should be allowed to intern unless he or she has completed some basic media skills courses." The students were evenly split on whether an "internship class" would be helpful, and they voted down the inclusion of a major research paper (59% to 27%) as part of the internship. [Numbers not adding up to 100% reflect no responses to that question, ed.] One student wrote in the comments section: "Additional papers seem only to serve as busy work for the student. They offer no additional professional experience and should be excluded from the program."

The pages of *Journalism Educator* are replete with articles on formats for running internships. Beneath all the logistical suggestions lies a measure of guilt (Or is it an administrative notion of accountability?) that a faculty member should earn his or her pay by reining back into the classroom for a validating experience interns who are already doing 10 to 15 hours per week on the job. But unless masscom educators fully understand the nature of the learning that occurs in internships, they will never design appropriate learning modules to bolster the experience.

The internship class is often a hybrid of a t-group and work orientation session, with students sharing on-the-job experiences and covering such topics as interpersonal relations, conflict resolution, interviewing skills and resume writing. Some colleges give credit not for the internship but for a collateral seminar taken during or after the internship.[13] In those instances where such a class is mandated, it would be appropriate to split the objectives and the grading into an experiential module and a classroom unit, thereby giving each pedagogical approach its due. In some disciplines this is a moot point, since internships are required for certification (e.g., practice teaching and clinical work in psychology and speech pathology). But internships in other disciplines usually do not occur in an organizational context where team work is an important factor in achieving goals.

Student attitudes affirm the theoretical model of a social context for field learning. Such learning occurs through a general orientation to the media company or agency, briefings by immediate supervisors, advice and help from other employees (peer learning), evaluation of tasks and finished products by supervisors, and general feedback during periodical employer-intern conferences. In addition to practical help, much theoretical and abstract knowledge is conveyed in order to make the intern a productive member of the communications team.

David Thornton Moore indicates that the significance of social relations in learning environments operates on two levels:[14]

— First, experiential learning programs must contribute to a student's self-confidence and sense of professionalism. (Of the Loyola respondents who had already been graduated and were now working, 90% agreed that internships provided a maturing experience, 87% agreed that internships increased their confidence, and 81% agreed that they were thinking and talking like professionals in the field.)

— Second, the learning environment must offer opportunities for interns to contribute to and alter the knowledge base that drives the organization's operations. (81% of the Loyola interns report having been given definite responsibilities [a pre-condition for conceptualizing objectives of tasks], deciding how they should be organized, proposing appropriate responses, and helping to infer conclusions from the process that will be useful in the future.)

In some instances the social context for learning in the workplace is very similar to learning in the classroom.[15] Both teachers and bosses sit at the top of a hierarchical learning pyramid in which students and workers must assimilate a fixed body of knowledge to pass tests and complete projects. There are even collegial work settings (not unlike a graduate seminar) which employ a flexible peer-oriented approach to the acquisition and use of knowledge.

In both the classroom and the workplace students also encounter and master new subject matter, learning how to expand their personal store of knowledge.[16] Moore cites Benjamin Bloom's breakdown of the mental work involved in learning, revealing a typical schema: knowledge, comprehension, application, analysis, synthesis, and evaluation.[17] All of these learning modes can be found in the workplace and in the classroom, though their convergence is not easily recognized. Part of the problem is that no vocabulary has been devised to articulate what one has learned from a work experience.[18] Is knowledge gained from internships somehow different from academically-based knowledge—practice vs. theory?

Loyola interns sensed one of the differences. Asked whether the internship program should be de-emphasized as opportunities for more practical hands-on experience (media lab, newspaper, student agency) emerged in the media courses, 91% of the responding interns said no. The idea of working professionals being brought onto the campus to work directly with students was also rejected by 85% of the respondents who felt internships provided more opportunities for learning. Students indicated that neither a professional activity (ersatz or real) on campus nor contact with professionals brought to campus could substitute for the workplace experience. This opinion was borne out by the unusually high evaluations Loyola students gave to the social environment of their internships:

- 85% agreed (46% strongly) that internships gave them a feeling for what it's like to be a communications professional,
- 77% agreed (32% strongly) that their bosses treated them like entry level professionals,
- 83% agreed (32% strongly) that their work as interns made a significant contribution to the company's mission,
- 74% agreed (30% strongly) that their supervisors took the time to teach them on the job,
- 83% agreed (40% strongly) that their supervisors were patient and caring, and
- only 4% claimed that the attitudes of co-workers somewhat interfered with their effectiveness on the job.

Once we have accepted the idea that experiential learning directly parallels academic learning (with gradations of emphasis), there should be no need for full-time faculty to impose the values of classroom methodology over workplace values. The on-site professional supervisor should be in a position to grade the interns. If such supervisors are not now so positioned, it is because masscom departments and schools are overwhelmed trying to keep up with the burgeoning student interest by expanding their catalogs of internship opportunities.

The students are very aware of the importance internships play in eventual job placement. In a recent study of masscom alumni at Rutgers University, 65% reported that their first communications jobs were the direct result of an internship.[19] The Loyola interns agreed (77%) that internships would be important to their future, and 79% stated that they wanted to build experience for their resumes. Perhaps it is a preoccupation with career programs, but student interest in internships extends into the high schools and is a factor in a choice of colleges by communications majors.[20]

With so many students banking on internships, problems of grading, standards and supervision have multiplied. How can the internship be evaluated (graded) for academic credit? And to what extent should the responsible faculty member rely on the judgment of the supervising practitioner?

Because faculty have been unwilling to rely on the judgments of the practitioners, students doing internships are often subjected to a sequence of academic hurdles marginally related to the internship experience. The simple fact is that the faculty sponsor grades non-internship related activities because he or she is in no position to grade the internship. Only the workplace supervisor is, and therein lies the crux of the problem and, perhaps, its solution.

We can see there are two factors mitigating the academic legitimacy of internships. Apparently these factors are related to evaluation and grading:

1. Internship programs are established without a clear sense of the nature of experiential learning and how to evaluate it.
2. The dichotomous values of the classroom and the workplace have led concerned academic faculties to create and evaluate activities often unrelated to the field work experience and presented as meaningful classroom activities.

By failing to perceive the continuum between communications internships and courses, faculty treat internships as entities wholly different from the traditional class offerings. Even in such enlightened internship programs as at the University of Alaska at Fairbanks, the only grade that can be assigned in an internship course is pass/fail.[21] But such stipulations, like Loyola's limitation that only one three-credit internship course can be counted toward graduation, is an explicit admission of the second-class status of internship courses and an implicit recognition that faculties have not adequately defined the cognitive aspects of experiential learning. Instead, each academic department should develop a cognitive plan for its own internship offerings. Without such a plan the function of the on-site internship supervisor is minimized.

Perhaps a more appropriate role for an internship supervisor would be the adjunct faculty member, most of whom tend to be active practitioners anyway. In fact, such status might be accorded the supervisor, provided he or she meets departmental criteria for an adjunct appointment, with appropriate rank and stipend. Such a step would overcome institutional policies that "will not acknowledge grades provided by anyone other than [a] faculty member."[22] Like any other teacher, the "field studies professor" (or another title) would be responsible for defining a body of knowledge that the intern should master, ranging from highly theoretical material to organizational data to knowledge of the communication enterprise's purpose, audience and clients. Testing would then be the prerogative of the field studies professor, as would be the assignment and grading of a major paper. In lieu of homework, the intern's field assignments could be graded and weighted.

Such an approach would foster a greater sense of responsibility and commitment by the internship supervisor, who would be both titled and paid. It would release the full-time faculty from direct supervision of interns and would provide a context for the masscom department or school to relate to the supervisor as a member of the faculty, requiring that he or she develop a syllabus and attend occasional meetings or seminars on the nature of experiential learning and the pedagogy of one-on-one teaching. In fact, several field studies professionals from each of the communications disciplines could rotate through a "Field Studies Curriculum Committee," perhaps chaired by a full-time faculty member.

This approach might limit the number of internships available since not all potential internship supervisors would merit adjunct faculty appointment or agree to its stipulations. And there may be some institutional rumblings due to additional costs. But tuition-paying students are entitled to a cognitive experience in an internship that is thorough, guided, and challenging.

Since fewer credit-bearing internships would result, the competition for them would increase thereby insuring that only the very best students would be enrolled in internships counting toward the major or the degree. Such an internship would become a de facto honors course.

This approach does not mean that other students would lack access to units of practical experience. Practicum or lab activities could still be developed around the student newspaper, various student magazines, campus radio and TV stations, a student-run advertising or p.r. agency, or a specialized college press. These campus-based experiences could be an extension of a classroom-based course.

Moving internship courses toward unquestionable academic legitimacy does not mean that departments and schools will have to scrap the bulk of internship opportunities listed in various looseleaf directories. Students unable to register for credit-bearing internships should have access to all remaining noncredit internships. An institution could still monitor internships as worthwhile or serious and certify to the internship provider that the student is a bona fide major. Beyond that the student would be responsible for negotiating the terms of his internship (hours, salary, duties, etc.) like any other part-time or temporary employee. When requested, faculty could provide letters of recommendation as for any job.

To be listed in non-credit internship books, a communications company would need to agree to a few minimal terms. First, they would offer the student an entry level professional position; at the internship's conclusion they would provide the student with an oral and written evaluation (perhaps on a college generated form); and if merited, they would write a letter of recommendation for the student's dossier in the placement office or for his departmental file.

There might be some concern that students who are doing unofficial internships would somehow put out less effort, which could damage the program's reputation among professionals and in the community at large. The Loyola survey revealed that 79% of the students interned primarily because they wanted "to build up experience for my resume." Another 77% felt it would be important to their future. These motives strike me as being as viable as the desire for a grade, and most students learn early that media employers rely more on resumes and work samples than on official transcripts. But perhaps the best argument for maintaining the zero-credit semi-official internship is the need for many students to use internships to test their interest in one of the masscom fields—at least that's what 79% of the Loyola respondents said they did.

Several conclusions and recommendations suggested by this literature review and survey are that:

— more faculty need to inform themselves on the cognitive value of experiential learning and the way it relates to classroom learning;

— before an internship is certified for academic credit, the on-site supervisor should be credentialed as adjunct faculty and develop clear learning objectives and evaluative procedures for the course;

— credit-bearing internships be available only to those students who are most likely to benefit from experiential learning outside the school;

— in addition to the credit-bearing internship (which could be distinguished by a term such as "practicum"), students should be helped to connect with informal internships that would appear on their resumes but not their transcripts;

— the separate "internship class" should be eliminated or at least restructured in order to defuse the conflict between academic and experiential learning objectives and evaluation.[23]

NOTES

1. Joan Daniels Pedro, "Induction into the Workplace: The Impact of Internships," *Journal of Vocational Behavior*, 25, No. 1 (1984), 80–95.
2. Bruce Garrison, "Post internship seminar can solve academic credit, grad-

ing problems of internship programs," *Journalism Educator*, 36, No. 1 (1981), 14–17.

3. John De Mott, "Post-internship seminar benefits J-students," *Journalism Educator*, 27, No. 2 (July 1972), 8–11.
   [Very often the administration of an internship program is foisted upon some unsuspecting junior faculty member who is usually untenured, ed.]

4. John De Mott, "Newspaper Internships in Education for Journalism: The Historical Perspective," Paper presented at the Annual Meeting of the Association for Education in Journalism (62nd, Houston, Texas, August 5–8, 1979), 29p.

5. Unpublished report of the Committee on Student Internships to the Loyola College Council (June 1987).

6. *Ibid.*

7. Jarice Hanson, "Internships and the Individual: Suggestions for Implementing (or Improving) an Internship Program," *Communication Education*, 33 No. 1 (January 1984), 53–61.

8. Garrison, 1981, *op. cit.*, p. 48.

9. David Thornton Moore, "Perspectives on Learning in Internships," *Journal of Experiential Education*. 6 No. 2 (Fall 1983), 40–44.

10. Sam G. Riley, "Some student assessments of newspaper internships," *Journalism Educator*, 38, No. 1 (Spring 1983), 8–10.

11. *Ibid.*, p. 9.

12. The Media Program surveyed (33% response) 148 alumni and students who had completed about 300 internships over a four year period starting in the 1983–84 academic year. The 3:1 ratio of female to male respondents approximated the gender ratio in the program. The surveyed group accounted for 94 internships, 40 of which were in public relations. The group included 6 current students, 13 seniors who had just been graduated, and 28 alumni. The students rated their answers to 84 questions on five-step scales ranging from "least important" to "most important" and from "strongly disagree" to "strongly agree."

13. Garrison, 1981, *op. cit.*, p. 17.

14. Moore, 1983, *op. cit.*, p. 43.

15. *Ibid.*, p. 43.

16. *Ibid.*, p. 42.

17. Benjamin Bloom, ed., *Taxonomy of Educational Objectives: Handbook I: The Cognitive Domain* (New York, Longman, 1956).

18. Moore, 1983, *op. cit.*, p. 40.

19. Hanson, 1984, *op. cit.*, p. 61.

20. Attendance at the Loyola College Media Program's presentation on college day to high school seniors and their parents quadrupled the year that all the internships (journalism, publishing, broadcast, advertising, public relations and graphics) appeared for the first time in the college catalog, each listed with its own course number.

21. Beverly James, "Interns go beyond OJT—link theory to the workplace," *Journalism Educator*, 41, No. 4 (Spring 1986), 42–43.

22. *Ibid.*, p. 42.

23. Portions of this article have appeared previously in a more comprehensive piece, "Masscom Internships: A Question of Academic Legitimacy," that appeared in the Winter 1988 issue of *Journalism Educator*. *JE* asked for revisions after the editorial work on the book had been completed. Significant survey data is included here that was deleted from that article.

5
THE VAGUE ACHES OF INTERNS

William Marling

The assumption that only pre-professional students who have acquired a foundation of communication skills are ready for an internship experience is challenged by successful programs run by liberal arts colleges and departments in the humanities. Students in one such program discovered that much media work is routine and dull and that much writing on the job is formulaic. Only after understanding the boring reality of adult life, did they learn to apply creativity and invention to routine tasks—to innovate by flexing their imaginations against the system's rigidity.

Three years ago a university invited me to come and run an internship program in "real world writing" offered through its English department. I guess I got hired because I had a long rap sheet in journalism and a PhD in English, a kind of academic pardon. I was flattered, but when I arrived I found the program more idea than reality. I was to carry it out; I was the "director." But I did not come fresh from the field. Ten years ago, true, I had interned at several newspapers and television stations; the chief memory I retained of those times was that there weren't enough journalists who thought critically about their writing or enough people encouraging them to do so.

The program shouldered other burdens of which I was unaware initially. Members of my department wanted it to buttress their classes in fiction and poetry writing, in film, in technical writing and advanced composition. The class would be our message to students that vocations waited at the end of a degree in English and thus save us from the financial consequences of an eroding base of majors. The dean hoped the program would "bridge the gap" between the university and its urban locale. As the art department had allied itself to the art museum, and the management school to industry, so would the English department meet the media and publishing industries through this program. The program would go downtown aggressively—become a placement agency with training wheels. It would show skeptics that English majors could do anything that journalism majors could, and also identify quotations from literary classics that journalism majors never learned.

The jobs end of the program worked out well; business was hungrier than we knew for students with a commando's mastery of the fundamentals, who were scrupulous about facts and eager to research new fields. But the program also had a classroom component, which is what I want to write about here, because for two years I was completely baffled by the conflict between the interns' expectations of the real world and the kind of writing that the real world needs.

There were initially only twelve interns, but they worked in sports promotion, Red Cross publicity, television news; at city magazines and cinema public relations; for weekly and student newspapers, rock radio news, the black community press; and for corporate public relations. There was no center. The problem became less, rather than more, manageable. Soon I had interns working for school boards, a redevelopment corporation in a Hungarian neighborhood, a modern dance troupe, and a news-and-talk radio station presided over by someone named Count Manalesco. My first task was to find common denominators, to focus on them, and then to work backwards toward the classroom, bringing learning to bear on experience. Or so I thought.

Since I wanted the interns to think critically about their work, I picked for that first semester a text with an abstract theme about the media. We read dutifully through chapters on media power and responsibility, advertiser pressures, public relations, and media ethics. They yawned. I was the only one interested in those topics, or the sole party thinking he knew how they applied to the workplace. One day near the end of the semester, I discovered that no one had read the assigned chapter. Half pleading, half desperate, I told the interns that, damn it, I wanted them to Be Ethical! Analyze! Think about what you're doing on the job! The evaluations I got at the end of the course, naturally, said that none of the reading related to the work. No one even mentioned being embarrassed by my outburst.

I was still way off the mark. They were hungry for the real world experience; I was still doling out academic abstraction and, moreover, theories that contradicted their day-to-day experience. As a student wrote, "What I wanted was a chance to use my skills, as well as a mild dose of the real world. I received a good measure of the latter, and was not particularly fond of it." There was something wistful about that comment that stayed with me.

The second time around I did no advance planning. At the first class meeting I asked the interns what they wanted to do in class. They told me: "Get Joe Sportscaster to talk." "Get an editor of a big daily paper." "Get the AFTRA president to explain why I can't touch the videotape equipment at work." "Get a headhunter to talk about jobs and salaries." I got them. Later I wished I hadn't. Some of the biggest media celebrities were monologuists of uninterruptable status. They had traveled so far from the crafts in which they started that they had forgotten the fearful heft of a pencil under deadline.

But between sessions with "guests" we talked about the interns "problems and projects." This went better, or kept everyone attentive anyway. The Red Cross intern told how her boss had fired her supervisor before her eyes. The sports promotion intern told about the security he arranged for skater Eric Heiden. The rock news intern asked what to do when the boss wanted her to smoke dope with him (that class went overtime).

But there was an undertone of cynicism, of disenchantment, that I did not know how to harness. I remember the day, however, that we crossed the divide. The intern in the university's sports information office announced that "downtown editors will grab any story on women athletes. They want to make it seem like they're giving fair coverage to both sexes." This prompted another public relations intern to say that "all editors are glad to use your stuff with their bylines on it. That's the exchange—we let them take credit for the story if they give us the publicity."

I sensed some admiration for this student in the class; he had passed some barrier, gotten beyond an initial cynicism about his workplace, and was a step ahead. After this, the Red Cross intern responded that he had been writing scripts for a local celebrity: "He just wants eight complete sentences, all beginning with 'discuss,' 'relate,' 'explain,' or 'tell about.' I'm to the point where I can knock off one of his scripts in about fifteen minutes." Eyes lit up around the room because, as I later realized, despair had just been reconceived as "craft."

We read something more vivid this semester, a collection of New Journalism pieces, and I spun out farfetched theories about the media that begged for contradictory examples from their experiences, I thought it went pretty well. Then came the evaluations:

> "The textbook idea should be scrapped."
> "Schedule two days a week to talk to the interns."
> "Two guests with conflicting viewpoints."

But the most frequent complaint was that I hadn't appeared personally at their work-sites once or twice in the semester to see them on the job. I thought of all those offices, spread out over 250 square miles, with interns working conflicting schedules (some at night), and I grew depressed. They wanted an additional sixty hours of visits and another sixty of special conferences. That I had met all those bosses and previewed all those jobs meant nothing to them when they coped day-by-day in a strange new environment. What they wanted was the reassuring presence of the teacher, the one who claimed the critical faculty was involved when they were filing papers and writing mundane press releases. They had discontents about the real world, to which I had intimated there were answers. Inside each of them was a small dread that was feeding on the discrepancy between the real world and what they had been told in school. All of their lives we had praised them for originality, even the most marginal originality; all of their lives they had been punished for copying, even for copying the best models. But in the workplace no one asked them to be original; in fact originality often raised eyebrows and led to the suggestion that they copy a suitable model. As a young women told me one afternoon, "I feel like a terrible phoney. The first time that I tried to abstract a few punchy and definite lines from a page-long press release, I thought that I could never do this with ease. I felt like a cheater. It seemed wrong."

The third semester I began to realize that their discontents arose not from the class but from the routine of adult life. I began the semester much the same as the second, but I guided the initial deliberations rather surreptitiously. I reduced the reading to *The Image*, by Daniel Boorstin. To counterpoint the theory of the text, I talked about specific sentences of the intern's work, sentences from press releases or news leads. Were these sentences fostering "image" or fighting it? We discussed the unseen constraints on these sentences and how, within those demands, the sentences might be rewritten. I invited fewer speakers, only those who demonstrated a willingness to share trade secrets and to quote starting salaries. The discussion of "problems and projects" continued but without the contagion of sudden firings and coercive drug use. That was contained and framed by the older interns, who were veterans now and able to dispense counsel.

I visited all work-sites again, as I had the previous year, to meet the new bosses. And I had papers now from previous students detailing each internship, so that each position had a history for me, one that I could invoke to explain or to complicate a student's complaints or questions about situations at work. When the interns discovered the papers, they wanted to know the history of the position before they began it.

Combined with a short list of speakers and a text of mesmerizingly simple theory, the job histories encouraged more criticism and analysis by the interns, though not about anything called "media writing." They started to think about their jobs, and themselves, because they did not want to accept what I had decided to make most logical: they were being routinized, being absorbed into the system. In each, I discovered, was this hidden fear that he or she would become a lifeless, methodical citizen after graduation. This feeling, Harold Rosenberg has written, "grows silently inside until you feel that there will be left of the original 'I' only a vague ache" ("Art and Politics," *Partisan Review*, 41 [1974], 381). By preying a little on this dread, I found I could promote critical thinking and better writing. In effect, I laid the significance of the stakes in the real world right on the table, for all to see. The real world is routinized, and the writing that it needs is largely formulaic, but its great successes are people who understand that creativity exists within and makes modifications on the proven formulas—people who think critically and infuse old genres with new vitality.

As one of my students wrote later, "Although I was growing more and more able to work within any given style of writing, I was also becoming more and more biased. I was learning to borrow, to adopt and modify the techniques and styles of others, but I strongly either liked or disliked their work. I wanted, at the same time, everything that I wrote to reflect me—it was a Mike C———production, even if my name wasn't on it."

The venerable press release seemed to most interns the Immovable Object of real world writing. "I thought there was no way to write one with a novel angle," wrote a public relations intern, "but I was put to trying, and in the process of trying to do it I found out how much more creativity there was in the process than I originally thought."

Poor working conditions were another annoyance that interns transmuted. "It was hard to write with people walking around behind me, looking over my shoulders," wrote one student. She turned her desk around a simple solution but one nobody in her office had tried. I understand that many desks are turned around in this office now. The interns, because they were temporary, were ideal candidates to introduce change in the workplace. After they left, I told them, regular workers would complain about them, even as they adopted their changes. And so a coffee pot appeared at one job, and plants graced the desks of another. For other interns, however, dealing with poor working conditions became a kind of battle scar. In the face of noise and distraction they now can achieve a self-absorption that I have only seen in metropolitan newsrooms. When they write on the microcomputers that our department maintains, they don't even pause as I stand behind them and read their work.

The veteran interns smirk when I push the dread button these days. They know about my own concerns for neatness, for deadlines, for strict parsing. They recognize the results of "routinization" in the teacher. But the smirkers are invaluable; for the new interns they are models of comparable age who are half-way to that state in which thinking-on-the-job is a viable way of life. This is what the interns have wanted from me all along—assurance that there is some path besides the Long March to Cipherdom if they venture out over the magic line of graduation. As one wrote recently, "I've discovered that I'm happier with some lack of predictability in my job than with the same secure but boring routine. This is perhaps the single most important lesson that I've learned in the last twelve months."

The accumulated history of each internship has become an important, unexpected cornerstone of the program. It means that few of the interns face completely new situations, which not only reassures but gives them a context in which they can place themselves at once. Each adds, almost competitively, to the file on the job to see who can best analyze the position. In conferences now I hear fewer complaints and I note more patterns being made. Some of the interns have already found that thinking critically is not entirely unrewarded in the real world.

What I have learned is that it does no good to camouflage the mundane and boring aspects of work. Every intern must be allowed to discover that routine, formula, and boredom are the common denominators and fundamental ground of the work world. Each must be allowed to preview the futility of the post-graduation world, to understand in a personal way that the "real world" does not need unalloyed "creativity," Only in this despair can a student's understanding be reordered. Originality, invention, creativity—these are tools against routine. But they are not the primary structure, as so many students go into the field believing. It does little good to forewarn, to discuss the problem ahead of time. I have learned to sense the downward swing, and when I see the new interns sitting silent, apart from the veterans—that's the day I begin to talk about graduation, and fear.

6
EFFECTS OF COLLEGE INTERNSHIPS ON INDIVIDUAL PARTICIPANTS

M. Susan Taylor

A methodological and analytical model for research assessing the value of internships, the study draws upon the disciplines of psychology, sociology and business to determine that students with internships had higher starting salaries and greater job satisfaction than non-interning students. In a follow-up study of how employers evaluated resumes, intern-experienced students were judged to be more qualified and more likely to get job offers than non-interns seeking the same entry level positions.

The benefits of internships, defined as structured and career-relevant work experiences obtained by students prior to graduation from an academic program, have been widely extolled by academicians, practitioners, and students themselves (Blensley, 1982; Hall, 1976; Ricchiute, 1980; Taylor & Dunham, 1980). Unfortunately, as noted by Super and Hall (1978), empirical support for the benefits of internships is not extensive. Much research consists of interns' retrospective reactions to their work assignments, which, not surprisingly, have tended to be favorable (Cole, Kolko, & Craddick, 1981; Davis, 1974). Although several studies have reported that internships yield high job satisfaction and favorable employment opportunities for participants, this research has rarely controlled for potential contaminants such as career goals and grade point average (Adler, Werner, & Korsch, 1980; McCaffery, 1979; McClam & Kessler, 1982). Nevertheless, despite a dearth of empirical support, the literature on job search and early work transitions suggests that internships may aid individuals in the difficult transition from school to work for at least three reasons: (a) greater crystallization of vocational self-concept and work values, (b) less reality shock, and (c) better employment opportunities.

CRYSTALLIZATION OF VOCATIONAL ABILITIES, INTERESTS, AND WORK VALUES

Internships are hypothesized to assist students in the crystallization of their vocational self-concept by facilitating the identification of vocationally relevant abilities, interests, and values (Hall, 1976). By performing job tasks relevant to the chosen vocational field, interns are expected to identify personally valued, work-related outcomes (e.g., co-workers pay, autonomy, and responsibility) and the vocational abilities and interests needed to attain satisfaction from the work arena. As a result, interns are likely to be more satisfied with their first jobs and more likely to remain in them than are students without such experience. Because the crystallization hypothesis has not been examined in previous studies, one objective of this research was to investigate its validity. Therefore, the following effects of internship experienced on participants' vocational crystallization are predicted. Hypothesis 1: Students with internship experience will differ from those without such experience with respect to (a) greater crystallization of vocational self-concept, (b) greater crystallization of values for work-related outcomes, and (c) higher levels of satisfaction with, and stronger intentions to remain on, the first job.

REALITY SHOCK

Interns also are expected to have an easier transition from school to work because they experience less reality shock on starting permanent jobs than do other students (Hall, 1976; Kramer, 1974). High levels of reality shock occur when individuals find that many of the work standards and procedures learned in school directly conflict with those required on the job. Consequently, they lose confidence in their preparation for work and experience high levels of anxiety that lowers their job performance, job satisfaction, and probability of remaining on the job (Kramer, 1974).

Research by Kramer (1974; Schmalenberg & Kramer, 1979) on student nurses suggested that internships may reduce the level of reality shock on the first job because participants experience these conflicts between work requirements and academic preparation while still in school and, thus, still exposed to both school and work cultures. Therefore, interns are more likely to resolve the conflict before starting their permanent jobs and feel less threatened at that time.

At least two studies have investigated predictions relevant to the reality shock hypothesis. Atkins (1980) examined a national sample of nursing graduates and found that former interns displayed higher job satisfaction and lower turnover on their first positions than did nurses without such experience. However, Atkins did not substantiate the reality shock explanation for these effects by examining nurses' confidence in their work preparation or the perceived conflict in work procedures and standards. Furthermore, a second study by Lindy, Green, and Patrick (1980) found that psychiatric residents with one year of internship experience performed worse on a measure of psychotherapy skills than did residents without internship experience. The authors attempted to explain their unexpected findings by proposing that exhausting and humiliating encounters experienced during the internship reduced the empathy of former interns. Thus, there is mixed support for the reality shock hypothesis in the literature, although it has not been thoroughly examined by previous studies. A second objective of this research was to further investigate the effects of internship experience on the reality shock syndrome. The following hypothesis was examined. Hypothesis 2: Students with internship experience will differ from those without such experience once they are on the first job with respect to (a) fewer perceived conflicts between the work methods, standards, and status quo procedures advocated by academic and organizational cultures and greater confidence in their preparation for work, (b) less anxiety and higher performance, and (c) higher job satisfaction and stronger intentions to remain once on the first job.

EMPLOYMENT OPPORTUNITIES

A third benefit of internships is hypothesized to be their positive impact on the employment opportunities students receive once leaving school (Henry, 1979; McClam & Kessler, 1982). Internships are thought to result in greater employment opportunities for two reasons. First, interns are expected to have greater access to informal job sources, that is, those that do not use an established third party to make contact between applicants and employees (e.g., work acquaintances and professional organizations) and, thus, are predicted to use these sources much more heavily than do other students who typically rely on more formal ones, such as the school placement office or newspaper ads. Informal sources have been found to generate higher quality (e.g., salary and type of position) and more satisfying job opportunities than the formal ones used extensively by students (Granovetter, 1974; Rosenfeld, 1975; Taylor, 1984). Second, employers are expected to evaluate the job qualifications of interns more positively and, thus, are more likely to hire interns than other students.

As a result of differences in job source utilization and perceived qualifications of the two groups, interns are expected to receive more job offers, accept higher salaried positions, and to be more satisfied with the accepted offer than are students without such experience.

The proposed impact of internship experience on labor-market opportunities seems quite intuitive. However, a literature search of relevant field studies identified only two studies that examined the employment opportunities hypothesis. Studying a sample of public administration graduates, Henry (1979) found that former interns took less time to attain their first position and, once employed, were more likely to have supervisory authority over 1 to 100 employees than were individuals without internship experience. It should be noted, however, that the study did not control for potential contaminants such as GPA [grade point average] or interns' receipt of job offers from their internship employers. Carroll (1966) examined the personal characteristics predictive of students' recruiting success and reported that the office work experience of business school graduates was directly related to the number of site visits and job offers they received during job search. On closer examination, the relation was found to be strongest for accounting majors whose office work experience consisted largely of accounting internships. Although correlational in nature, Carroll's research did control for many potential confounds such as career objectives, grades, and marital status. Thus, there is empirical support for the hypothesized relation between internship experience and employment opportunities, although previous research has not investigated the full set of dependent variables associated with the employment opportunity hypothesis.

A final objective of the present research was to provide a controlled test of these relations by examining the following hypothesis. Hypothesis 3: Students with internship experience will differ from those without such experience with respect to (a) more frequent use of informal job sources, (b) receipt of more job offers, acceptance of a higher salaried position, and greater satisfaction with accepted position, and (c) higher employment ratings and a greater probability of hire.

POTENTIAL MODERATING VARIABLES

Two of the three hypotheses discussed previously, regarding crystallization and reality shock, propose that internships stimulate psychological changes in participants (e.g., clarification of vocational self-concept, conflict, and anxiety). However, previous researchers have suggested that the effects proposed by these two hypotheses may be moderated by at least three variables: the similarity of work tasks performed during the internship to those found in entry-level positions in the chosen field, the amount of autonomy experienced on the internship, and the nature of the supervision received.

In the case of work task similarity, if interns do not perform work similar in nature and complexity to that of full-time entry-level positions in the vocational field, they would not be expected to achieve greater clarity of vocational self-concept or to experience substantial conflicts in work methods and procedures. Furthermore, it seems likely that some employers overstate the complexity of job tasks in order to recruit interns.

In the case of autonomy, researchers have found that jobs that allow incumbents a significant degree of self-direction (autonomy) tend to increase their ability to cope with the intellectual demands of complex situations (Kohn & Schooler, 1978) and their sense of personal efficacy (Brousseau, 1978, 1984; Kohn & Schooler, 1982). Similarly, it appears likely that such positions would increase individuals' opportunities to explore their vocational interests, values, and so forth, and enhance their ability to resolve potential conflicts between the procedures and standards advocated by school and work.

Finally, both Kramer (1974) and Schein (1968) have noted the importance of the supervision experienced when a new employee enters a work organization. In general, effective supervision is seen as being supportive of the newcomer and thereby increases, rather than lowers, self-esteem, demonstrates high work standards and competence, provides frequent feedback, and develops the individual through coaching. Seemingly, individuals exposed to effective supervision during their internships also would experience better opportunities to explore their vocational values and interests and be more likely to resolve work conflicts prior to beginning their permanent jobs.

Thus, prior research and writing have suggested that the degree of work similarity, autonomy, and effective supervision received will positively moderate the effects proposed by the crystallization and reality shock hypotheses. No moderating effects are proposed for the employment opportunity hypothesis because it is dependent on referrals and perceived qualifications rather than on characteristics of the assignment itself. Because of the difficulty in controlling the work complexity, autonomy, and supervision experienced by interns working in different positions and organizations, these variables were examined as potential moderators in the study.

STUDY 1

METHOD

SAMPLE

A total of 67 students, 32 interns and 35 cohorts, from a large midwestern university participated in Study 1. The small discrepancy in group sizes was not planned but has considerable precedent in

Table 1 Descriptive Statistics for Intern and Cohort Samples

Variable	Intern	Cohort
Age	23	23
Credits toward major	56	62
Grade point average	3.27	3.21
Marital status		
Single	30(94%)	33(94%)
Married	2(6%)	2(6%)
No. of months of relevant part-time work experience	4	4
Sex		
Female	18(55%)	15(43%)
Male	14(42%)	20(57%)

prior research on internships (Atkins, 1980; Henry, 1979; Lindy, Green, & Patrick, 1980).[1] Intern and cohort groups did not differ significantly with respect to age, credits toward degree, GPA, marital status, or work experience related to field of study. Descriptive statistics for the two samples are shown in Table 1.

PROCEDURE AND RESEARCH DESIGN

In selecting participants, an internship was defined as

A position held within an established organization while completing the college degree which required approximately 200 hours of work within an 8–15 week period and the performance of job tasks similar in nature and level to those carried out by college graduates employed in the relevant field of study.

Students having prior internship experience were not included in the study.

Interns and cohorts were obtained by contacting faculty advisors in academic departments that encouraged, but did not require, internships for their students. The use of departments requiring internship experience would have prohibited the assembly of a cohort group. At least six interns were taken from each of the following academic departments: business, engineering, industrial relations, interior design, and journalism. Students were asked to participate in a study of the school-to-work transition. Only one individual, an intern, declined to do so. Participation was voluntary, but individuals received from $5 to $8 for completing each of the four questionnaires used in the research. Once an intern agreed to participate in the study, faculty advisors were asked to assist in locating a matched cohort.

A quasi-experimental design, pre- and postmeasures with control group, was used for the study, inasmuch as participants could not be randomly assigned to experimental conditions. Questionnaires were administered at the following times: (a) preinternship—immediately before beginning the internship or during its first week, (b) postinternship—at the end of the internship, (c) job search—immediately prior to the students' graduation from the academic program, and (d) postwork—after working on the new job for 8 weeks. Cohorts provided data at the same measurement point as their interns for the first three measures and at a comparable time for the fourth measure. Participants who failed to return the questionnaires within 2 weeks received follow-up phone calls.

Sample sizes remained approximately the same throughout the first three measurement points. However, because funding that supported the research expired after a 1-year period, participants who failed to find employment within 2 months after college graduation were excluded from the fourth (postwork) measurement. This policy reduced the total sample size to 30 for the fourth measurement period.

MEASUREMENT OF VARIABLES

Several instruments were developed for the research because established measures were not available. A principle factoring method with iteration and a varimax rotation was performed on items written to tap relevant constructs in order to confirm the factor structure (Nie, Hull, Jenkins, Steinbrenner, & Bent, 1975). Cronbach's (1951) alpha is reported as an index of internal consistency. The alpha reported is the mean value across all measurements.

Variables were calculated as the mean of all items included in a scale. Except where noted, high scores indicate high levels of the variables. Intercorrelations between dependent variables ranged from −.70 to .60, with a median of .28. Table 2 shows the measurement periods at which variables were assessed.

CRYSTALLIZATION HYPOTHESIS

Four variables were used to examine the hypothesized effects of internships on individuals' identification of vocal abilities and work values.

Table 2 Measurement Points for Dependent Variables Assessed in Study 1

Variable	Measurement point			
	Pre-intern	Post-intern	Job search	Post-work
Crystallization of vocation self-concept	X	X		
Values for work outcomes	X	X		
Job satisfaction				X
Intention to remain on job				X
Conflict in work methods or standards	X	X		X
Conflict with the status quo	X	X		X
Confidence in work preparation	X	X		X
Anxiety				X
Job performance				X
Autonomy of internship		X		
Effectiveness of supervision		X		X
Work similarity		X		
Use of job sources			X	
No. of job offers			X	
Salary of new job			X	
Satisfaction with job offer			X	

* These variables were assessed only for interns.

CRYSTALLIZATION OF VOCATIONAL SELF-CONCEPT

Crystallization of vocational self-concept was assessed with a short form of the Vocational Rating Scale (VRS; Barrett & Tinsley, 1977). Developed to assess the clarity and certainty of self-perceived patterns in vocational abilities and interests, the VRS has demonstrated high internal consistency reliability ($a = .94$) in previous research and has been related to students' confidence in their vocational decision (Barrett & Tinsley, 1977), the number of job offers received during job search, and satisfaction with accepted position (Taylor, 1985). The 24 items used in this study displayed a coefficient alpha of .86.

VALUES FOR WORK OUTCOMES

The crystallization of work values was assessed by examining pre- and postinternship changes in the reward value section of the Temperament and Values and Inventory (Johansson & Webber, 1976). The instrument was designed to assess individual differences in work reinforcement hierarchies that are relevant to career choices. It includes 97 items that assess the importance of various rewards for individuals' happiness. The measure yields seven dimensions of work values: (a) social recognition—sensitivity to the friendliness and respect of others in the work environment, (b) managerial/sales benefits value for fringe benefits usually associated with managerial and sales promotions, (c) leadership—desire to be responsible for hiring, firing, leading, and directing people as well as making major decisions, (d) social service—value for activities relating to the helping of others, (e) task specificity—desire to work on tasks in which performance standards are well-defined and in which one receives clear feedback about work progress, (f) philosophical curiosity value for activities that explore the meaning of the laws of nature, scientific discoveries, the meaning of life, and so forth, and (g) work independence—the importance of being one's own boss, scheduling work time, and deciding how work should be done. In this research the seven subscales yielded coefficient alphas of .84, .67, .64, .85, .74, .77, and .70, respectively. No criterion-related validity data have been reported by the instrument's developers.

JOB SATISFACTION

Individuals' overall satisfaction with their new job was assessed with the short form of the Index of Organizational Reactions (Dunham & Smith, 1979). The instrument assesses satisfaction with eight job facets: amount of work, career opportunities, co-workers, organization, physical conditions, pay, supervisors and type of work. It is supported by an extensive research base that includes evidence of internal consistency reliability, as well as construct and predictive validity (Dunham & Smith, 1979). The 20 items used for this study displayed a coefficient alpha of .72.

INTENTIONS TO REMAIN ON JOB

Individuals' intention to remain on the new job was used as a surrogate measure of turnover for the research because individuals were studied only through their second month on the job. Behavioral intentions have shown a consistently strong relation to actual turnover in much prior research (Mobley, Griffeth, Hand & Meglino, 1979).

The Staying or Letwing Index was used to assess behavioral intentions in this study. The index asks about participants' intentions to remain with their present employer. The six items used in this study yielded a coefficient alpha of .93.

REALITY SHOCK HYPOTHESIS

In addition to the job satisfaction and intention to remain on the job—variables described in the previous section—five variables were used to examine the reality shock hypothesis.

CONFLICT BETWEEN METHODS AND STANDARDS OF WORK AND SCHOOL

Four items were used to tap perceived conflict between the standards and methods advocated by the work and school environments. The items asked students how closely professionals in their field followed methods and practices taught by textbooks and professors, how different the expected methods used at work to be from what was learned in school and how useful what was learned in school would be on the job. These items yielded a coefficient alpha of .81.

CONFLICT WITH THE STATUS QUO PROCEDURES

Two items were used to assess students' expectations concerning employers' reactions to conflicts between the organizations' work procedures and those used by students. The items were of a Likert form and stated (a) that employees would prefer one to use the best way of doing the job even if it conflicted with the status quo and (b) that students would get credit for pointing out more effective work procedures. The alpha coefficient for this scale was .58. A high score reflected a low level of conflict.

CONFIDENCE IN PREPARATION FOR WORK

Students' confidence in their work preparation was measured with three items asking about their level of preparation to perform a full-time job in the major field of study, confidence in performing well on the first job, and coworkers' likely evaluation of their work preparation. The coefficient alpha was .60. High scores are indicative of low levels of confidence.

ANXIETY

Level of anxiety on the first job was assessed with the IPAT 8-Parallel Form D Anxiety Banery (Scheier & Canell, 1973). The battery was developed as a measure of free floating anxiety, independent of other personality factors. Test developers have provided evidence of construct validity and alternate form reliability. In this study, the instrument yielded a coefficient alpha of .77.

JOB PERFORMANCE

Level of job performance was measured by individuals' self-assessments of their overall job performance using an eight item scale developed by Sundstrom (1977). Items ask individuals to rate their performance on timeliness, mistakes, quality, quantity, accuracy, coworker relations, and overall effectiveness. The measure yielded a coefficient alpha of .73.

The use of self-ratings to assess performance is consistent with conclusions by Carroll and Schneier (1982); on reviewing the literature, these authors concluded that self-ratings may provide valuable performance information and contain less leniency than do supervisory ratings. They advocated use of self-ratings for performance appraisal under conditions of high trust in superior-subordinate relationships. Such conditions seem irrelevant for this study because participants were aware that ratings would be kept confidential and would be used only for research purposes.

POTENTIAL MODERATING VARIABLES

Three potential moderators of the crystallization and reality shock hypotheses were examined.

WORK SIMILARITY

The similarity of work performed on the internship to that of full-time, entry-level positions in the field was measured with four items asking whether the internship tasks were similar in nature and complexity to those in entry-level jobs. The coefficient alpha of these items was .69.

AUTONOMY

The degree of autonomy experienced in the internship was assessed by three items asking about the extent to which individuals were permitted to do the job on their own, use their own discretion, and exercise independent thought and action. The coefficient alpha for this Scale was .73.

SUPERVISION

The effectiveness of the supervision experienced in the internship was assessed by nine items that asked about the supervisor's competence, supportiveness, and willingness to help interns improve their performance and value as a source of performance feedback. The coefficient alpha for this scale was .89.

EMPLOYMENT OPPORTUNITY HYPOTHESIS

Two sets of variables were used to test the employment opportunity hypothesis: individuals' use of job sources and the equality of employment opportunities.

USE OF JOB SOURCES

Individuals' use of informal job sources was assessed by asking how frequently they used a combined index of informal sources (direct applications, friends or relatives, and professional organizations). The coefficient alpha was .66.

NATURE OF EMPLOYMENT OPPORTUNITIES

The employment opportunities experienced by participants were assessed by the number of job offers received, starting salary of accepted offer, and satisfaction with accepted job. Satisfaction with accepted job was measured on two dimensions: (a) satisfaction with position—the nature of the position, the organization where employed, and the level of the position in the organization, and (b) extrinsic satisfaction with pay and with geographic location. The alpha values of the dimensions were .69 and .67, respectively.

ANALYSES

Data were analyzed using multivariate and univariate analyses of variance and covariance (MANOVAS, ANOVAS, and ANCOVAS, respectively). In cases in which multiple measures of variables were collected (e.g., vocational self-concept, work values, conflict in work methods and standards, work-school conflict, conflict with status quo, confidence in preparation for work), the earliest measurement of the variables was used as a covariate. Except for the work value scales (in which crystallization was operationally defined as a change in either direction), directional hypotheses were proposed and one-tailed tests were used to examine them.

Effects of the three moderating variables—work similarity, au-

Table 3 Group Means for Crystallization Hypothesis

Variable	Intern M	Cohort M	F value
Crystallization of vocational self-concept	3.93	3.63	5.14*
Value for work-related outcomes[a]			1.60
Job satisfaction	3.89	3.85	0.07
Intention to remain	3.78	3.53	0.64

[a] Value is appropriate F yielded by multivariate analysis of covariance test conducted on the seven work values.
* $p < .05$ ** $p < .01$.

tonomy, and effectiveness of supervision—were assessed by dividing the intern sample at the medial value for both variables and examining the group of interns scoring above the medial value for autonomy and effective supervision. A series of ANOVAS (or ANCOVAS for multiple measurement variables) were performed to compare the sub-sample of interns ($n = 15$) with their cohorts.

RESULTS

CRYSTALLIZATION HYPOTHESIS

Hypothesis 1 predicted that students with internship experience would display greater crystallization of their vocational abilities and interests and of their value for work-related outcomes during the internship period than would cohorts. Interns also were expected to report higher job satisfaction and stronger intentions to remain on the new job once they were employed. Results provided partial support for the hypothesis. The ANCOVA performed on the crystallization of vocational self-concept was significant, $F(1, 61) = 5.14$, $p < .05$. However, the MANCOVA analysis performed on the seven work values did not yield significant results. Furthermore, the ANOVAS performed on individuals' job satisfaction and their intention to remain in the organization were not significant (see Table 3).

REALITY SHOCK HYPOTHESIS

The reality shock hypothesis predicted that interns would experience fewer value conflicts and display more confidence in their work

Table 4 Group Means for Reality Shock Hypothesis

Variable	Intern M	Cohort M	F value
Conflict in procedures and standards	2.91	2.81	0.00
Conflict with the status quo	2.29	2.20	0.40
Confidence in work preparation	3.04	2.95	1.82
Job performance	5.58	5.29	0.02
Anxiety	0.81	.84	0.23

preparation, less anxiety, and higher performance. This hypothesis was tested with ANCOVAS using the postinternship measures of conflict and confidence as covariates. The hypothesis was not supported because the ANCOVAS revealed no significant effects for conflict experienced during the internship period or once participants started to work (see Table 4).

TESTS OF POTENTIAL MODERATORS

The ANOVAS and ANCOVAS were conducted on the subsamples of interns (and cohorts) selected because of their high scores on the moderating variables. Because this study was a preliminary examination of all three hypotheses, the costs of a Type II error was considered higher than that of a Type I error. Therefore, given the reduced sample size available to examine the moderator hypothesis, a significant level of .10 was used. Results revealed little support for the role of work similarity or supervision as moderating variables. However, when assignment autonomy was used as a moderator, weak but consistent support was found for parts of the crystallization and reality shock hypotheses.

In the crystallization case, interns displayed a significantly greater crystallization of their vocational self-concept, and stronger intentions to remain on the job ($p < .10$) than did their cohorts (see Table 5). However, no differences were found between the groups on work values or overall job satisfaction. For the reality shock hypothesis, interns tended to report fewer conflicts with the status quo, higher job performance, and (as noted earlier) a greater intention to remain on the job. No differences were found for conflicts in work methods and standards, confidence in work preparation, anxiety, or job satisfaction.

Table 5 Group Means for High Autonomy Interns and their Cohorts

Variable	Intern M	Cohort M	F value
Crystallization hypothesis			
Crystallization of vocational self-concept	3.95	3.72	2.34*
Work values			0.63[a]
Job satisfaction	4.05	3.81	1.06
Intention to remain	4.02	3.66	1.82*
Reality shock hypothesis			
Conflict in methods or standards	2.75	2.71	0.11
Conflict with status quo procedures	2.44	2.02	2.25*
Confidence in work preparation	2.92	2.92	0.00
Job performance	6.08	5.39	2.47*
Anxiety	0.80	0.77	0.06

EMPLOYMENT OPPORTUNITIES HYPOTHESIS

Hypothesis 3 predicted that interns would use informal sources more frequently than did cohorts. Interns also were expected to receive more job offers and higher starting salaries and to express greater satisfaction with their accepted positions. Because moderating effects were not predicted for this hypothesis, it was examined using the full sample of interns and cohorts. The hypothesis was partially supported. Interns reported using the composite of informal sources significantly more frequently than did the cohorts, $F(1, 54) = 4.61$, $p < .05$ (see Table 6). Furthermore, the informal source variable was significantly correlated with job salary for both the intern and cohort groups ($r = .52$, $p < .01$, and $r = .43$, $p < .03$, respectively). In addition, the MANOVA performed on the number of job offers received, starting salary, and satisfaction with new position variables was significant, $F(4, 16) = 3.97$, $p < .05$.[2] Interns received significantly higher starting salaries and, not surprisingly, expressed greater satisfaction with the extrinsic rewards associated with the new job. However, the two groups did not differ significantly on the number of offers received or in their satisfaction with accepted position (see Table 6), nor did the percentage of students accepting jobs by the time of

Table 6 Group Means for Employment Opportunity Hypothesis in Study 1

Variable	Intern M	Cohort M	F value
Use of informal sources	.057	0.23	4.61*
Job offers	2.45	1.90	1.11
Starting salary of position	$24,440	$19,030	5.50**
Extrinsic satisfaction	4.64	3.70	13.13**
Position satisfaction	4.39	4.23	0.51

* $p < .05$ ** $p < .01$ for the predicted one-tailed test.

graduation differ significantly for the intern (39%) and cohort groups (35%).

STUDY 2

METHOD

OVERVIEW/PROCEDURE

Study 2 was conducted to provide additional evidence concerning the impact of internship experience on employment opportunities, inasmuch as the expiration of funding required terminating the study before many students found jobs. Organizational recruiters interviewing students at a large midwestern university were contacted by mail and asked to participate in a study of the college applicant evaluation process. Recruiters provided demographic information and evaluated three student resumes. They were informed that their responses would be kept confidential and were promised a copy of the research findings. Recruiters who did not respond in a 2-week period were sent a follow-up letter.

SAMPLE

A sample of 128 recruiters participated in the study, yielding a response rate of 51%. However, because several recruiters did not see three items inadvertently printed on the backside of pages, a smaller subsample of 101 recruiters providing complete data was used for the study. The typical participant was a 33-year-old man (77%) with a bachelors degree, 4 years of recruiting experience, and 7 years of tenure with the recruiting organization. A majority of the recruiters were employed by manufacturing (25%), insurance (18%), banking (15%), or retail organizations (11%) and worked in personnel (41%) or actuarial (10%) positions.

INDEPENDENT VARIABLE

Three resumes were constructed to manipulate internship experience. They were based on actual resumes obtained from campus placement offices. All depicted a slightly above average, undergraduate student majoring in accounting, mechanical engineering, or personnel management and provided information about career objective, education, extracurricular activities, GPA, and work experience. For example, career objectives expressed the desire to obtain a position in personnel staffing, financial analysis, or thermal systems that would provide increasing responsibility, high interest, or would make good use of the applicant's abilities. Extracurricular activities included professional organizations, fraternities/sororities, intramural sports, and hobbies such as reading science fiction. Grade point average was varied slightly around 3.30 on a 4-point scale. Work experience included two to three summer and part-time work activities that were not related to the student's major field of study (e.g., lifeguarding, waiting tables, short-order cook, clerical aide).

Internship experience was manipulated by substituting one summer of major relevant work experience for one of the summer work experiences described in the previous paragraph. The experience included the performance of job tasks in one major function (e.g., analyzed career development opportunities) and the observation of other major functions (e.g., observed grievance procedures, attended disciplinary hearings). All other information was held constant across the resume conditions.

RESEARCH DESIGN

An experimental simulation was used to evaluate the impact of internship experience on recruiters' evaluations of students' job qualifications and the probability of various hiring actions. A single experimental factor, internship experience (i.e., absence vs. presence), was used. In order to increase the generalizability of findings across different internships, participants were randomly assigned to one of the internship conditions for each of three resumes (accounting, mechanical engineering, and personnel management). Because resumes differed on many dimensions (e.g., sex, major career goal, extracurricular activities) besides work experience, it seems unlikely that participants' receipt of three resumes caused them to readily identify the purpose of the research, cell sizes ranged from 56 to 70.

DEPENDENT VARIABLES

JOB QUALIFICATIONS

Applicants were evaluated on their job objective, professional activities, extracurricular activities, leadership, and work experience. Recruiters were instructed to compare applicant's qualifications for a position in their organization with those of other students interviewed. The coefficient alpha for this measure was .67.

HIRING ACTIONS

The probability that a recruiter's organization would take various hiring actions on a resume also was measured. Items asked about the likelihood of keeping the resume on file, referring it to the relevant department, having the candidate come in for an interview, having the applicant visit the work site, extending an offer, and so forth. The coefficient alpha for this variable was .71.

ANALYSES

Analysis of variance was used to analyze the data. The three resumes were treated as constructive replications and analyzed separately.

RESULTS

The final employment opportunities hypothesis predicted that interns would receive higher employment evaluations from recruiters and would have a greater probability of hire. Students with internship experience were evaluated as being significantly more qualified than were students without internships in all three resume conditions, $F(1, 96) = 40.67, 42.40,$ and $45.33, p < .01$, respectively (see Table 7). Recruiters also indicated that the probability of hiring actions was significantly greater for interns in one of the three resume conditions and tended to be greater in a second condition, $F(1, 96) = 5.48, p < .05; 0.44, ns;$ and $3.72, p < .06$, respectively. In combination, these results provide strong support for the hypothesized effects of internships on employment evaluations and the probability of hire.

Table 7 Group Means for Recruiter Evaluation in Study 2

Variable	Intern M	Cohort M	F value
Job qualifications, Resume 1	3.18	2.51	40.67***
Hiring actions, Resume 1	3.22	2.62	5.58**
Job qualifications, Resume 2	2.99	2.32	42.40***
Hiring actions, Resume 2	3.73	3.35	0.44
Job qualifications, Resume 3	3.21	2.50	45.33***
Hiring actions, Resume 3	3.71	3.08	3.72*

$*\, p < .08.\ **\, p.05\ ***\, p < .01.$

GENERAL DISCUSSION

This research used two relatively rigorous designs (pre- and post-measures with matched cohorts and an experimental simulation) in order to investigate hypotheses concerning the effects of college internships: (a) greater crystallization of vocational self-concept and work values, (b) less reality shock once on the first job, and (c) better employment opportunities when compared with matched cohorts. Although initial results provided support for only the employment opportunity hypothesis, somewhat different findings emerged when the amount of autonomy experienced on the internship was used as a moderator variable.

Consistent, albeit weak, differences emerged from the moderator analyses. High autonomy interns showed significantly greater benefits than did their cohorts on many of the hypothesized crystallization and reality shock variables. These findings are important ones because of their potential utility for reducing the difficulty of students' school-to-work transition (Taylor, 1985). The consistency of the moderator results suggests that the relevant question may not be whether vocational crystallization and decreased reality shock are benefits of internship, but rather, under what conditions they are benefits. Thus, it seems very important to replicate the research on a larger sample that permits stronger tests of hypothesized moderators.

Relatively strong support for the employment opportunity hypothesis emerged from both studies in this research. Interns reported using informal job sources significantly more heavily, received more positive evaluations from organizational recruiters, accepted higher salaried positions, and expressed greater satisfaction with the extrinsic rewards of their accepted position. Each of these findings indicates that interns have a distinct advantage over their peers in the labor market. Although these results are quite intuitive, internship experience has not been linked to job search methods, starting salary, or satisfaction with new position by prior research. Thus, one implication of the findings may be that the time and effort invested in an internship, as opposed to the earlier completion of the academic degree, is cost effective for many students in the long run.

In combination, the two studies presented here provided partial support for all three hypothesized benefits of internships. However, in evaluating these findings, several methodological weaknesses of the research bear mentioning. Readers should note the relatively low internal consistency reliability coefficients found for several measures used in the study. Because there seems to be no noticeable association between the significance of results and the reliability of measures and because the reliability of most scales exceeded the .70 criteria recommended for preliminary research by Nunally (1978), it does not appear that the lower internal consistency reliability had a substantial effect on the results.

It is also important to recognize that individuals were not randomly assigned to conditions in Study 1 and, thus, may have differed on other variables affecting vocational self-concept, reality shock, and labor market opportunities. Nevertheless, obvious potential confounds such as age, career goals, grades, sex, stage in academic program, and work experience were controlled. This fact strengthens the internal validity of the results.

In addition, sample sizes for the job search and postwork periods clearly reduced the power of the relevant statistical tests performed on measures assessed during these periods. A power analysis conducted on data from the postwork period indicated that, even if differences between the two populations means was equal to $1 \ 1/2 * SDs$ of dependent variable, the probability of rejecting the null hypothesis would be only about 50%. Thus, the power issue is an important one in this research. Power concerns were the basis for a decision to use a higher probability level for testing moderator effects. Although the use of a .10 level of significance for the moderated tests may be questioned, the threat of a Type II error appeared serious enough to warrant such a course of action.

Finally, readers should note the possible bias introduced by the amount of relevant work experience cohorts reported having in the study. Although great care was taken to select cohorts without prior internship experience, both interns and cohorts averaged 4 months of part-time, relevant work experience. The likely impact of this work experience would be to obscure hypothesized group differences on the crystallization and reality shock variables. Thus, interns may experience even greater benefits when compared with less experienced cohort groups.

Aside from methodological limitations, it is relevant to note that this research did not examine all of the mechanisms through which interns may benefit from their work experience. For example, interns may sharpen social skills that subsequently assist them in interviewing successfully for full-time work. They also may acquire technical skills (e.g., conducting a job analysis) that increase their value to potential employers. In addition, the very fact that an individual is selected for a highly competitive internship may benefit him or her because of the resulting assumptions that prospective employers make about the intern's job qualifications. Finally, many interns may subsequently accept permanent positions from their host organizations, although this was not the case in the present study. Only two interns accepted positions from their employers in this research. Nevertheless, each of these mechanisms generally would be expected to result in greater employment opportunities for internship participants and may, in fact, have accounted for some of the opportunity effects found here.[3] Therefore, they seem worthy of investigation in future research on internships.

In conclusion, further research is needed to replicate these findings on larger student samples over a longer postemployment period. Future research also should examine potential advantages of internships other than those studied here, and further investigate logical moderators of the internship effect (e.g., effectiveness of supervision, work similarity, and work challenge). Special consideration should be given to the design of studies with sample sizes that permit powerful comparisons between interns and cohorts, as well as between different types of internship experiences (e.g., between journalism and personnel internships).

NOTES

1. The size of the two groups differed because one intern reversed his decision to participate after his cohort had agreed to join the study and because, in two cases, interns could not be matched to one cohort as closely as desired with respect to grade point average and relevant work experience. Thus, they were matched with two cohorts.
2. Sample size was reduced for the salary and satisfaction variables because

many students had not found jobs by college graduation, the time when the third measure was collected.
3. The author is indebted to an anonymous reviewer for making these points.

REFERENCES

Adler, R., Werner, E. R., & Korsch, B. (1980). Systematic study of four year internships. *Pediatrics*. 66. 1000–1008.

Atkins, P. B. (1980). *The relationship of nurse internships to longevity of first employment, job satisfaction and cost effectiveness*. Unpublished doctoral dissertation, University of San Francisco. (Order No. 8110585)

Barrett, T. C., & Tinsley, H. E. (1977). Vocational self-concept crystallization and vocational indecision. *Journal of Counseling Psychology* 24, 301–307.

Blensley, D. L. (1982). Internships: A personal account. *Journal of Accounting, 154,* 48–49.

Brousseau, K. R. (1978). Personality and job experience. *Organizational Behavior and Human Performance,* 22, 235–252.

Brousseau, K. R. (1984). Job-person dynamics and career development. In K. M. Rowland & G. R. Ferris (Eds.), *Research in personnel and human resources management* (Vol.2, pp. 125–154). Greenwich, CT: JAI Press.

Carroll, S. J. (1966). Relationship of various college graduate characteristics to recruiting decisions. *Journal of Applied Psychology, 50,* 421–423.

Carroll, S. J., & Schneier, C. E. (1982). *Performance appraisal and review systems.* Glenview, IL: Scott, Foresman.

Cole, M. A., Kolko, A. J., & Craddick, R. A. (1981). The quality and process of the internship experience. *Professional Psychology, 12,* 570–577.

Cronbach, L. J. (1951). Coefficient alpha and the internal structure of tests. *Psychometrika, 16,* 297–334.

Davis, R. M. (1974, June). Practitioners' perceptions of their internships. *Counselor Education and Supervision,* 303–305.

Dunham, R. B., & Smith, F. J. (1979). *Organizational surveys.* Glenview, IL: Scott, Foresman.

Granovetter, M. S. (1974). *Getting a job: A study of contracts and careers.* Cambridge, MA: Harvard University Press.

Hall, D. T. (1976). *Careers in organizations.* Santa Monica, CA: Goodyear.

Henry, N. (1979, May-June). Are internships worthwhile? *Public Administration Review.* 245–247.

Johansson, C. B., & Webber, P. L. (1976). *Temperament and values inventory.* Champaign, IL: National Computer Systems.

Kohn, M. L., & Schooler, C. (1978). The reciprocal effects of substantive complexity of work and intellectual flexibility. A longitudinal assessment. *American Journal of Sociology,* 84, 24–52.

Kohn, M. L., & Schooler, C. (1982). Job conditions and personality: A longitudinal assessment of their reciprocal effects. *American Journal of Sociology,* 87, 1257–1286.

Kramer, M. (1974). *Reality shock: Why nurses leave nursing.* St. Louis, MO: Mosby.

Lindy, J. D., Green, B., & Patrick, M. (1980). The internship: Some disquieting findings. *American Journal of Psychiatry*, 137,1, 76–79.

McCaffery, J. L. (1979, May-June). Perceptions of satisfaction in the internship experience. *Public Administration Review*, 241–244.

McClam, T., & Kessler, M. H. (1982). Human services internships. *Journal of College Placement*, *42*, 45–47.

Mobley, W. H., Griffeth, R. W., Hand, H. H., & Medino, B. M. (1979). Review and conceptual analysis of employee turnover processes. *Psychological Bulletin*, *86*, 493–522.

Nie, N. H., Hull, C. H., Jenkins, J. G., Steinbrenner, K., & Bent, D. H. (1975). *Statistical package for the social sciences*. New York: McGraw-Hill.

Nunally, J. C. (1978). *Psychometric theory* (2nd ed.). New York: McGraw-Hill.

Ricchiute, D. N. (1980, July). Internships and the local practitioner. *Journal of Accounting*, 35–46.

Rosenfeld, C. (1975). Job seeking methods used by American workers. *Monthly Labor Review*, 8, 39–42.

Schein, E. (1968, March). The first job dilemma. *Psychology Today*, 29–31.

Scheier, I. H. & Cattell, R. B. (1973). *IPAT 8-Parallel Form D Anxiety Battery*. Champaign, IL: Institute for Personality and Ability Testing.

Schmalenberg, C., & Kramer, M. (1979). *Coping with reality shock*. Wakefield, MA: Nursing Resources.

Sundstrom, E. (1977). Interpersonal behavior and the physical environment. In L. Wrightsman, *Social Psychology* (2nd ed., pp. 510–549). Monterey, CA: Brooks-Cole.

Super, D. E., & Hall, D. T. (1978). Career development: Exploration and planning. *Annual Review of Psychology*, 29, 33–72.

Taylor, M. S. (1984). Strategies and sources in the student job search. *Journal of College Placement*, *44*, 40–45.

Taylor M. S. (1985). The roles of occupational knowledge and crystallization of vocational self-concept in students' school to work transition. *Journal of Counseling Psychology*, *32*, 539–550.

Taylor, M. S., & Dunham, R. B. (1980, October). A program for planned student and personnel practitioner interactions. *Personnel Administrator*, 35–37.

III. OVERVIEW

7
UPDATE: BROADCAST INTERN PROGRAMS AND PRACTICES

Milan D. Meeske

A survey of 319 institutional members of the Broadcast Education Association reveals great variance in the organization, requirements, and administration of broadcast internships. The lack of uniform structure may pose problems for sponsoring organizations that accept interns from more than one school.

Nearly all of the radio-television departments polled in a recent nationwide survey say they offer a professional internship program. This reflects the importance of professional experience in the curriculum and the willingness of schools to give academic credit for work done outside the direct supervision of faculty. Other findings:

- The majority of schools do not require their students to take an internship
- Only a few schools have paid internships for all their students.
- Most broadcast educators do not feel that internships exploit students as cheap labor.

I sent a questionnaire to the 319 two- and four-year schools that are institutional members of the Broadcast Education Association (BEA). I received replies from 207 (65 percent) of the schools

All but 2 of the schools (99 percent) have a formal broadcasting internship program in their curriculum. A 1982 study found that 91 percent of the broadcast programs had formal internship programs.[1] In one of the two schools that reported not having internship programs, the broadcast program was new and would soon have an internship program. The other school said it offered paid programs through its cooperative education office.

The number of students who intern in the programs ranges from as few as 5 a year to more than 100. This is a function of both enrollment and geographical location. Many schools offer internships during the academic year when students also take classes and must intern in the local area. However, summer internships are often completed in another city.

Two-thirds of the schools will not permit students to repeat an internship (same location and job). Some who said they permit students to repeat internships do so only up to a given number of credit hours or if a student is advancing in work experience.

More than 50 percent of broadcast students intern with radio or television stations, but students also intern with other media, including cable TV systems (20 percent), industrial video operations (17 percent) and broadcast related businesses such as advertising agencies and non-profit organizations (8 percent).

Students usually aren't permitted to intern until they reach a given point in their program. Half of the four-year schools require students to be juniors, while 40 percent require them to be seniors. Fifteen of the 22 two-year schools that replied will not let students intern until they are sophomores. Twenty percent of the respondents report internships for graduate students.

Many schools have a GPA requirement for interns, from 2.0 to more than a 3.0 on a 4.0 scale. Two schools require more than a 3.0. A common pattern is to require different GPA figures for overall coursework and major coursework. For example, a school may require a 2.75 overall GPA and a 3.00 GPA in major coursework to qualify for an internship.

Students must also meet other criteria to qualify for internships. Nearly 60 percent of schools require the completion of specified courses, and 30 percent require that prospective interns be evaluated by faculty members. Many schools require a combination of qualification criteria.

The amount of credit students can earn for internships ranges from 1 to 15 hours. The 15-hour figure, and others close to it, are generally used when students intern full-time for an academic term. Half the schools say students can earn 3 credit hours in a term, while a third permit student to earn 6 hours.

The total number of credit hours permitted for internship credit varies widely. Several schools said they award no more than 3 hours of internship credit, while several schools report having no limit. The most frequent figure cited was 3 hours of credit (27 percent) followed by 6 hours (24 percent).

The number of work hours required in an academic term varies according to the amount of credit. A typical plan, for instance, requires students to spend 3 hours interning for each hour of credit. This obligates interns to 9 or more work hours per week.

Sixty percent of the schools give letter grades for internships, while 40 use a pass/fail approach. Three schools said they don't give grades.

Faculty members use a number of ways to determine grades. Almost two-thirds rely on student reports, but 58 percent also use letters from industry supervisors. Just over one-third of the respondents make visits to the internship site while another 16 percent have their students submit research papers.

MANDATORY OR PAID?

Only 20 percent of the schools require students to take internships. Respondents cited several reasons for keeping internships optional. Some said not all students are academically deserving of internships. Others said the difficulties of administering internships for all majors is prohibitive. This is particularly true in schools that have a large number of students interning.

Only 10 schools report having paid internships for all students. Half of the schools said that up to 50 percent of their internships are paid and eight schools reported that 50 to 100 percent are paid.

The amount of pay varies; it is often minimum wage. Some employers pay a stipend on the premise that interns are not employees, and stations are thus not obligated to provide employee benefits like insurance and unemployment.[2]

Schools often use more than one method to initiate internships. Three-fourths said students find internship positions and then work out arrangements with faculty. Many schools prefer to have faculty work out internship arrangements to avoid situations that take advantage of students.

Internships are supervised in a number of ways. At a third of the schools, the department chairperson designates one faculty member as internship coordinator, who is given release time, usually one course per term. Where a faculty member supervises interns in the summer session, extra pay is sometimes supplied in lieu of release time.

One-quarter of the schools assign the job to faculty members on top of their course load. In that case, students may be supervised by their academic adviser or a faculty member with expertise in the students' area of interest. Not surprisingly, some of the complaints about internships were directed at this method of assignment.

The third most common method of supervising internships is to assign the job to an administrator. In some cases, the departmental chairperson supervises all internships, while in other cases the chairperson assigns the job to an assistant chair or a similar administrative person. Several schools reported that internships were handled by their cooperative education office, by graduate students or by staff members.

Several methods are used to build internship supervision into a faculty member's teaching load. If the faculty member coordinates all internships, the typical pattern is to reduce the load by one course per term. In some cases a faculty member must supervise a specified number of interns before being given release time. One school, for instance, reduces the load by one course when an individual supervises 10 or more interns. Other plans reduce the load by credit hour. Supervising three interns, for example, may equal one credit of the faculty member's assignment.

Do broadcast educators feel that internships lead to exploitation of students as cheap labor, perhaps to the detriment of academic work? Three-fourths of the respondents said internships do not take advantage of students. Many said close faculty supervision keeps the problem to a minimum, and others felt there is no exploitation when students are paid. Several who said there is exploitation felt that the job experience makes for a fair tradeoff.

PROBLEMS

Faculty members identified a number of problems with internship programs. The problem most frequently mentioned was the variation of the quality of internships, a direct reference to the amount of planning, or lack of it, by stations. Respondents also noted the lack of feedback from stations, the tendency to place interns in low-level, routine jobs and conflicts with labor unions.

While there are occasional problems with internship programs, the predominant feeling among respondents is that the advantages to the students, schools and employers outweigh any problems.

Internship programs vary in structure, a fact that might be a problem, especially to broadcasters who must deal with several sets of guidelines and requirements when accepting interns from more than one school. It is unlikely, however, that schools will adopt any uniform structure. Each program is shaped by the beliefs and experiences of its own faculty, and variations in structure result. This means that faculty supervisors must be alert to variations in the marketplace and be careful to educate industry supervisors to the requirements of their own program.

NOTES

1. Roger Hadley, "Policies and Practices: Internship Programs Across the Country," *Feedback*, 24 (1983), 14–16.
2. John M. Hyde, Jr. and Alfred W. Owens, "Interns: The Ivory Tower At Work," *Communication Education*, 33 (1984), 374.

8
INTERNSHIP PRACTICES IN PUBLIC RELATIONS

Robert Kendall

A survey of public relations programs at 286 colleges and universities found a great variance in how the respondents converted internship hours into credits. Most popular internships (descending order) were media, corporations, non-profits, public relations firms and advertising agencies. Least utilized were government, educational institutions, small businesses, trade associations and religious organizations. The survey uncovered problems with grade inflation, prerequisites and competency of industry sponsors. The survey projected 15,000 interns nationwide in journalism programs, 4,000 of which were in public relations.

The term "internship" is the preferred designation for an academically governed work experience. Indeed, by tabulating the phrases used by public relations educators who responded to this survey, a surprisingly workable definition emerged: An internship is media-related work experience at an on-the-job location, supervised by a professional practitioner, involving a student enrolled in an academically organized program requiring full-time work which provides salary and credit during a specified term (quarter or semester).

Other terms describe variations on this definition. "Practicum" is preferred for part-time campus media work but may mean the same as "internship" or "in-class work" or "nonpaid internship." "Cooperative work experience" most often describes alternating terms of work and school, but may mean a lower-level repeatable internship. No significant recurrence of other terms emerged from 115 responses to a mail questionnaire sent to 286 programs listed in the 1979 *Journalism Educator*.

METHODOLOGY

POPULATION

The most reliable information about public relations should come from faculty members who supervise interns. Because of the present structure of public relations education within journalism programs, the roster listed by AEJ in the January 1979 issue of *Journalism Educator* was selected as the primary cluster. To identify the internship supervisor within each program, two cover letters were prepared, one for the program administrator and the other for the intern supervisor. The first requested the aid of the administrator in forwarding the questionnaire to the proper person or persons for each internship program in the unit. The second requested the cooperation of the intern supervisor by completion of the instrument, and forwarding any printed material used in the internship program.

SAMPLE

The relatively small size of the population, 286, would dictate a probability sample of 50 percent, assuming that all programs offered an internship. Since there is evidence that not all programs do indeed offer internships, a response of less than 50 percent, i.e., 115, might approach the acceptable minimum. However, since responses were dictated by other than random selection the results should be projected to the total population with caution.

The research plan calls for follow-up mailings in an attempt to achieve a complete census of internship practices. The present report covers data from 115 respondents out of a total mailing of 286.

INSTRUMENT

The questionnaire evolved out of intensive study of the literature on internships and consultation with faculty members who had experience with internship supervision. Five drafts of the instrument eliminated most problems in wording and in structure.

A decision to include all internships offered in journalism programs rather than just public relations arose from two considerations: Many programs, especially small ones, make fewer distinctions between public relations and other media work experience; also, public relations internships can be better understood in the context of allied media internships. Most items were closed-ended types to make a discouragingly-long questionnaire less formidable. Open-ended items were used to elicit definitions of terms, and comments were encouraged in the margins and at the end. Check-type responses and 1-to-5 intensity ratings for "least-most" ranges were used to yield a mean rating for each sub-item to indicate "importance" or "frequency." Mean scores thus yielded an average importance rating or frequency of use rating that makes the information more meaningful than simple tabulation.

Table 1 Work Hours Required for 5 Quarter Credits

Frequency Rank	Number of Mentions	Minimum Work Hours Required
1.	10	40
2.	9	10
3.	7	6
4.	5	3
5.	4	9,12,15
6.	3	4,20
7.	2	5,8
8.	1	7,13,22,33

ADMINISTRATION

The survey questionnaire was mailed Aug. 20, 1979 to 286 journalism programs listed in the January 1979 *Journalism Educator*. Only responses received through Nov. 1, 1979 have been included in the tabulations.

Computer frequencies, mean score tabulations, cross-tabulations as provided in the *Statistical Packages for the Social Sciences* software program were used for analysis of the data. University of Florida keypunch staff transferred responses from returned questionnaires to IBM data cards and verified all responses. Four cards per case were used.

Respondents indicated that more internship positions exist than students can fill, and expressed great interest in participating in a national exchange listing of internships available. Internship practices in AEJ programs generally appear sound, with respondents reporting adherence to academic standards and conformity to the demands of professional practice.

FINDINGS

The greatest variation in internship practice comes in the number of hours of academic credit awarded for the number of work hours required. A mode of five minimum quarter hours and three minimum semester hours required an average of 20 work-hours per week, but practice ranged widely from this norm. In the quarter system, five hours of credit is the predominant pattern, accounting for 90.5 percent of cases. But required work hours for the five credits range from 3 hours to 40 hours.

Table 2 Worked Hours Required for The Mode of 3 Semester Credits

Frequency Rank	Number of Mentions	Minimum Work Hours Required
1.	8	10
2.	4	15,40,6
3.	3	8,9
4.	2	12
5.	1	13,20,22

Forty hours of work earned one quarter-hour of credit at two institutions and six credits at two others. Closer to the norm, six credits required 36 work-hours in one case, and four credits required 20 work-hours in another or one credit for five to six hours.

In semester system, three credits were the most common minimum (38.3 percent of respondents).

Forty work-hours also earned six credits in five cases, five credits in four cases and one or two in three cases each.

Other common patterns ranged from one credit for three hours work (seven cases), but also four, five, seven, nine, ten and 33 work-hours for the same one semester hour of credit. Two credits required six, seven, 10, 36 and 40 work-hours. Twenty work-hours earned six credits in three cases and eight in another.

Commonly, salary was permitted in addition to credit, 83 respondents reported. Salary was required in addition to credit at 28 institutions, but 18 reported salary is not permitted with credit. Only 10 reported that salary is required when credit is not available—a type of "required employment".

Students qualified for internships most often by completing prerequisite courses (85 responses). Sixty reported that students must complete either the third (40) or second (30) year. Applicants at 36 programs must qualify by achieving an acceptable grade point average, at a mean GPA of 2.63.

Policy statements governing internships were rated on a scale of 1 (least)—5 (most) in order of "importance" by (N = 92 +) respondents: "Available to qualified students only," M (mean) = 4.28; "Counts as credit toward major, but not required," M = 3.59; "Encouraged as elective for all students," M = 3.50; "Required of majors," M = 2.59; "Required for graduation," M = 2.48. The pattern of practice tends toward admitting only qualified students to internships, and tends away from making a requirement for graduation of all students.

In selecting internships sites, prior faculty control was the stronger pattern. On a scale of 1–5, preferred policies, by mean score, were: "Arranged by student but approved by faculty before work begins," M = 3.42; "Approved by faculty then arranged by student," M = 3.07; "Arranged entirely by faculty in advance," M = 3.03. Less common patterns were: "Work may be completed prior to faculty approval," M = 1.36; and "Academic credit may be received for work prior to college enrollment," M = 1.20. Responses ranged from 97 to 108. There seemed to be a slight pattern of allowing credit for nonacademic working experience, but the tendency is toward academic control.

Supervision policies tended toward formalized procedures, reports, guidelines and approved professionalism of the supervisor rather than ad hoc arrangements, Rating of policies on a 1–5 scale by mean score: "Faculty required reports; supervisor gives daily direction," M = 4.20; All parties follow printed guidelines, M = 3.50; Faculty approves professional experience level of job supervisor," M = 3.30; "Formal agreement approved and signed by all parties," M = 3.00; "Faculty makes job site visit for advance approval," M = 2.50; "Faculty approved educational background of supervisor," M = 2.30.

Requirement patterns for internships differed somewhat from requirements used in grading. Final comprehensive reports from the intern and supervisor with copies of all work produced, a record of daily activities and a personal conference reports constituted the most common pattern. Weekly reports, classroom reports, supervisor weekly reports and examination drew the least rating in importance for internship requirements.

Organizations employing interns by frequency included media, corporations, nonprofit (service) agencies, public relations firms, and advertising agencies, in that order, with government, educational institutions, small business, trade association and religious organizations ranked in that order least frequently.

Job responsibilities of interns found newsgathering and news release writing tied for most frequent, with feature writing next. Informal research, report writing, speech or scriptwriting were next in frequency, with formal (scientific method) research least frequent.

For specific publications, job assignments found employee and external publications named most frequently, with brochures, promotional materials, advertising and annual reports in declining frequency. In all publication assignments, writing, editorial, and layout-pasteup duties were most frequent, while photography, working with the printer and distribution were less frequent assignments.

Special events duties ranked "assisting with shows, exhibits and open house" most frequent; preparing AV presentations, scheduling of activities, conducting tours followed, in that order. Full responsibility for events, making presentations or speeches and fundraising ranked least frequent. Forty-four to 65 responded to this block of questions.

Grading fell into two groups, those using A through F and those using Satisfactory or Unsatisfactory. The S-U grade is much less common than letter grades; 82 responded with A-F compared to 18 for S-U. Mean scores of reported average grades yielded 64.2 percent A, 27.4 percent B, 12.1 percent C, 4.1 percent D, and 4.5 percent F. Satisfactory drew 72.4 percent and Unsatisfactory 16.1 percent; 8.5 percent reported incomplete grades.

Most internships take place within 50 miles from campus, which 60.4 percent reported; 38.8 percent were reported from 50 to 300 miles from campus, 15.2 percent reported on-campus internships and 12.7 percent internships were reported placed "beyond the adjacent state."

If a nonrandom sample could be projected to the 286 listed programs, the total number of internships reported for the past year would exceed 15,000 (sum of means 53.3 × 286 = 15,243.8), for all journalism program majors. For public relations alone, the figure would exceed 4,000 (15.6 × 286 = 4,461.6). The mean score and number reporting by sequence are:

	mean	n
Advertising	10.2	54*
Print Journalism	22.2	93
Broadcasting	18.7	79
Public Relations	15.6	80
Other	9.2	27

(*Unlike the other programs, 10 percent of advertising programs are outside journalism schools or departments so this number is unrealistically small. Fourteen respondents reported a mean of 9.9 internships completed in a field other than the student's major).

Legal considerations about internships drew a small number of responses for "areas in which you have encountered legal questions." Labor union rules were mentioned first (38 responses), the Wage-Hour Law (Fair Labor Standards Act) drew 35 responses; workmen's compensation (33), and contract obligations (23 responses). Twelve indicated "other."

The reported values of internships emphasized that they: "Provide demonstrable experience for future employment" first, and "Weed out those unsuited to a public relations career" last. In between were "Provides trial employment; and Builds rapport between professional and academic department."

Faculty intern supervisor duties ranked "counseling prospective interns, developing internships opportunities, approve sites, determine final grades and conduct correspondence" as most common. Least-noted duties included "determine requirements, maintain standards and design forms (application, etc)." The supervisor had, on the average, administered the intern program 7.3 years. Primary job assignments of supervisors were teaching (reported by 81) and administration (dean, etc.) reported by 34. Four have other duties and two are public relations directors. Thirty-three reported two faculty members teaching public relations, 31 reported one public relations teacher, 22 reported three, eight reported four, two reported five, and one reported eight teachers of public relations at their institution. Twenty-seven faculty supervisors included an internship in their own academic program, 79 did not.

The mean enrollment reported for academic departments responding was 360. The mean college or university institutional enrollment was 13,767, and the mean city population where the institution was located was 183,847.

CONCLUSION

"Internship" is by far the preferred term for academically governed work experience. It serves well to convey what both educators and practitioners mean. It would seem worthwhile to promote the use of the term over other terms.

The "consensus definition" derived from survey responses appears to be a good starting point toward a standard definition: "An internship is media-related work experience at an on-the-job location, supervised by a professional practitioner involving a student enrolled in an academically organized program of full-time work which provides salary and credit during a specified term (quarter or semester)."

Standardization of other terms in common usage could not fail to strengthen the relationship between the classroom and professional practice. Such terms as practicum, cooperative work experience, field work and apprenticeship lend confusion when they mean different things to people in the same discipline. Encouragement of certain standard terminology will enable educators to provide uniformly more competent employees to the demanding world of public relations.

We might agree on the following meanings: Practicum means a part-time media experience, taken as part of a course, that may be repeated for minimal academic credit. Apprenticeship means probationary work experience with minimal academic governance. Pro-am means an internship served in close association with a single practitioner. The program should cover the full range of the practitioner's duties for a short period.

A major problem associated with internships is that the number of credits available does not match the normal term load. To take an internship, students must enroll for a low number of credit hours and fall behind in their progress toward meeting degree requirements. On the other hand, offering a full term of academic credit for a single internship would weaken academic standards in the eyes of the accrediting body in journalism. A system with an internship related to a classroom course seems to offer a viable compromise. Such a system as Ohio State's works well, with interns placed close at hand. Perhaps a follow-up course could be used for more distant sites.

High concentrations of academic credit for internships tend to displace other academic work. Perhaps a recommendation from ACEJ to limit the number of credit hours available for internships might help hold the line for sound academic policy. Some institutions are under pressure to attract students in a declining enrollment period and the temptation may be great.

Whether salary should be standardized seems appropriately beyond the interests of this body. Some programs would suffer if salary were required, but as the reputation of internship programs grows, the possibility of salaried positions increases. Salaried internships should certainly be encouraged; an increase of paid internships might be tied to achieving the standards we are considering here.

Qualifications for internships as now practiced suggest formalizing these standards: 1) minimum prerequisite course, 2) senior standing, and 3) a standard GPA minimum. Supervision policies also suggest minimum standards: That faculty require reports from both student and supervising professional, that all parties follow prepared guidelines, and that perhaps a signed contract should be standard. Other considerations, such as the professional experience level and educational level of the practitioner, should be addressed also.

Perhaps requirement patterns for internships should be combined with supervision policies. Minimum standards might specify that copies of all work, with a record of daily activities, be submitted in a comprehensive final report. At that time, a personal conference between faculty and student should be held. If the program combines the internship with a related class, class reports could logically be included in basic requirements. Weekly supervisor reports and an exam are low-priority requirements, according to responses and also according to practical considerations.

The range of organizations offering internships seems beyond the scope of standardization, as are the types of job responsibilities. A careful reading of responses on job assignments suggested that a wholesome balance of public relations responsibilities is the common pattern.

Grading of internship experience reflected grade inflation to a considerable degree, with 64.2 percent A and 27.4 percent B, etc. Sound academic policy might suggest the S-U system as a preferred alternative. [See "A Perspective on Internship Grading Problems and a Solution" in Section IV, *ed.*]

The small number of responses on internships and the law may reflect a false sense of security. The pattern of practice indicated the possibility that there is some lack of compliance with the Fair Labor Standards Act. The greatest problem lies in nonpaid internships and with organizations engaged in interstate commerce. These might involve all areas noted: contracts, wage-hour law, workmen's compensation and union rules.

Respondents indicate more opportunities for interns exist than student can fill, and a great interest in a national listing of opportunities presents an immediate and compelling challenge.

9
PRACTICA AND INTERNSHIPS FOR TECHNICAL WRITING STUDENTS

Lionel D. Wyld

Three types of experiential learning for college students are described: internships, externships and workships. Internships are viewed as particularly germane to the post-graduate environment. Faculty are urged to develop various forms of experiential learning across a variety of disciplines that feed into technical writing. Numerous on-going programs are used as examples.

There are basically three types of employment open to college students. These three may be briefly described and categorized as follows:

Internships: Post-graduate work in the student's major field and often at a job site with which there is at least some potential for employment following the internship.
Externships, (Pre-internships): Undergraduate work in one's major field or area of interest; not usually at a location at which the student will necessarily seek employment upon graduation.
Workships: Undergraduate or graduate employment not related to the student's major career goals and not location-pertinent.

Each of these may have relevance to students of technical writing, although the first two bear the most consideration in relation to a student's academic program and career goals. The first category comprises the more-or-less pure internship, based upon the classic definition of an intern as an advanced student or recent graduate undergoing supervised practical training. Co-op programs, Jan-Plans, and other school-arranged intersession work periods are examples of "externships" or pre-internships. The last category includes all other work/study financial aid and student employment. Examples include library clerks or shelvers, dining room helpers, dormitory RAs, laboratory assistants, and the like, as well as off campus employment both during school semesters and at vacation times. In each of these situations benefits accrue, in varying degrees, for both student and employer, and if the employment situation has provision for academic credit, the externship or workshop can be academically as well as financially rewarding for the student employee.

GRADUATE INTERNSHIPS

Internships are important in many fields of endeavor, and internships are mandatory in some of the leading professions, preeminently of course in medicine and related areas. The law field has its own requisite apprenticeship, in many respects like the internship in medicine. Similarly, too, do certain fields of engineering, oceanography, and—more close to our own area of emphasis and interest—journalism. Even the lowly (and low paid!) cub reporter is really serving a kind of internship. In such a demanding field as technical communication, it is only natural that internships can well serve as the necessary bridge between academic study/degree and the real-world career.

A post-baccalaureate internship offers good experience. The summer internship program in technical writing and editing at the Naval Underwater Systems Center (NUSC)[1] is a leading example of this type; the one and two semester program offered at Argonne Research Laboratory is another. Since the NUSC program has already been the subject of three articles—one by a former intern in the program (*The Technical Writing Teacher*, Winter, 1975), the second by a supervisory editor at the Center (*Technical Communications*, First Quarter, 1977), and one by the present writer (*Journal of Technical Writing and Communication*, vol. 8, 1978)—I need not discuss nor describe this program in detail here, except to say that it is an interesting and, I feel, a valuable program, perhaps even a unique one (for this field) in the United States. The requirements have been straightforward: the candidate summer employee (the intern) must be enrolled in a graduate program in technical or scientific writing or be a graduate of one. Interns' undergraduate programs have varied widely: NUSC has had interns whose undergraduate majors ranged from the more obvious ones in English or journalism to those in biology, astrophysics, and classical literature. Only two persons who came in to the summer program have held bachelor's degrees in the field of technical communications itself (one in technical writing per se, one in bio-communications).

In a co-related field, Lottie B. Applewhite, a technical publications editor at Letterman Army Medical Center, has outlined a graduate program including an academic affiliation and a residency (on-the-job) affiliation in the technical/biomedical communications area. The result is a master's degree program with a concurrent communications residency.[2] Another newly proposed program at Miami University (Ohio) incorporates an "internship" as a requirement within the two-year period of study of the degree of Master of Technical and Scientific Communication. The arrangement may be more of the practica sort, since it is planned not as a requirement of post-graduate certification (as in the case of the medical internship) but is, rather, an integral part of the pre-professional training. A similar mandatory requirement for engineering students has proven highly successful at the University of Louisville's J. B. Speed Scientific School. This engineering program, with three "cooperative internships," straddles the externship/internship areas, since the five-year program includes the usual undergraduate major but results in a master's degree for the successful student. The highly organized program apparently also results in good matching of interns with career employment sites. An interesting aspect of the Speed School program—and one which is particularly relevant to technical writing teachers—is its requirement of courses that teach communication skills: technical reports, business letters, and other speech and writing techniques.[3]

INTERSESSION PROGRAMS AND PRACTICA

Intersession programs have been around for some time, their general purpose to provide real-world work experience (and sometimes academic credit) during periods when a college is normally closed between semesters.

Bennington College's requirement in this regard is an outstanding example of one of the older programs. In Bennington's case, each student must work (and be judged by a supervisor in the employment situation) during the period when the college is shut down in mid-winter. While the predominant factor in the Bennington program is gainful employment experience, intersession job situations frequently reflect a student's academic interest and career goals, and, even in cases where they do not, other considerations (such as proximity of the job location to a major museum or art gallery for an art major) play an important part in the employment arrangements.

Jan-Plans, or variations thereof, are somewhat newer to the academic scene, though the purpose is essentially the same as in the Bennington model. The expression "Jan-Plan" derives from the most common form these programs have taken, offered for the approximately three-week long period between semesters, usually in January, from the close of the fall semester examinations to the beginning of the spring term. The original Jan-Plan at Cazenovia College, to cite a leading example from the late 1960s, required student compliance but gave no academic credit. Jan-Plans were graded simply Pass or Fail; if satisfactorily completed, the PASS was entered on a student's record as a graduation requirement, much the same way colleges like Hamilton used the requirement of oral and written proficiency in a foreign language as a prerequisite to a student's receiving his A. B. Cazenovia College's first Jan-Plans, for which I served as faculty mentor, included such individual projects as journalism internships on a Malone, New York newspaper and an internship in yearbook editing. In the latter, a student who had been editor-in-chief of her high school yearbook returned, with the concurrence of the high school faculty advisor, as a consultant/advisor to the incumbent editor.

Despite my use of the word "internship," these early Jan-Plans more properly fit the externship category. In sociology, quite viable and valuable externships were arranged: all applicant Cazenovia students were placed as temporary employees in city and regional social service agencies to gain practical experience, with one day a week spent on campus focusing on a mutual discussion of problems encountered.

I cite this example because it seems to me that a similar program, for two or three weeks' duration, might prove especially valuable (and interesting) to college students in technical writing. The literature documenting the various instances of career-related work arrangements for technical writing (or communication) students indicates that an increasing number of colleges and their faculty are doing just that. James Zappan of the University of Michigan used the term "mini-internship" to describe a course developed for Western Michigan University; in this case the work situation was within the university itself and involved students in other divisions of the university for four or five weeks.[4]

The University of Rochester offers complete courses, designated "practica," on an intern-type basis. One in child psychology, for example, entails about eight hours per week of work at a nearby Family Mental Health Clinic. Students write a term paper on the overall experience and submit it at the end of the semester. Regular academic credit is given, the same as in a conventional classroom course.

In the mid-1970s externships were discussed by an NASF (National American Studies Faculty) workshop at Roger Williams College, which has actively sought training arrangements with local industry and other employment sources for its students. Journalism (including radio and television), an area which was the subject of a Roger Williams community seminar, has proven a difficult one in which to place degree candidates. The radio station or the television studio does not have the luxury of time to cope with an on-the-job training process; they need persons who can already "read the news," handle the sports, write up and present the features for the day, etc. They cannot afford, for both professional and financial reasons, to take air time to train college students.

Yet, I suspect there are countless uncharted off-campus sources conveniently near most colleges, where interested students could be placed. Technical writing instructors and their students should seriously investigate such opportunities.

CO-OP PROGRAMS

A co-op program allows students to work for a specified period (usually a semester) and study for a similar period, alternating until graduation. The co-op program is thus a series of apprenticeships that carry throughout a student's undergraduate study. It prolongs the time to complete a program, but the advantage in addition to the financial arrangements which ease the tuition—is that by the time the degree is conferred, considerable real-world experience and on-the-job training have resulted. Although co-op programs have been common with engineering schools and those devoted to other technical programs, cooperative education is gaining wider acceptance, according to a *Chronicle of Higher Education* article.[5] For example, Northeastern University, among the largest of co-op institutions, offers a program whereby their students are required to work one out of every four academic periods. The university placement tries to place all their students in jobs pertinent to their career fields, if at all possible.

Industry has not shown much interest in technical writing co-ops, though companies employing technical writers often, ironically, have co-op arrangements with one or more universities for their engineering and science employees. The problem is essentially the same as that with the journalism aspirants cited above. To give training on the job to inexperienced college students as technical writers or editors is neither economical nor practical for industry.

WORKSHIPS AND OTHER EMPLOYMENT

Undergraduate or graduate employment may be closely tied in with a student's academic program, and may indeed be a requirement; or it may be an arrangement largely or solely left to the student who seeks remunerative work either part-time when classes are in session or during times when the college is closed for vacation periods.

Work/study programs are a common means of financial aid for many college students. Most colleges offer their undergraduates various ways to earn money to help defray their college costs and to earn extra money through employment at campus-based agencies: the library, dining service, housing office, laboratories, and the like. At many institutions, particularly in urban areas, some opportunities exist for off campus employment as well. When the student can find employment in his or her prospective field, a viable externship program has been provided to the benefit of student and employer alike; if that same process includes academic credit, so much the more rewarding for the student.

SUMMARY

It seems entirely feasible that some viable arrangement for practica or other externships can be developed for the technical writing student. College and university faculty in technical communications programs ought to seriously consider suitable placement areas by investigating possible employment situations for their technical writing students with technical/scientific and government laboratories or other technical agencies. At the same time, professional society interest ought to be fostered. The subject of writer/editor internships for students in communication areas was addressed at the 6th International and 45th National Convention of the American Business Communication Association, held in Washington, D.C., in December 1980, where various programs and the need for career-relevant, honest work assignments (as opposed to "mere work") were aired. Other academic forums, like the Modern Language Association and the College English Association have similarly broached the subject, as has the Society for Technical Communication; but much more widespread discussion in the academic community, along with comment from employer representatives, is needed.

College faculty can do much by helping to place technical writing students (or other majors who may thus be introduced to the field of technical writing or editing) as editorial clerks or writer-editor trainees. Thus, teachers of technical writing can serve as career counselors and liaison between classroom and field. At the very least, they can apprise local industry, perhaps by a small leaflet or flyer, of the availability and interest of their students for such work activity. As a matter of fact, preparing such an informative flyer might prove to be an excellent and practical assignment in a technical writing class!

NOTES

1. Begun in 1972 and conducted each year through summer 1978, the program was suspended due to funding constraints. Regular summer employment opportunities in technical publications continue to be available, however.
2. See Lottie B. Applewhite, "A Residency Program for Technical/Biomedical

Communicators: A Master's Degree Program with Concurrent On-The-Job Training," *Journal of Technical Writing and Communication*, 9:2 (1979), pp. 127–140.

3. Joseph H. Pierce and Ray J. Birmingham, "The Cooperative Internship Program: Giving Students the Best of Both Worlds,"*Engineering Education*, January 1981, pp. 288–293.

4. James P. Zappan, "A Mini-Internship in a Professional Writing Course," *Journal of Technical Writing and Communication*, 8:2 (1978), pp. 89–95.

5. Beverly T. Watkins, "Cooperative Education, with Built-In Benefits for Students and Employees, Gains Acceptance," *The Chronicle of Higher Education*, May 26, 1981, p. 3.

10
ACCOUNTING INTERNSHIPS AND SUBSEQUENT ACADEMIC PERFORMANCE: AN EMPIRICAL STUDY

W. Robert Knechel and Doug Snowball

This study compares the academic performance of interns and non-interns and concludes that the two groups have similar grade point average overall and in the major. However, interns performed better when taking courses directly related to their career track.

Supervised practical experience is an important preparatory step for a variety of careers (such as medicine, law, journalism, and education). The first formal programs providing practical experience to accounting students were established more than 70 years ago. Under such programs, students are awarded degree credit for supervised work performed in an accounting position.[1] Degree credit awarded for accounting internship programs is based on the assumption that the student's education is enhanced by internship experience. However, there is little empirical evidence available to support this assumption. The purpose of this paper is to provide some evidence concerning potential educational benefits of internship programs. Specifically, it assesses the impact of internship experience on subsequent academic performance.

POTENTIAL EDUCATIONAL BENEFITS OF ACCOUNTING INTERNSHIPS

Because internship experience is rarely a required component of an accounting degree program, the continued popularity and size of internship programs indicate that they are perceived as beneficial to both students and employers. Student participation may be influenced by financial considerations, job search strategies, and overall career evaluation concerns. Employer participation is probably motivated most strongly by recruiting and staffing considerations. These motivating factors mean that the "market approval" of internships does not necessarily indicate that internships provide incremental educational benefits to the student.

The accounting literature has identified a number of potential educational benefits of internships that may justify awarding degree credit. The AAA Committee on Internship Programs [1952] cited such benefits as: (1) exposure to accounting techniques and problems not encountered in a classroom environment, (2) enhanced understanding of the business world, and (3) improved ability to evaluate and assimilate classroom experiences. Increased motivation to master subject material on returning to school also has been cited as a benefit of internships [AAA Committee on Faculty Residency and Internship Programs, 1955]. Lowe [1965] reported that a significant majority of former interns indicated that their participation clarified points of theory that they had previously studied, increased the meaningfulness of some courses, and warranted the granting of credit. Koehler [1974] also concluded that internship programs have educational merit. He asserted that internship programs motivate students to work hard early in their programs (to enhance their chances of being offered internships) and result in improved grades upon returning to school.

INTERNSHIP EFFECTS ON SUBSEQUENT ACADEMIC PERFORMANCE

Internships may affect subsequent academic performance through the motivation and/or knowledge base of students. Student's general motivation (that is, their willingness to exert more effort in their studies) may be enhanced because they are refreshed by their break from classroom routine and are more cognizant of the relationship between their degree studies and later professional success. On the other hand, returning to the classroom may be anticlimactic, especially if the student is close to graduation or if the internship has resolved career or placement uncertainties. Whether the general motivation of students is raised or lowered, moreover, likely will be affected by positive or negative aspects of their particular internship experience.

Regardless of the overall motivational impact upon students, there may be a differential motivational effect across courses taken after the internship. In other words, students may focus their attention and effort on those courses now perceived to be more important to their chosen area of specialty, with less effort exerted in other areas. If student motivation does become more focused, performance in accounting courses would be expected to be enhanced by their internship experience, possibly at some expense to performance in nonaccounting courses. This differential focusing effect may also extend to specific accounting courses.

In addition to the motivational implications, internship experiences may provide students with an expanded knowledge base that aids performance in related coursework. For example, if students primarily serve as auditing interns, they may find their experiences and new knowledge to be of direct benefit in mastering the material presented in formal auditing courses, including other accounting courses.

Koehler [1974] examined the academic performance of 226 students who participated in internships. He compared each student's grade-point average at graduation with the grade-point average immediately prior to the internship. Koehler concluded that students tended to improve academically following participation in an internship program. Increases in grade averages, both cumulative and accounting, of the former interns were more common than grade decreases. Unfortunately, the results were not tested for statistical significance, nor did Koehler use a control group of noninterns. The absence of a control group means that the grade improvement cannot safely be attributed to participation in an internship.

The present study represents an extension and expansion of the initial work by Koehler [1974]. Two features of this study are explicitly designed to obtain more meaningful and generalizable results. First, a control group of non-intern students were selected to eliminate competing explanations of changes in academic performance. Second, performance in specific subject areas was considered to provide insight into effects of differential motivations and the differential substantive knowledge provided by internship experiences.

RESEARCH METHOD

This study was conducted at the University of Florida, which has had an active internship program in accounting for more than a decade. A matched-pairs approach was employed to compare the academic performance of former interns with the academic performance of non- intern students possessing comparable academic records. Random assignment of students to treatment (internship participation) and control (nonintern) groups was not possible since students and intern employer jointly determine internship participants. Selection criteria used by accounting firms are such that intern and nonintern groups will probably differ along certain important dimensions. To overcome these problems, a matching procedure was used. The internship group was identified from records kept of intern placement; the control group was formed by identifying a "match" for each member of the internship group. The matching process was based on overall grade-point average (GPA) and seniority in the degree program.

The intern group consisted of 108 students who registered for intern credit during the period Fall 1978 through Spring 1984.[2] All interns were placed with public accounting firms and, almost without exception, performed audit-related duties during their internship.[3] A matched sample of 108 students was selected for the control group. The matching process employed three criteria. First, the nonintern had to be enrolled in school during the term that the matching intern was completing his or her internship. Second, the grade-point average of the nonintern immediately prior to the internship term had to be within 0.15 of the intern's GPA. Third, there could be no more than 12 hours difference in the total hours completed immediately prior to the internship term by the intern and nonintern.[4] If a suitable matching nonintern could not be identified, the internship student was dropped from the treatment group.[5] A check was made to ensure that no member of the control group participated in an internship at any time prior to graduation. Each nonintern (control) subject was matched to only one intern subject.

The *absolute* mean difference between subjects on the cumulative GPA dimensions was .042; the *absolute* mean difference on the completed hours dimension was 4.248 hours. The 108 intern subjects had an overall mean GPA of 3.366 and had completed an average of 112.61 hours prior to commencing their internship. The corresponding measures for the control group were 3.375 (GPA) and 112.25 (hours completed).[6]

Formal academic transcripts were obtained for the 216 students. The hours completed and grades earned between the start of the internship term and graduation from the undergraduate program were gathered for each subject. Accounting courses were examined individually while other courses were classified as either business (nonaccounting) or general (nonbusiness).

RESULTS

This section first presents the effects of internship experience upon subsequent overall performance in undergraduate studies. To assess motivational forces underlying performance, we then report results separately for accounting courses, business courses, and nonbusiness courses. Finally, to assess possible effects of substantive knowledge gained from internships, we report performance results for three individual accounting courses. The dependent variable in all cases related to grades earned in courses taken after the internship term but prior to graduation from the undergraduate program. The analy-

Table 1 Summary Statistic for Grade Data

VARIABLE	INTERNS			NONINTERNS		
	N	Mean	S.D.	N	Mean	S.D.
Post-internship grades earned in:						
All courses	108	3.179	.511	108	3.198	.662
Business courses	81	3.296	.551	95	3.410	.583
Nonbusiness courses	65	3.537	.525	79	3.639	.442
Accounting courses:						
All	107	3.119	.561	101	3.059	.660
Non-auditing	101	3.065	.576	91	3.100	.684
Tax	36	2.958	.669	49	3.092	.839
Systems	47	3.309	.576	64	3.195	.652
Auditing	74	3.284	.763	83	3.030	.786

ses are based on analysis of covariance (ANCOVA) models with fixed effects. The following independent variables were included in the final model:

INDEPENDENT VARIABLES	EXPLANATION
INTERN	Primary treatment factor: interns versus noninterns
PREGPA	Grade-point average prior to the internship term (covariate)
PREHRS	Hours completed immediately prior to internship term (covariate)

The covariate variables are used to remove any random variations that may be due to confounding factors, and to increase the power of the test statistics for the effect of interest (i.e., INTERN).

OVERALL PERFORMANCE

Overall post-internship performance is summarized in Table 1. Contrary to prior research [Koehler, 1974], it was found that the overall GPA level dropped after the internship term.[7] The decrease in overall GPA was significant different from zero ($p < .05$) for both the intern and nonintern groups. The GPA earned in post-internship

Table 2 Significance Levels for Factors In ANCOVA

FACTOR	POST-INTERNSHIP GPA	COURSE GRADES		
		Accounting	Business	Nonbusiness
Main Effect:				
INTERN	.5572	.4368	.2909	.3232
Covariates:				
PREGPA	.0054	.0001	.0001	.0001
PREHRS	.8793	.0922	.6969	.4347
R^2	.0376	.2718	.2325	.1131
FACTOR	NON-AUDITING COURSES	ACCOUNTING COURSE GRADES		
		Auditing	Systems	Tax
Main Effect:				
INTERN	.9502	.0126	.1378	.6606
Covariates:				
PREGPA	.0001	.0001	.0001	.0001
PREHRS	.0556	.5854	.3257	.2014
R^2	.2655	.2088	.2031	.3187

coursework by the internship group (3.179) was lower than that earned by the noninternship group (3.198), but Table 2 shows that thedifference was not statistically significant.

PERFORMANCE BY SUBJECT AREA

Post-internship performance was analyzed separately by subject area, with courses being classified as accounting, business, or nonbusiness. The presumption was that students would approach accounting, business and nonbusiness courses differently depending on the perceived relation between performance in these courses and subsequent career success in accounting. The perceived relation, which should be weakest for nonbusiness courses and strongest for accounting courses, may be magnified or altered by internship experiences. Descriptive statistics for these variables, presented in Table 1, are consistent with our expectations. That is, the post-internship GPAs of interns were higher than GPAs of noninterns for accounting courses (3.119 vs. 3.059), but were lower for business courses (3.296 vs. 3.410), and nonbusiness courses (3.537 vs. 3.639). However, the ANCOVA for these course categories (Table 2) indicated that there were no statistically significant differences between the intern and nonintern groups.

PERFORMANCE IN INDIVIDUAL ACCOUNTING COURSES

The direction of differences between the performance of interns and noninterns in the various course categories, though not statistically significant, is consistent with the view that internship experiences may lead to more narrowly focused motivations. Alternatively, the differences, at least in accounting, could also be affected by substantive knowledge gained from the internship experience. This second explanation was examined more closely by separately analyzing post-internship performance in three undergraduate accounting courses normally taken during the senior year of study. As Table 1 shows, many students took auditing, systems, and tax after the internship term. Given the content of these courses and the activities that characterize internship experiences, it can be expected that substantive knowledge gained by interns will not be equally applicable to the three courses. Such substantive knowledge would probably be most relevant to auditing and less applicable to other accounting courses, particularly tax.

Tables 1 and 2 present a summary and analysis of performance in specific accounting courses. Performance in non-auditing courses (which includes tax, systems, and a few less frequently taken accounting courses) taken after the internship was slightly higher for noninterns than for interns (3.10 vs. 3.065). Results for the tax course alone also indicate that noninterns performed better than interns (3.092 vs. 2.958). The pattern was reversed in the systems course where interns outperformed noninterns (3.309 vs. 3.195). These differences were not statistically significant, but the direction of these differences is consistent with the view that customary internship experience is more related to systems work (e.g., via audit applications) than tax work.

Results for the undergraduate auditing class, presumably the course most closely related to internship activities, support our predictions about post-internship performance. The auditing grades provided the only clear evidence of superior performance by the intern students. The intern group had a mean auditing grade of 3.284 compared to a mean of only 3.030 for the interns. Table 2 indicates that the difference is statistically significant ($p < .0126$).[8] In general, the results for the separate accounting courses are consistent with those for business and nonbusiness courses in the sense that interns performed worst in courses not directly related in internship experience and best in courses where substantive knowledge could be carried over from internship experience.

SUMMARY, CONCLUSIONS, AND LIMITATIONS

Accounting internships have become increasingly popular among both students and accounting firms over the last decade. Results reported in this paper suggest that while internships may help students master the material presented in a narrow set of accounting courses, there are no clear broad-based or synergistic benefits for subsequent academic studies in general.

The specific findings of the study may be summarized as follows:

1. There was no significant difference between interns and non-interns with respect to the overall GPA earned in courses completed after the internship period. Contrary to Koehler [1974], the cumulative GPA of interns (and noninterns) declined significantly after the internship period.
2. No significant differences between the two groups were found for performance in total nonbusiness, total business, or total accounting courses taken after the internship period. However, the pattern of GPAs earned in these course categories suggests that the relation of courses to the student's chosen career may affect the degree of motivation of intern students in particular.
3. The undergraduate auditing course was the single area in which interns performed significantly better than noninterns. The auditing course is the most directly related to internship experience. The superior performance of the interns could be due to substantive knowledge benefits of internships and/ or narrowly focused motivational forces (i.e., the interns are now more interested in this particular topic area).

Though the issue of post-internship performance was examined with greater rigor than in prior studies, this study has limitations that should be recognized and could lead to further research. First, the data pertain to students at a single institution and may not generalize to other institutions. Second, negative motivational effects may be amplified when students are close to graduation (a so-called "senior-itis" effect). Since most students in our study were within a semester of graduation upon returning from the internship, there was insufficient variation in our samples to adequately test this factor. Third, other potential motivational effects may not be completely randomized between the intern and nonintern groups and may be confounding the results. For example, intention to enter graduate school may increase some students' motivations at the end of their undergraduate career.[9] Fourth, the matching procedures may cause regression effects. It is unlikely that our results were so affected since we found a significant internship effect for auditing, but no significant effect for other courses. Our use of matching variables as covariates also provides some protection against regression effects.

A final limitation is the confounding of motivational and knowledge-based effects, particularly in the auditing course. We attributed the general decline in GPAs to a general decrease in student motivation, since knowledge-based benefits should not lead to a *decrease* in grades. Where interns earn higher post-internship grades than noninterns, however, this could be due either to experience-generated knowledge or narrow motivational effects or both. Isolating these two effects by obtaining direct motivation measures would be a worthy element of future research in this area.

The above limitations notwithstanding, this study's findings offer no support for the view that clear cut, synergistic academic benefits accrue to students who participate in internships. The results suggest that the academic benefits of internships are narrowly confined. Moreover, the results imply that there may be negative motivational effects upon returning to school We recognize that there may be positive educational benefits from internships that we did not address and that are not captured in grades earned in subsequent academic coursework. Nevertheless, arguments extolling the virtues of internship experience should be viewed with caution in light of the evidence presented in this study.

NOTES

1. Of the institutions reporting that an internship program was available to students, Schmutte [1986] found that 80 percent offered degree credit for participation.
2. This is not an exhaustive list of students gaining internship experience over the period. A significant number of interns chose not to register for internship credit because the hours were not needed for graduation. We also excluded interns who were not officially majoring in accounting (e.g., Business majors) or for whom there was no acceptable matching control subject.
3. The internship program is highly structured. Students must have completed specific accounting courses (introductory, intermediate, and cost) prior to the internship, and must complete at least one of the required accounting courses after the internship term. Students usually plan their program such that they will be left with 12–15 hours (including one or two required accounting courses) of coursework to complete after the

internship. Students generally must go out of town to complete their internship. The only course that is taken during the term is the internship itself. Since the internship is graded on a pass/fail basis, the internship term has no effect on GPAs.

4. The choice of maximum acceptable differences for the GPA (.15) and the completed hours (12) variables was not wholly arbitrary. We sought to minimize differences between matches without precluding matches where the difference was do to a single term's work. Thus, 12 hours was chosen since that is the average course load for a single semester. The GPA cutoff of .15 approximates the maximum GPA change that can occur during a single semester for an accounting senior whose grades are one level lower than normal (based on previous performance).

5. The matching criterion for GPA was difficult to satisfy since a large proportion of students with high GPAs participate in the internship program. As a result, our final sample included a slightly smaller proportion of students with exceptionally higher GPAs than the total intern population. The matching process obviously produced a nonintern sample with higher GPAs than the total nonintern population. We dropped approximately 16 percent of our original list in arriving at our intern sample of 108. Maximization of the quality of the matches was the only reason interns were dropped from the sample.

6. The nature of the institution, characteristics of the accounting program, and some specific testing provided reasonable assurances that variables such as student gender, transfer students, part-time study, other work experiences, course loads, and types of courses completed would not underlie the differences observed for intern and nonintern groups. SAT/ACT scores were not available for all students in our sample (especially those in the early years of the study). Aptitude-related differences should be captured in our pre-GPA variable which, in any event, would be more recent than available standardized test scores. With respect to transfer students, GPAs do not include transferred grades, and hours completed include transferred credits only up to a maximum of 64 semester hours. Transfer students must complete all required accounting courses at our institution.

7. To determine if our samples were unrepresentative of the general population of accounting students in this respect, we randomly selected an additional 100 students who graduation who graduated in 1982, 1983, 1984, or 1985. We found that 64 of the students had lower GPAs at graduation than at one year prior to graduation. Only 36 students saw their GPA increase during their senior year. The average GPA change for the 100 students was $-.037$.

8. In some cases, only one member of a matched pair was included in the analysis. These situations arose when one member of the matched pair completed the auditing course prior to the internship term. An alternative analysis for auditing grades was performed on only those pairs of students where both the intern and the matching nonintern took the auditing course after the internship term. This additional matching procedure reduced the sample size to 61. The results were virtually identical to those reported

in Table 2 and are not included in the paper. A similar analysis was not possible for the tax and systems courses due to insufficient observations.
9. Our experience indicates that candidates for the bachelor's degree either enter the profession or enter a graduate program at the same institution shortly after receiving the bachelor's degree. We tested to determine if intention to attend graduate school was a significant covariate, since such intentions may motivate a student during the latter stage of the undergraduate career. We defined GRAD as a dummy variable equal to one if the student actually went to graduate school at the University of Florida (or zero otherwise). GRAD is a surrogate measure of student intentions. Since GRAD only includes students who came back to subjects as graduate students. We re-performed the ANCOVA analysis with GRAD as a secondary treatment factor. Significant main effects for GRAD were obtained for overall course performance ($p < .0123$), performance in accounting courses ($p < .0196$), and performance in nonauditing courses ($p < .049$), in all of which students classified as GRAD were superior. There was also evidence of an INTERNxGRAD interaction in the systems course ($p < .0763$) and the tax course ($p < .0492$). We suspect that these interactions may reflect differences in the typical career paths for students interested in the tax or audit area. Specifically, we believe that students interested in the tax area are disproportionately represented in the graduate/nonintern cell while students interested in auditing are disproportionately represented in the nongraduate/intern cell. These results must be carefully interpreted due to the previously noted potential measurement error in GRAD, but may be a source of interesting future research.

REFERENCES

American Accounting Association, Committee on Internship Programs, "Report of the Committee on Internship Programs," *The Accounting Review* (July 1952), pp. 316–323.

――――, and American Institute of Accountants, Committee on Faculty Residency and Internship Programs and Committee on Accounting Personnel, "Statement of Standards and Responsibilities Under Public Accounting Internship Programs," *The Accounting Review* (April 1955), pp. 206–210.

Koehler, R. W., "The Effect of Internship Programs on Subsequent College Performance," *The Accounting Review* (April 1974), pp.382–384.

Lowe, R. E., "Public Accounting Internships," *The Accounting Review* (October 1965), pp. 839–846.

Schmutte, J., "Accounting Internships: The State of the Art," *Journal of Accounting Education* (Spring 1986), pp. 227–236.

IV. RUNNING INTERNSHIP PROGRAMS

11
SIX INTERNSHIP MODELS

Bruce Garrison

Six models of internships common to journalism/mass communications programs are enumerated, ranging from the non-credit loosely supervised internship to the internship required for graduation. While accreditation guidelines have limited internship credit to 10 percent of those allowed toward the major, little progress is reported in setting uniform standards for internship courses. Both a national clearing house and national standards are needed.

Throughout the liberal arts and elsewhere, professional field experience for students is common. We find internships in political science, in education, in interpersonal communication, and, of course, in mass communication.[1]

These programs vary in purpose and standards of development, theoretical design, and process. In the area of mass communication there is considerable variation in the goals and types of internship programs for undergraduate and graduate students of the 1980s. Academic organizations such as The Association for Education in Journalism and Mass Communication have grappled with the problems of internship programs.[2]

Generally unsuccessful attempts to organize national, regional, and local internships have been made. The Intern Research Group, one organization which was created to collate information about internship programs offered to students by mass media organizations, has published a directory annually since 1975, listing both internships and temporary media positions for students.[3] The state of the mass communication internship is not perfect by any standards. Those teaching in journalism education and related areas are seldom in agreement over policy that would bring consistency to regulation of internships. Professionals also disagree on the student internship, further complicating the matter.

One of the major concerns about internships is their contribution to the overall academic program of the student. Highly professionalized academic programs readily endorse them. More theoretically based academic programs often scoff at internships and encourage them only to the extent that students work in internships as extra-curricular activities. The Accrediting Council on Education in Journalism and Mass Communications (ACEJMC) says internships should not comprise more than 10 percent of total major hours.[4]

In the conflict arises the concern for academic credit. Among mass communication programs there are at least six different models for internships, ranging from those which do not consider internships at all.

There is no doubt, of course, that a properly structured internship can benefit all persons and institutions involved. The student grows professionally. The student's institution develops contacts with the professional community. A mutual awareness of the missions of the school and the host company develops as well. And the host acquires an employee for vacation replacement, additional assistance in strained departments, and the possibility of a permanent, full-time employee if the internship is successful.[5]

MODELS HAVE EVOLVED

In the area of mass communication internships, six models or formats have evolved in the academic environment as a means of incorporating the internship into the department's overall program:

MODEL 1

In this model, the department offering internships in broadcasting and journalism does not grant academic credit for the student's internship experience. There is not an available means nor a policy toward endorsing academic credit for summer work or work done concurrently with the usual academic calendar.

The curriculum committees which prevent such developments generally subscribe to the philosophy that granting credit will dilute the overall quality of the program. Furthermore, many institutions are already crowded in terms of required courses and cannot consider offering internship credit as a required course of majors or minors. Others institutions, considering direct internship credit as elective credit, have not done so as a policy decision, believing that students should not be permitted to earn credit for work not performed in the classroom under faculty supervision and direction. Seeking quality in the program, these departments do not want decisions on student performance in the hands of professionals not in the academic environment.

MODEL 2

Schools and departments working with this approach also do not offer direct academic credit for the internship experience. However, the attitude toward the internship is not as absolute in those departments fitting Model 1. The schools and departments will generally permit students serving internships to enroll in an independent study course or research courses. But these programs because of various restrictions and policies above departmental level which prevent course credit, have found this to be an acceptable means of circumventing the system.

Model 2 students, depending on the department and the instructors involved, are permitted to work in internships with varying levels of control for one to three hours of academic credit. The instructor here has two options involving the internship. First, the instructor can simply set work requirements for the internship and no other requirements for the "course." Second, the instructor can require additional academic work to be done concurrently with the internship professional work. Traditionally, this has been a term paper-research project or other type of analysis. At some schools, this has included a "diary" account of activities without the benefit of analysis or study of what the work experience has meant.

Often students in Model 2 schools lose the application of classroom theory in their internship experience. However, many institutions have made this format work when demand for internships and credit from students has been low. When there is greater demand, other models may be more appropriate.

MODEL 3

Schools and departments offering Model 3 use a seminar approach and differ from Models 1 and 2 in several ways. However, the Model 3 programs do not offer direct academic credit for internships either. The primary difference lies in creation of a post-internship seminar for student interns for what can be considered indirect academic credit.

This post-internship seminar is ideally set up as a class with a faculty member assigned as a part of his or her regular class and to teach the course or seminar. In the seminar, students discuss and study mass communications, utilizing common internship experiences or at least bringing in common elements of internship experience that enable them to function in the course at a more advanced level. The course is limited usually to seniors.

Although the structure of such a course may vary, it is typical for these courses to require research or other analytical work as well as other assignments beyond the actual internship experience. Usually these seminars require internship work off campus and do not allow practicum credit or work on school publications or campus broadcast stations to meet prerequisites.

The goal of such a seminar is to provide an intellectual exercise broader than a normal upper division course in terms of scope and depth of study.

This sort of seminar has been used with success at Northern Illinois University[6] and is now in its beginnings at Marquette University.[7]

MODEL 4

The fourth internship model is the specific seminar-type course designed for direct academic credit within the curriculum of a program in communications or mass communications. This course, like the three other models discussed above, is voluntary, and this post-internship seminar is for elective credit only. It is not required. A number of universities with programs in mass communications, such as the Department of Communications at the University of Miami, offer direct credit for internships.

Most universities limit the number of hours a student can earn in this situation, usually setting a ceiling of three hours to meet ACEJMC guidelines. Some programs will offer from one to three credit hours, depending on how much time the student and host of the internship can schedule in a semester while school is in session or how much can be arranged during summer.

There are two approaches here, just as there are in Model 3, toward arrangement of internship courses. The first approach subdivides the students into sections according to specialization sequences, such as news-editorial, advertising, public relations, film, broadcast production, broadcast journalism, community journalism and so on. The second approach mixes students of all sequences in the same seminar under the philosophy that a student's journalism education is enriched by exposure to the internship experiences of all fields.

MODEL 5

This model is much like Model 4 in the fact that it provides students with the opportunity for direct internship credit within the curriculum of the school. This distinction between Model 4 and Model 5 is that the programs using Model 4 do not require an internship as an overall departmental or sequence requirement to graduate. Model 5 programs do require such an internship. Wayne State University in Detroit and Northwestern University have a tradition of requiring all journalism students to serve from three credit hours (Wayne State) to nine to 12 credit hours (Northwestern) of internship before graduation.[8]

MODEL 6

In this model, the university or college department requires the student to complete an internship before the overall requirements for graduation are considered completed. This is not an academic requirement in the sense that it forces the student to take three to twelve semester hours for credit, as Model 5 does. It requires the internship, but it does not include it in curriculum hours requirements for majors; nor does it figure into the student's grade point average in any manner. This type of program is not in wide use, to the author's knowledge, but it remains a distinct possibility in management of interns from the institution's perspective.

NO STRONG GUIDELINES

De Mott has written widely about mass media internships, noting that "while the internship idea has thrived until the last few (1980–81) years or so, no set of guidelines has emerged, no standards have been compiled as benchmarks for those wishing to establish new programs or improve existing ones. The ways in which college and universities conduct journalism internship programs differ widely."

De Mott points to these major differences:

(1) Internship experience is required for graduation by some schools and programs but not by all.
(2) Academic credit is given for internship experience by some schools and programs, but not by all.
(3) Students are paid for their work under some internship programs by some employers, but not all students are paid in all positions.
(4) Some schools and departments of journalism delegate all supervision of interns to newspapers or other internship interests. Others require a faculty role.[9]

Perhaps it is this wide variation and wide range of academic control and quality that should concern us the most. Any attempts, however, by organizations to unify it seem to be fruitless. The Association for Education in Journalism and Mass Communication has unsuccessfully grappled with the matter for a number of years, including a lengthy discussion of an AEJMC committee report at the annual convention at Boston University in August 1980 that led to a tabled decision on acceptance of the report.

Lack of consensus within AEJMC is typical of the lack of discipline-wide consensus journalism education faces. Until those who teach and those who host the internships can reach agreement, and until those members within the two groups are in agreement on the goals, there can be no real progress.[10]

A point which cannot be argued is one raised earlier. The benefits are broad for the student and the host as well as the institution which provides the student. Both professionals and educators have sought to bring this early glimpse at the real world journalism to their best students. And it helps professionals gain an understanding of what mass communications and journalism education try to achieve.[11]

STANDARDS NEEDED

It is clear there is a great variety of approaches in placing the internship into the mass communications academic program. There is an equally wide variety of means for handling academic credit. There must be a nationwide effort to standardize internship administration and experiences. Greater effort should be channeled toward coordination of internship opportunities in the mass media such as that being done by the Mass Media Internship Group.

While journalism education depends on them a great deal already, it might be that a foundation or other organization could grant funds for creation of a clearing house for internships in the mass media for mass communication and journalism programs. This new organization, which would be centrally located, could then be the filtering point for internship information on a national basis and manage regional centers as well. Such an organization would serve all mass communication much as the annual Magazine Internship Program of the American Society of Magazine Editors (ASME) coordinates many of the major national magazine internships each year.

Clearly, such a group or organization would require the complete support and cooperation of all academic groups such as the AEJMC, Broadcast Education Association, the Accrediting Council on Education in Journalism and Mass Communication, the American Society of Journalism School Administrators, and the International Communication Association. It would require support of the professionals through organizations such as the American Society of Newspapers Editors, the Society of Professional Journalists/Sigma Delta Chi, Radio and Television News Directors Association, and others. It will require support and active assistance of student organizations also—such as student chapters of Society of Professional Journalists/Sigma Delta

Chi, Public Relations Student Society of America, and so on. In short, it would be a major coordination activity for this new organization. And it would follow that uniform standards would be necessary. Whether these standards would be across all mass communications areas or be set up for each area could be debated as standards are established. As mentioned, some organizations have proposed such standards and have had varying responses to them. It may be an impossible dream, but as much as could be possible, it would assure quality in the long run—especially if academic credit were involved.

NOTES

1. See Bernard C. Hennessy, *Political Internships*: Theory practice, *Evaluation*, Penn State Studies, University Park, Pa: Penn State University, 1970; Mary R. Wright, "Teaching Centers: A Study in Professional Development," paper presented to Association of Teacher Educators, annual convention, Los Vegas, Nevada, February 1978; Robert Barger, et al., "Program to Operationalize a New Training Pattern for Teaching Evaluation Personnel in Education: Final Report," National Institute of Education (Dept. of Health, Education, and Welfare), Research Foundation Ohio State University, Columbus, Ohio, June 1973.
2. Bruce Garrison, "Post Internship Seminar Can Solve Academic Credit, Grading Problems of Internship Programs," *Journalism Educator*, April 1981, pp. 14–18, 48.
3. Ronald H. Claxton, *The Student Guide to Mass Media Internships (1982)*, Internship Research Group, Department of Journalism, University of Wisconsin -Eau Claire, Eau Claire, Wis., 1982.
4. Accrediting Council on Education in Journalism and Mass Communications, *Accredited Journalism and Mass Communications Education, 1981–82*, published by Accrediting Council on Education in Journalism and Mass Communications, Columbia, Missouri, 1981, p. 9.
5. Robert A. Brown,"Shop Talk at Thirty: Training Interns," *Editor and Publisher*, Oct. 16, 1980, p. 56.
6. For a discussion and description, see John De Mott, "Post-Internship Seminar Benefits J-Students," *Journalism Educator*, July 1972, pp. 8–11.
7. See Garrison, *op cit.*
8. Rich Femmel, "Why Not make Internships Mandatory for Everybody?" *Journalism Educator*, October, 1978, pp. 17–19.
9. John De Mott, editor, *Internship Programs: A Manual for News Executives*, American Newspaper Publishers Association Foundation, p. 5, available from American Newspaper Publishers Association, P.O. Box 17407, Dulles International Airport, Washington, D.C., 20041, published in 1981.
10. See Garrison, "Post-Internship Seminar."
11. De Mott, *Internship Programs*, p. 5.

12
SUGGESTIONS FOR IMPLEMENTING (OR IMPROVING) AN INTERNSHIP PROGRAM

Jarice Hanson

With more than 1,000 colleges and universities already offering internships, the pre-professional disciplines, such as those in mass communications, move inexorably toward including and expanding internship programs. In establishing such programs, high priority should be assigned to issues of practicality and academic standards. Many smaller departments and liberal arts colleges are ill equipped to provide the "skills" courses required to bolster an internship experience, and there is a danger that internships can be substituted for academic classes. The Rutgers Model is put forth as exemplary, one that elicits a high degree of student initiative and responsiblity and reduces participation by eliminating students who are merely dabbling in work experiences.

Internships, or opportunities for students to receive course credit for applied education in the working world, are often valuable experiences for students who hope to test the application of theoretical material learned in the classroom to specific field experiences. Internships give students a chance to see what realities await them before they find themselves competing for jobs in areas in which they have little or no practical understanding or experience. Employers too, benefit from a close involvement with a young person who is often eager to please, and willing to do almost anything for a line of "experience" on his or her resume.

With recent cutbacks in student loans accompanying the rise in the cost of an academic education, a greater demand has been placed upon the college or university to prepare students for the working world. In his 1980 book, *On Higher Education*,[1] David Riesman discusses the need for alternative programs which make the college or university adaptable to contemporary needs, and suggests the option of creating programs which give "credit for off-campus involvement."[2]

Even the popular media have recently begun to suggest internships as a way for students to gain practical, firsthand knowledge about certain fields, while gaining a competitive edge over other graduates.[3]

Over one thousand colleges and universities in the United States now offer some type of internship program,[4] and many departments of Communication, Mass Media, or Journalism are finding that their curriculums lend themselves to the establishment of such a program in their schools. But before attempting to establish such a program at any college or university, it is necessary to consider a number of factors. While the practice of such a program may appear to be appealing and academically sound, the amount of time necessary to insure the proper administration of an ongoing program is overwhelming. Similarly, any institution currently involved in the maintenance of an internship program could benefit from periodic reexamination to strive for the best possible working relationship among students, employers, and participating faculty members.

The suggestions outlined below may be useful to any department or school considering implementing an internship program, but they also provide a framework for monitoring existing internship programs. These suggestions and the commentary accompanying each section are the result of a three year program at Rutgers University, in which the Department of Communication[5] actively redefined its own internship program. In this period, the program grew from accommodating three-to-five students per semester to accommodating fifty-to-sixty students per semester. This rapid growth in the internship program required the Rutgers faculty to consider several alternatives for the administration of the program. Therefore the "Rutgers Model" will be used to illustrate the components of the program as they evolved at Rutgers.

PRELIMINARY CONSIDERATIONS

Before instituting any new program of study, the department and academic institution should consider the program's practicality and academic integrity as well as the economy and the resources available to the department. Once an internship program is established, students and cooperating employers will have a number of questions regarding their individual expectations and experiences. The philosophy of the program must therefore serve as the foundation for a strong program which can be adapted to the needs of individuals. If such is to be the case, each faculty should come to some agreement on the following elements:

PRACTICALITY

Some departments should not even try to institute an internship program unless the courses offered in the major give students the skills necessary for an internship experience. Those institutions which rely on Communication-related departments for the administration of a number of service courses to the school, usually do not have the resources to establish an ongoing program. However, departments which offer special skill-related courses such as editing, layout, writing for the media, administrative or counselling skills, may find that their programs are easily adapted to specialized internships. A Rutgers Communication major chooses one of six tracks to focus on: Public Relations/Advertising, Organizational/Administrative Communication, International/Intercultural Communication, Mass Media, Interpersonal and Group Communications, or Speech Communication and Advocacy. While the greatest number of majors engaged in internships comes from the Public Relations/Advertising or the Mass Media tracks, special internships in other tracks have been facilitated. Often the Speech Communication and Advocacy track draws a number of students interested in continuing their educations in law school. Many of these students engage in internships with local politicians or lobbying groups. Students in the Interpersonal/Group track sometimes find themselves working as peer counsellors within the school, as aides in the counselling offices of local Senior Citizen groups, or in religious centers. Organizational/Administrative students have occasionally been placed with community organizations such as the Boy Scouts, the Teen Arts League, or the local Civic Improvement Committee.

ACADEMIC INTEGRITY

Once an internship program is deemed a practical consideration, matters of academic integrity and course credit should be considered. While the philosophy and/or mission of the academic institution may dictate how much time may be spent in the field or how the awarding of credit may be handled, there are usually three alternatives to consider. Alternating programs: Many colleges or universities which stress career preparation will develop full-time internships, called alternating programs. In this program, a student spends one full semester at the field site, five days a week, and then returns to the school as a full-time student the following semester. The number of credits usually totals the number the student would receive if engaged in full-time study at the institution. If the student is participating in an internship in another geographic area, the student's tuition might be adjusted to reflect the costs incurred for the internship experience.

Columbia College in Chicago, Illinois, is one institution which prepares students for careers in the media arts.[6] Because of the total involvement expected by students in the internship program, the school feels that only an alternating type of program will give the students the full range of experiences at the site. All students enrolled in the program are required to attend mandatory intern meetings and expected to attend seminars held at the school. Because Columbia College puts a great deal of emphasis on experience-based learning, the school also has been able to develop a strong support system of cooperating employers.

Liberal Arts schools also facilitate alternating internship programs, but usually do not have the resources to extend an experience-based program to a large number of students at any given time. Sometimes the location of the academic institution will determine the practicality of having alternating internships. While there may be some internships, like the Newspaper Fund or Voice of America Internships,[7] which would require students to be away from the academic institution for a full semester, most of the internship experiences could fall into one of the categories below.

Parallel programs: A parallel program is one in which the student is concurrently enrolled in courses at the academic institution while spending a limited period of time in the field. While the student may not be able to take advantage of the full range of a site's experiences in a parallel program, this type of internship often works better as an adjunct to the curriculum, and gives the faculty a greater amount of control over the program.

Rutgers University takes the position that an internship experience may be valuable, but that it does not take the place of classroom instruction. Accordingly, the Department of Communication opted for a parallel program of internships, with limited course credit available for the experience. While students in the program may receive three credits per semester for one or two days in the field (with a written component, to be discussed later), these credits may not be used in place of the required number of elective credits necessary for the Communication major. By allowing students to participate in internships which give them credit toward graduation, but not toward the major, students are assured of having at least a minimum number of credits taken in the department. It was discovered too, that this policy helped eliminate a number of students who were not sincerely motivated to participate in an internship experience. Likewise, the proximity of New York City to the University afforded a number of possible internship sites, making commuting daily only a modestly expensive burden. Thus the limitations imposed upon the students neither jeopardize the academic integrity of the course of study, nor do they cause undue financial stress.

Independent Study: Many institutions which are either unsure of the support they will be able to provide an internship program, or which question the validity of an internship program as it relates to the course of study, may find that an Independent Study approach to internships is the best approach. In this type of program, students propose to work as "volunteers" at an internship site, and then put together a written paper or project under the sponsorship of a faculty member. Course credit is sometimes assigned according to the type of paper or project contracted for. Usually students will receive anywhere from one to four credits, though special arrangements may be made for independent studies which last longer than one semester.

In addition to the working relationship between the student and the faculty member which often serves the mentoring process well,[8] an independent study with an internship-like field placement allows the student with special interests to develop his or her focus on a special basis. When independent study programs are successful over a number of semesters, an alternating or parallel internship program can be instituted easily, providing the department can handle the numbers of students who may wish to participate.

ECONOMY

While the location of the school might suggest the economic viability of an internship program to the department or course of study, another matter which needs to be considered is that of paid or subsidized internships. While internships are usually non-paid experiences, some employers will offer students some financial remuneration. Though many schools have individual rules regarding the payment of students for off-campus work, the guidelines for interns are not always clear. With the current economy, it may be unfair to expect students to participate in internships which do not at least pay their expenses. Faculties should be aware that some companies cannot legally have non-paid students working for them in any way, for reasons which usually revolve around the company's accountability to stockholders or to state labor laws.

When rules regarding payment of interns raise questions for the academic institution and the employer, a useful publication may be the *Employment Relationship under the Fair Labor Standards Act*[9] which states that while employees must be paid, interns who act as trainees need not be paid.

RESOURCES

The availability of internship sites and employers is often dependent upon the location of the school, but perhaps the greatest resource to consider is the availability of faculty to administer the program. The responsibility for making the internship a rigorous academic activity falls to the faculty coordinator. While large institutions committed to an internship program usually have the funding available to hire someone who is responsible for the internship program, most liberal arts schools do not have this luxury. Therefore, the administration of an internship program usually falls to one faculty member who may or may not have released time from classes, or to a number of faculty members possessing strengths relating to specific internships.

At Rutgers it was decided that the number of students in the internship program was too large, and involved too many different types of internships for any one faculty member to administrate effectively. Therefore, one person became responsible for interviewing students, setting up employer interviews, fielding questions from prospective employers, and administering the record keeping functions of maintaining the program. Other faculty members with strengths in the different fields were responsible for guiding the research and grading the written projects required of all interns. This approach has proven effective because it reduces the ambiguity for interested students and employers, as well as insuring individual guidance for students from faculty members who are aware of the current trends in the field.

WHO ARE THE PARTICIPANTS?

STUDENTS

One of the first determinations to make when considering the implementation of an internship program is outlining the criteria for determining which students and employers are eligible to participate. Of course students should be required to complete all preliminary courses pertaining to their fields of interest before their internship experiences begin, and therefore, internships are usually restricted to juniors and seniors.

Motivation is also a large part of making the internship experience a valuable one, and it is also one of the hardest factors to measure. Criteria such as grade point averages or prior experience do not often give the faculty member enough information to determine whether or not an individual student is ready for a field experience. Many institutions require prospective interns to submit letters of recommendation from former employers or other teachers. The securing of letters requires prospective interns to plan ahead for an internship, thereby eliminating students who do not regard the internship experience worthy of planning and preparation, but it does not in itself provide definitive information about the student's capabilities.

Perhaps more effective is the student's statement requesting an internship, followed by an in-depth interview with the faculty coordinator. The student's statement should include reasons for the student's interest in a particular placement, as well as the goals he or she hopes to accomplish. If a written paper is required, the student should summarize the direction he or she hopes to take.

At Rutgers, students interested in the internship program first receive a handout stating the policies of the department and the requirements for the student. Next, the student must make an appointment with the faculty coordinator, at which time the student presents his or her statement and résumé and answers questions which help determine the student's readiness for a field placement. Because internships at Rutgers are treated as a job placement simulation, students know that their written materials must be neatly typed, and that they should show up for the interview appropriately attired for the type of placement they desire.

One of the reasons this method has been so successful at Rutgers is because the internship program there is so competitive. There are always more students desirous of internships than there are placements, and the amount of time a student must invest in applying for a competitive internship really acts as a deterrent to students who are merely bent on escaping classroom learning.

Many institutions however, must recruit students for the internship program. One of the best ways to recruit students is to have former interns come to classes to speak about their own experiences. Another effective method which has occasionally been used in institutions which have public relations or communication education students, is to develop an internship within the institution in which two or three students become responsible for publicizing the program in campus media (and sometimes holding question and answer periods for interested students), and/or in which communication education students actively develop programs for the development of related skills (such as résumé writing workshops, interviewing seminars or career counselling sessions).

A question relating to the active recruitment of students centers on the amount of control the faculty coordinator hopes to exercise. When internships are highly publicized, or dependent upon the efforts of other students, the faculty sacrifices some of the control. Therefore, particularly in the initial stages of any internship program, it is probably better to publicize internships on a smaller level (say, within the department) and administer the program to only a few students who have been concerned enough to keep up with the deadlines and the flow of information.

For programs which depend upon the student's ability to find his or her own field placement, there is a helpful paperback called *The Internship Experience*.[10] This book supplies excellent information to students who are trying to find their own field placements with little guidance from the faculty. But again, under such circumstances the cooperating faculty member has little control over the placement.

EMPLOYERS

Locating prospective employers to participate in the internship program is usually not difficult, though it may be time consuming. To start, a form letter may be mailed to the personnel divisions of major corporations or organizations within a given area. Finding potential employers may also be facilitated by consulting other faculty members who have individual contacts, or by making contacts through the school's Alumni Relations Office.

Along with the letter which introduces the program, its goals, and items such as the skills students may be expected to have, evaluation procedures, deadlines for an organization's application for an intern, school policies on financial remuneration, security and insurance,[11] the letter should provide the name of the faculty member to contact for more information, and the hours in which that faculty member may be reached. Nothing can frustrate a potential employer more than attempting to phone someone who is never in his or her office when the employer is trying to offer a service.

Since the reduction of the CETA program, several employers have turned to internship programs in local colleges and universities for free labor. When interviewing prospective employers over the phone or in person, it is best to get them to talk about the needs they have for specific interns before elaborating on the particulars of the internship program. In this way, it is often possible to determine whether the employer is likely to exploit the intern, or be unable to give proper supervision to a student in his or her charge. If the employer has considered his or her needs adequately, he or she would provide a job description on paper, to aid in student placement as well as to outline to the employer what to expect.

Most academic institutions have policies regarding the evaluation of off-campus instruction, and the employer should be informed of those policies. Often institutions will not acknowledge grades which have been provided by anyone other than a faculty member, and given the trouble an employer would have in grading someone with no understanding of the grading system of the university or college, this is often a good policy.

An employer's evaluation might take the form of a letter or recommendation which could go the student and the faculty coordinator, or it might take the form of an "exit interview."

Perhaps one of the best approaches is to have the employer respond to a form which asks questions about the student's maturity, cooperativeness, knowledge of procedures, motivation, and responsibility. When the form is mailed to the faculty coordinator and is treated as a confidential correspondence, the employer is more likely to be candid and treat the evaluation more seriously than a less formal, oral evaluation.

THE FACULTY COORDINATOR'S RESPONSIBILITIES

The faculty coordinator's job requires a strong commitment to experiential learning. When each student has a slightly different set of expectations, problems seem to surface daily. Also, the effort expended to develop internships for the next semester while administering the ongoing semester leads to a never ending struggle against time.

One of the most time consuming activities is maintaining the records for the internship. When one person is responsible for a large number people, it is difficult to send evaluation forms to employers, address the needs of the periodic phone callers for information, and evaluate prospective interns with an eye for their academic growth.

A method recently introduced at Rutgers has cut the amount of time devoted to record keeping in half, by making the interns responsible for keeping records of faculty discussions about research, employer and student evaluations. When a student begins the internship, he or she is given an information packet stating the deadlines for completion of the research project, the dates for personal conferences with the internship coordinator, and the evaluation forms. When the student comes to the faculty member for a consultation, the faculty member dates and signs the form. Likewise, when the student gives the employer the evaluation form which will be mailed directly to the faculty coordinator, the employer signs and dates the cover sheet on the student's packet. The student then becomes responsible for the maintenance of his or her own record, and suffers the consequences if the responsibility is not carried through. Again, the idea that an internship is only for responsible, mature students, is affirmed.

The faculty coordinator may also have to deal with a large number of students who hear about the internship program but who should not be allowed to participate. At Rutgers, majors from disciplines other than Communication try to arrange internships in television studios, public relations, etc. every semester. At one point, a Dean's wife inquired whether she could register for three credits of independent study with the Communication Department, so that she could participate in an internship with a local video production house. Because internships are so time consuming, it is best to restrict them to majors only, otherwise the academic integrity of the program as an adjunct to the curriculum will be lost.

The most difficult time period to administer the program is during the summer, when it is less likely that a faculty member will be in the office for the entire duration of the student's internship. It is advisable to have a faculty coordinator responsible for summer internships if the number of students warrants supervision, or it may be necessary to arrange the period of the intern's field experience for a week or two into the new semester so that he or she may benefit from the discussions about performance by the employer and faculty coordinator. Once the intern has left the field placement, it is difficult to find constructive criticism from employers who may be busy training new interns, or who are less likely to give time to someone who is no longer actively involved in the company.

If time and resources are adequate, it is a great help for the faculty member to observe the intern at work. In this manner, the student is impressed by the seriousness of the internship experience, while the informal meeting of all three parties involved encourages commitment by the employer as well as maintains a public relations tie between field placement and academic institution.

Students need to know when they must start planning for an internship, and how they will be evaluated. Also, the faculty coordinator sometimes forgets that an internship may well be a student's first academic experience outside of the classroom. Sometimes extra guidance may be necessary to provide a modicum of structure to what the student views as a seemingly unstructured experience.

EVALUATING THE INTERNSHIP

As mentioned above, it is helpful for the faculty coordinator to receive some form of evaluation from the employer regarding the student's participation at the field site. It is also very helpful to allow the student to evaluate the internship experience and the employer, so that future discussions between the employer and faculty coordinator may be guided by a student's perception of the experience. Finally, the student evaluation is helpful to the faculty coordinator when interviewing potential interns for the same placement or for periodic review of the individual field site for placement of other interns.

Giving the intern a letter grade for the experience is somewhat difficult at times, but perhaps the best criterion upon which to base a grade is the fulfillment of the purpose of the internship within the academic department. Some internships in schools which stress classroom education, but which facilitate internships out of concern for potential student employment, do not grade internships at all, but treat them as "pass/fail" options. This is a very practical approach to the administration of alternating internships, particularly when the student is operating in a field site some distance away from the academic institution.

Parallel internships or independent studies, however, are often regarded as different types of educational experiences which should be graded. Because it is often difficult to measure how much the student learns during an internship, students are usually required to submit some from of written paper or project. One of the most common written forms is a journal which outlines the intern's tasks and responsibilities daily. But this type of project does little to inform the faculty coordinator how the intern has assimilated classroom education with the field experience.

At Rutgers, each intern is responsible for turning in an extended research paper or project, which deals with some aspect of the internship which the student would like to know more about. Therefore, a student working in a cable television facility might research legislation regarding the establishment of the cable industry, public access, or satellites as used by the cable industry. A student working in an organization might develop a project detailing the hierarchical structure of that organization complete to job descriptions and experience needed; or develop a program for use by the organization, such as a day-care center or a fitness program for employees. In fact a number of the projects undertaken by Rutgers interns have not only been used as tools for grading the intern, but as aids to the sponsoring organizations or employers as well.

CONCLUSION

The commitment of an institution to the establishment and continuation of an internship program cannot be taken lightly. Every individual student and employer needs guidance from the faculty coordinator, and each coordinator must have the time and the support system to administer the program properly. Faculty coordinators must

	Number of Seniors Participating	Number of Seniors Receiving Jobs
Public Relations/Advertising	18	12
Mass Media	8	5
Interpersonal/Group	3	2
International/Intercultural	1	1
Organizational/Administrative	3	2
Speech Communication and Advocacy	1	0

Number of graduating Seniors in the Department of Communication receiving jobs as a result of their internship, Spring Semester, 1982.

have a strong commitment to experience-based learning, or the administration of the program can become tedious.

Each faculty needs to recognize the place of the internship program with the curriculum at the academic institution involved, and develop guidelines accordingly. While an internship program can be a useful tool for training students for careers, and giving some assistance in difficult economic times, it may also strengthen ties between the academic institutions and the community.

Internships are often stepping stones to careers for students. The table below indicates how many seniors engaged in the internship program at Rutgers University actually found employment after graduation as a result of the internship experience. While the internship program may be difficult and time consuming to administer, the results speak for themselves.

NOTES

1. David Riesman, *On Higher Education* (San Francisco: Jossey-Bass Inc., 1980).
2. Riesman, pp. 71–76.
3. See for example: "Partners," *American Education*, 16, No. 5 (1980), 55–58; "Beyond Student Teaching," *Educational Digest* 1, 45, (1979), 49–50; "Internships: a Head Start on a career," *McCalls*, 108 (1981), 55; "Jobs that let you learn. . . . " *Mademoiselle*, 87, (1981), 144 + .
4. Dan Bardy, "The Coop Experience: Getting the Best of Both Worlds," *Training Today*, The Magazine of the Illinois Training and Development Association, (November 1981) 2.
5. Formerly the Department of Human Communication, the department became called the Department of Communication when the University began its reorganization July 1, 1981. The Department of Communication now has approximately 700 majors.

6. Columbia College, The Columbia College Chicago Cooperative Education and Internship Program, (Chicago: Columbia College, 1981).

7. Information regarding the Newspaper Fund's Internship Program may be obtained from: The Newspaper Fund, P.O. Box 300, Princeton, N.J. 08540. Information regarding the Voice of America Internship may be obtained from the Voice of America, Washington, D.C.

8. Gerald M. Phillips, "The Peculiar Intimacy of Graduate Study: A Conservative View," *Communication Education*, 28, No. 4 (1979), 339–345.

9. *Employment Relationship under the Fair Labor Standards Act*, White House Publication 1297 (Rev.) (Washington, D.C: U.S. Department of Labor).

10. Lynne Schafer Gross, *The Internship Experience* (Belmont, California: Wadsworth, Inc., 1981).

11. Matters related to security and insurance are important to discuss with potential employers. Most universities and colleges will not assume responsibility for broken equipment, or injuries sustained by the intern while on the job. Few companies will assume responsibility for anyone who is not employed by them, but who becomes injured while using the company's equipment.

13
A PERSPECTIVE ON INTERNSHIP GRADING PROBLEMS AND A SOLUTION

Andrew Ciofalo

Problems with the administration and evaluation of internships are rooted in the "student revolution" that swept most campuses in the Vietnam War era. In all disciplines challenges were made to the traditional academic approach to the dissemination of knowledge. In mass communications, in particular, campus-based experiential learning units (student newspaper, campus radio station, etc) became political and economic liabilities to schools and departments. In the mad scramble to divest of on-campus media, internships were hastily conceived and prematurely launched as substitute vehicles for experiential learning. Beset by a host of problems, one of the most vexing (and symptomatic of the malaise) is the question of internship grading. Grade inflation, long suspected as a factor in the popularity of internships [see articles herein by Bruce Garrison and Robert Kendall, ed.], was confirmed by a study of internship grading patterns at Loyola College (Maryland). A simple change in grading procedure resulted in lower grades and, ultimately, fewer students opting for internships.

Problems in grading and evaluating student performance in internships must be resolved despite the continuing larger debate among masscom faculties over their academic legitimacy.[1] There would have been no urgency in the 1950s when few students engaged in internships and those that did were permitted to do so either because of their excellent academic records or to fulfill requirements for graduate programs in journalism.[2] But now the proliferation of communications internships[3] challenges the pedagogy of undergraduate communications curricula and raises some critical questions.

First, is the increased accessibility of internships a by-product of increased careerism among students? Second, have the students discovered that their classroom experiences do not prepare them to meet the high standards of the professions? And third, are internships simply easy courses yielding high grades that raise the communications major's grade point average?

The first two questions belong to the larger debate over legitimacy, but the question of grading and evaluating internships is one that can be answered quickly and with immediate results, as we have discovered in Loyola College's Media Program.

The problem with grading has not emerged solely because of the number of students taking internships has grown exponentially. There is also a subtle historical residue left from the temporary shift when masscom's experiential learning base moved from on-campus activities to off-campus internships in the 1960s.

Internships did not begin to proliferate in most professional disciplines until late in the 1960s.[4] They appeared in conjunction with the student-consumer movement and lowered academic standards resulting from student-led opposition to the Viet Nam War. Given that dubious birthright, it is no wonder that even well-conceived and well-managed internships like The Field Studies Program at the University of California, Berkeley were retrenched[5] in the wake of the budget-crunching inflationary recession at the beginning of this decade [1980s].

While the "student revolution" had a direct effect in other disciplines, giving rise to internship programs, it devastated existing experiential learning in mass communications. Journalism programs, in particular, used to deliver practical experience to their majors through a direct affiliation with campus newspapers and other media. But militant students and politicized advocates of "new journalism" seized editorial control of these instruments, creating liabilities for journalism schools and departments, whose faculties and budgets were vulnerable to institutional retribution for the excesses of campus-based media. Wisely or not, J-schools and departments either divested themselves of or terminated working agreements with the student press, leaving a large gap in faculty supervised opportunities for practical experience. Internships became the alternative in order "to take up the slack in practical experience."[6]

There is a major difference, however, between on-campus and off-campus experience. Full-time faculty are directly involved in the former and only marginally so in the latter. Yet full credit for "experiential learning" was reapplied from one format to the other, despite the fact that the role of the faculty was reduced to that of gatekeeper, monitor and/or clerk.

The transfer of primary responsibility for the internship grade to a non-faculty entity (the editor) challenges the academic credibility of the major and whittles down the doctoral standing of the discipline as it seeks a special place at the cusp between the humanities and social sciences.

Accordingly, among masscom faculties there is a nascent sentiment that could potentially swell into a backlash to decertify internships, if not to eliminate them altogether.[7] However, like Coca-Cola, it is difficult to take a successful and widely accepted product off the market. Instead, one might consider reducing the appeal of the internship by altering one of its most attractive features—the easy grade—as Loyola's Media Program did.

Having spent four years speaking to prospective communications majors at Loyola College, I have never ceased to be amazed at the interest in media education shown by Loyola underclassmen and high school seniors. Until the 1986–87 academic year, a fully-developed communications curriculum never appeared in the college catalog. All that was available was a truncated half-major in media that a student was able to combine with a half-major in almost any other discipline. Yet enrollments increased five-fold to 180 in four years.

The one evident change was the sudden expansion of the Media Program's internship opportunities in 1983–84. The internships were given high visibility in the college catalog, each with its own course number under journalism, broadcast, advertising, public relations, publishing and graphics.

Private interviews with prospective freshmen by media faculty and admissions officers and open questions on college visitation days revealed a universal interest in the internship program. Although this evidence is anecdotal, it seems that the variety of available media internships, coupled with a liberal college policy on internship education, provided the primary fuel for launching entering freshmen and others into the media split-major. The lack of courses and technical facilities at the time did not deter the first rush of interest.

Obviously there is a danger that masscom and other professional disciplines will succumb to the "sexiness" of internships as enrollment builders, or simply respond to student demand without fully understanding the nature of experiential learning. But the danger that most visibly undermines respect for the discipline is grade inflation, and Loyola found internship grading to be a primary contributing factor.

In examining the grades college-wide for Loyola interns a pattern emerges that indicates internships result in grade inflation. What is the value of a course and what does it tell us about a student's performance and ability if the grade is usually an "A"?[8] The internship experience at Loyola College during the 1985–86 academic year offers some startling consistencies in grading practices across most disciplines offering internships. (Some disciplines sponsoring one or two internships were excluded from the study as being atypical.)

During that period, 77 college-wide internships were run without requiring a weekly class meeting. The GPA (4.00 = A) for internship courses by discipline averaged out as follows:

Fall 1985

Poli Science:	4.00
Writing:	4.00
Business:	4.00
English:	4.00
Media:	3.84
Fine Arts:	3.67

Summer 1986

Business:	4.00
Sociology:	4.00
Media:	3.67

Spring 1986

Poli Science:	4.00
Psychology:	4.00
Theology:	4.00
Media:	3.79
Fine Arts:	3.71

The Writing/Media Department addressed the problem of grade inflation by making a simple change in its evaluative procedures. Instead of asking internship supervisors to assign a final grade, we asked them only to rate intern performance in 20 categories, using a 1 (outstanding) to 5 (poor) numerical rating system. (We had noticed that supervisor ratings generally did not reflect their recommended grades.) The result was that the overall GPA for media interns fell to 3.0, which is what one would expect from upperclassmen taking advanced electives in their majors.

By breaking down the evaluation into as many categories as possible, the Media Program insured that idiosyncratic low ratings in a few categories would not skew the final grade. The 20 categories we use actually guide the internship supervisor step by step through the evaluative process. The evaluator's focus is thus shifted from the consideration of an overall grade to a highly specific appraisal of each attribute that indicates a successful professional performance. And by assigning a graduated numerical rating to each attribute, we have reduced the assignment of a final grade to a simple mathematical averaging that students are accustomed to and understand.

This system, besides bringing down the GPA for internship courses, has eliminated the inevitable grade challenges by internship students receiving anything less than an "A" from supervisors who never administered a test or graded a piece of written or graphic work. The following are the numerical averages and their letter grade equivalents:

1.00 to 1.25 = A
1.26 to 1.75 = B+
1.76 to 2.00 = B
2.01 to 2.25 = B−
2.26 to 2.75 = C+
2.76 to 3.00 = C
3.00 to 3.25 = C−
3.26 to 4.25 = D
4.26 to 5.00 = F

The categories the Loyola communication students are rated on include:[9]

— promptness
— resourcefulness
— maturity
— interest in job
— ability to learn
— creativity
— writing skills
— editing skills
— graphic skills
— photography skills
— speed
— accuracy
— ability to communicate
— ability to organize
— ability to work with others
— ability to work under deadline pressure
— ability to contribute to the organization
— understanding of organizational procedures
— acceptance and constructive use of criticism
— promise of success in the profession

Registration for media internships was down from the usual 25 to 8 for the Fall 1987 semester, indicating that grades may have been a factor in the extensive participation in the internship program. A survey of 148 Loyola interns (32% response) seemed to support this contention.

The respondents represented a proportional mix of graduates and current students spanning the first four years of the internship program. Almost half the students (43%) admitted that an "easy grade" was a factor in their decision to register for an internship. (Loyola

communication students average two internships during their bac-
calaureate careers, ranging from a single internship to four.)

The two highest-rated factors cited by the surveyed communications
students as "important" reasons for doing an internship were motivated by practical and career-oriented thinking. Most students (79%)
used internships to test their interest in one of the media fields and
78% used internships to build a base of experience for inclusion on
their resumes.

Thus it is apparent that students are not taking media internships
for what they can learn but rather for very utilitarian reasons. It is
astonishing to witness seniors who have received a "B" for an internship course pleading for a higher grade because, as one said, "How
can I explain this on a job interview?" While most students say they
aren't looking for an easy grade, the Loyola experience indicates that
a more realistic grading policy could result in reduced internship
enrollments. That would narrow the internship base down to the more
serious and better students who then could be directed to higher
quality internships. Eliminated from the internship scene, at least
from a college certified internship experience, would be the weaker
internships and those dilettantes that are attracted to them.

NOTES

1. Bruce Garrison, "Post internship seminar can solve academic credit, grading problems of internship programs," *Journalism Educator*, Vol. 36, No. 1
   (April 1981), pp. 14–17.
2. Alan Scott and Vernon Bowen, "Publishers and Students Favor Summer
   Internships Plan," *Journalism Quarterly*, (June 1949), pp. 197–99.
3. Garrison (1981), *op. cit.*
4. John De Mott, "Newspaper Internships in Education for Journalism: The
   Historical perspective," paper presented at the annual meeting of the Association for Education in Journalism, (August 1979).
5. Jon Wagner, "Integrating the Traditions of Experiential Learning in Internship Education," *Journal of Experiential Learning* (Fall 1983), p. 9.
6. Warren K. Agee, "Trends in the Development of News-Editorial Curriculums," paper presented to the newspaper division of the Association for
   Education in Journalism, (1966), p. 13.
7. Garrison (1981), *op. cit.*
8. *Ibid.*
9. Categories adapted from Lynne S. Gross, *The Internship Experience*, (Belmont, California: Wadsworth Inc. 1981).

14
INTERNSHIP PROGRAMS—
BRIDGING THE GAP
Terry A. Madoch

There are a number of ways for business and higher education to interface, but the most successful has been through the use of internships. Elmhurst College (Illinois) offered a program for "selective seniors" and found that both businesses and student benefitted at a number of levels from involvement in internships. Ten suggestions are put forward for building a successful business internship program.

Business organizations are consistently complaining about the lack of qualified, dependable, and productive employees. And educators express concern about providing relevant curricula. Obviously these two concerns are not only complementary, but are actually inseparable. Programs can be designed to meet the needs of both. Examples of successful cooperative ventures presently being undertaken include faculty/employer conferences, career days, utilization of actual ongoing case studies by academia, utilization of business people as resources in the classroom, and cooperation with governmental agencies such as the Small Business Administration.

All these ventures address themselves to the issue of bridging the gap between schools and the business world. However, one program in particular—internships—has been especially successful.

To illustrate a specific example, over the past three years, I have been responsible for developing and coordinating the Internship Program for the Center for Business and Economics of Elmhurst College [Elmhurst, Illinois]. Since the program began, more than 60 percent of all placed interns have been offered full-time positions by the companies with which they served their internships. We have placed approximately 35 to 40 students a year.

Students come from different majors in our curriculum and are selectively screened by our center and the participating organizations. They are placed with a variety of organizations throughout Chicago and the western suburbs. Anywhere from 35 to 40 organizations have been participating in the program on a continual basis and the list of interested organizations is constantly growing.

The Internship Program at Elmhurst is designed for "selective seniors," the purpose being to provide an experience which integrates classroom learning with actual business experience. For the student intern, the benefits gained from involvement in the program include: sound training for entry level job(s) coupled with academic credit; having a testing ground for academic preparation, career aspirations, and self-concept; and a possibility for full-time employment upon graduation with the internship organization, or practical experience for gaining other employment opportunities.

For the employer participating in the program, the following benefits are realized:

- the addition of a qualified and well-prepared, part-time employee;
- a source for recruiting employees;
- a resource for special projects; and
- an opportunity to "groom" potential full-time employees.

Not only does such a program serve the employment needs of both the participating organizations and the students, but it can be viewed as an investment in the future. The resulting working relationship enhances communication channels, thereby leading to the development of additional programs.

The following offers 10 suggestions for building a successful business internship program. These guidelines are substantiated and supported by an ongoing successful program.

1. The program should be related to, and focus on, local employment opportunities.
2. The program must be totally committed to and supported by both the educational institution and the faculty.
3. The program must have the ongoing involvement and cooperation of the participating organizations. This provides for continuity, marketability, and maximum benefits to all participants.
4. The program should involve only interested, qualified and conscientious students. Students should be selectively screened by the educational institution and the participating organizations regarding their interests and abilities.
5. Participating organizations must provide structured, meaningful job experiences. Development of such experiences

should be a cooperative effort of the organization and the coordinator.

6. Student interns should be supervised by a management individual at the organization. Provisions for directions, feedback, and evaluation of performance are essential.

7. Written and agreed upon training plans enhance the experience. Agreements should include performance objectives developed and accepted by the employer, student, and coordinator.

8. Some intern compensation (minimum wage, or salary based on company policy, union regulations, etc.) is strongly suggested to make the experience realistic.

9. During the internship, students should be provided with opportunities to interact and share their experiences with regular employees.

10. An individual faculty member should have responsibility for the program and be available to market, coordinate and monitor the program on a continual basis.

"How do we make our business curriculum more relevant?" "How can we better meet the employment needs of our organization?" Both questions can be answered with one response—internships. The result of such a shared, cooperative venture can bridge the barriers separating theory and practice.

15
POST-INTERNSHIP SEMINAR CAN SOLVE ACADEMIC CREDIT, GRADING PROBLEMS

Bruce Garrison

Arguments that internships-for-credit dilute the over-all academic program have led to discipline-wide consideration of the "academic abuse of internships," but without much in the way of concrete steps or recommendations to resolve the situation. In the absence of national standards, many high quality institutions devise interesting approaches to the problem. Marquette University's solution is offered as one of the viable models. No credit is given directly for the internship, but students wanting credit can take a follow-up seminar as a collateral requirement.

Critics of internship programs that grant academic credit to students often argue that the overall academic program becomes diluted. The problem, then, is to provide a strong program with viable internship opportunities without endangering the quality of the curriculum. No journalism educator wants an internship program which harms the academic package offered by his or her institution's journalism unit.

Concerned nationally about the quality of internships, the Internship Committee of the Association for Education in Journalism proposed a series of 13 guidelines for internships to the Executive Committee of AEJ at the Boston convention in August 1980. The report was a response to a resolution at the 1978 Seattle convention to study the matter of credit, economic and academic abuses, and other aspects of internships. At the Boston convention, however, the resolution to approve the report generated considerable attention and discussion by members of AEJ. After debate, Resolution 6 was tabled, leaving the AEJ stance on internships in uncertainty for at least another year. The original report of the Internship Committee was summarized in the fall, 1980 issue of the *AEJ Newsletter*.

The discussion at the business meeting of AEJ at Boston indicated extensive interest in internships and a desire to learn successful methods of controlling academic abuse of internships. A number of observations were made by the committee, among them that there is considerable range in views on the credit question, and that a "very high percentage (of programs) require internship credit as a condition of graduation."[2]

Although tabled and still in the consideration stage, the report presents guidelines which could become the model by which internship programs in journalism education in the 1980s are based.

But they raise some important questions which must be addressed. The single most important question is not new, centering on whether work experiences should be granted academic credit. Obviously, the AEJ Internship Committee guidelines, and the majority of universities with internship programs in this country, condone granting academic credit for internships.

Hugh Cowdin, writing in *Journalism Educator* in 1978, stated that a survey conducted by the American Society of Journalism School Administrators (ASJSA) found that 53 of 55 (96.4 percent) responding schools had formal intern programs. And of that total responding, 52 (94.5 percent) granted some form of academic credit for the internship experience. While one must consider that only 55 of the 128 member schools in ASJSA responded in the survey, the figure, even considering those not responding, represents almost half of the entire membership of ASJSA which grants academic credit for internships.[3]

A survey conducted by Women in Communications, Inc., (WICI) found equally high proportions of schools granting credit. The data in the WICI study in 1978–79 indicated "nearly all interns earn credit, but only 15 percent of the responding universities require an internship for graduation." The study also found that about half of the interns interviewed received credit and a salary.[4]

Thus, schools which do not grant academic credit for internships are likely to be harder to find as the new decade passes. With the recommendations of the AEJ Internships Committee and the figures reported by Cowdin, the trend is clearly toward granting credit. In fact, Richard Femmel suggests that internships should be required of all majors, as is done at Wayne State University, another urban university, located in Detroit. Femmel implies that there is internship credit built into the curriculum as a required course or courses for all majors.[5]

While there are obvious advantages for requiring an internship program in an urban environment—such as a proximity of a major media market and greater numbers of opportunities for students seeking internships—the College of Journalism at Marquette clearly stops short of granting credit for an internship and requiring internships of all majors. Just as required internships have been a tradition at

Wayne State University, Marquette has maintained that internships should not be given direct academic credit in an already packed-tight curriculum—even as an elective course or as elective credit.

De Mott offers another reason for not granting direct academic credit for the journalism internship. He argues, "Since the experiences of summer interns differ so greatly, and the average school or department of journalism is seldom in a position to oversee a student's summer activity satisfactorily, there is a natural reluctance to grant academic credit."[6]

At the point when the college decided that a formalized internship program would be desirable, the Marquette faculty set up an Internship Committee to reevaluate the college's policy on internships.[7] After a two-semester series of meetings and thorough study of literature such as *Journalism Educator* articles and the much lengthier *ASJSA Roundtable No. 80* on which Cowdin's article is based,[8] the committee recommended the college maintain its long-term position that credit not be given to students.

Instead, the faculty approved in September 1979 a formal internship program which only grants academic credit for a course taken by students after the internship has been completed. As in many other intern programs, the burden of locating and completing the internship stays with the student. After the internship summer, for example (although only a few students at Marquette serve internships in the fall or spring semesters, the program is flexible and can meet their needs), the student then decides to petition to take the course designed as a readings and research seminar on experiences based on the internship—in effect, using the internship experience as a prerequisite for the course and eligibility for the three semester hours academic credit granted for the elective course.

This type of indirect credit intern program was tested successfully by De Mott at Northern Illinois University in an earlier experiment.[9] It also has worked out well since 1975 at the University of Wyoming where an adequately supervised concurrent internship program is made impossible by the state's low population density, the great distances between communities, the lack of any media concentration in the state, and limited faculty members and time.

Despite the many advantages of internships to students and school, the Marquette internship program does not grant credit solely for the internship per se. Furthermore, credit is not given for work on school publications (which is provided at some institutions as "practicum".) Whether students receive wages or salary during the internship makes no difference. (However, Marquette faculty generally feel students should be paid. Students are not encouraged to accept positions and perform professional level work without compensation. In short, the college philosophy is that students should not be required to pay high tuition costs for academic credit granted for the opportunity to gain practical experience.)[10]

After a Marquette student completes an internship, he or she obtains an agreement with a faculty member to enroll in the new seminar course for either two or three semester hours with approval of the Field Study Committee and of the dean of the college.

These limitations or qualifications are stated:

(1) Evidence must be offered by the student which demonstrates the capability of completing a study or inquiry based on the internship, given the semester time limitation and the student's personal resources.

(2) The study must be broader in scope and depth than a normal course and must not be in an area ordinarily covered by a regularly offered course.

(3) The work must be an intellectual exercise, one in which certain results can surface from the inquiry.

(4) The project cannot be limited to the internship experience; the internship is only the foundation for the study.

The course became part of the curriculum in the fall semester, 1980. It remains, therefore, in early testing stages. The first group of student interns eligible for the course petitioned for approval of applications and served internships during the summer 1980. They represented various sequences of the college—news-editorial, advertising-public relations, broadcasting, and film.

Students in all sequences are eligible but must enroll with a professor with specialization in the appropriate area. An advertising specialist on the faculty, for example, would not teach the course to students who served news-editorial internships. The course was designed to be taught in small group situations. However, the possibility of fully organized courses (with a minimum number of students approved by the dean) giving faculty a course load credit, is strong but dependent upon student enrollment.[11]

The course description for the 1980–81 bulletin says:

Independent study related to professional work (including internships) in journalism taken in semester following the professional experience. Minimum 3.0 GPA and approval of Field Study Committee and Dean required in semester preceding internship or other professional experience. Junior standing, Jour 14 (advanced reporting, a sophomore level course).

In the Marquette internship class, instruction emphasis is placed in the area of analysis of the internship experience. In its 1980 report the AEJ committee only encouraged "collateral reading, research, and/or special projects" related to the internship. Marquette feels that extension of the internship experience should be required in the spirit of intellectual development. The problem here is maintaining high quality in such papers and projects. Without proper instructional attention and guidance, these papers are often reduced to diaries and other far less-than-analytical activities and contribute little or nothing to the student's scholarly development and intellectual growth. While the new program at Marquette is being tested for the first time this year, the faculty intends to view the course as a complete theory course with the normal high performance standards.

The Marquette course is expressly designed to avoid the abuses of some practicum and independent study courses which are too often automatic high grade courses and more frequently in this era of grade inflation, an "easy A" course. The Marquette internship program is strongly academic in nature and should provide solutions to many of the problems which have been discovered over the years. And in an era of proliferation of internship programs, it is an alternative which deserves serious consideration as an option without opportunity for academic credit abuses.

NOTES

1. The report, published in the *AEJ Newsletter* of January 15, 1981, summarized the Internship Committee's recommendations for consideration at the 1980 convention at Boston University. The AEJ membership voted to table the resolution, 60–32, August 13 at the convention. The major recommendations in the committee's proposal are reprinted in the box accompanying this article.
2. Internship Committee Report to the Association for Education in Journalism Executive Committee, December 1, 1979, pp. 1–2.
3. Hugh P. Cowdin, "More and more schools offer internship credit," *Journalism Educator*, October 1978, Vol. 33. No. 3 pp. 13–17.
4. "Journalism Education: WICI Survey Examines College Internship Programs," *Southern Newspaper Publishers Association SNPA Bulletin*, June 30, 1980. pp. 1–2.
5. Richard Femmel, "Why not make internships mandatory for everybody?" *Journalism Educator*, October 1978, Vol. 33, No. 3, pp. 17–19. For a complete list of references regarding internships, see John De Mott, "Journalism Student Internship Programs: An Annotated Bibliography", presented to the Association for Education in Journalism, annual meeting, University of Houston, August 1979. See also an historical review of internships by De Mott, "Newspaper Internships in Education for Jour-

nalism: The Historical Perspective," a paper also presented at the AEJ meeting in Houston, 1979.

6. John De Mott, "Post-internship seminar benefits J-students," *Journalism Educator*, July 1972, Vol. 27, No. 2, pp. 8–11.

7. Policy at that time had been to strongly encourage students to seek internships and to support their searches in all possible ways, but not to grant credit. An informal program under the supervision of an administrative assistant to the dean of the College of Journalism had long been in effect and had been quite successful in assisting students in placement for internships. But there was no formal program, with contractual agreements of less rigid restrictions, with the search burden on the student.

8. Hugh Cowdin, ed., "Academic Credit for Internships," *Roundtable No. 80*, American Society of Journalism School Administrators, June 1978.

9. De Mott, "Post-internship seminar," p. 9.

10. As a private school, Marquette's tuition is comparatively high compared with public institutions. The full-time tuition (12–18 hours) for students for 1980–81 is $1,810 per semester.

11. At such schools as the University of Wyoming, the post-internship seminar is not segregated according to sequences. News, advertising, public relations, community journalism and broadcast majors attend the same seminar. The faculty there contend that each student's journalism education is enriched by exposure to the internship experiences of students in all fields. In addition to written reports and packaged presentations, each student is required to deliver a two-hour oral report and internship analysis to the seminar class during the semester. Seminar oral and written performance is the sole basis for the grade.

16
COORDINATING THE HOSPITALITY INTERNSHIP

James F. Downey and Linsley T. Deveau

A survey of internship policies at universities reveals widely divergent practices and standards in hours required, credit given, amount of faculty supervision, and collateral student requirements. Examples are drawn from 68 hospitality-education programs.

Whether we call the program industry experience, field work, internship, externship, or a practicum, the most worthwhile education a student can receive in a hospitality program coordinates industry-acquired techniques with academic reinforcement. The more experience students receive, the better prepared they will be to assume responsibility in the industry. Moreover, most hospitality education programs pride themselves on their ability to include this industry interface in their curricula.

Our industry places a great deal of emphasis on what is learned on the job, compared to what is taught in the classroom. Accordingly, we sought to answer the following question: To what extent are we providing students experience outside the classroom? We also wondered about the quantitative and qualitative dimension of an educationally based supervised experience in which students must participate. In this article, we will report on the results of a survey we conducted to investigate these issues.

ARE YOU EXPERIENCED?

In a 1986 survey, we received 68 responses from the more than 145 four-year hospitality-education programs in the U.S. Our purpose was to assess the degree to which industry experience at the non-managerial level is provided for students as part of the hospitality program.[1] In addition, the survey examined the particular dimensions that such a course or requirement entailed.

We asked respondents to report on:

- Total industry-experience hours required,
- Academic credit earned,
- Student-reporting requirements,
- Employment coordination,
- Coordinator or director supervision, and
- Anticipated changes in industry experience courses or requirements.

OBJECTIVES

Although guidelines and procedures for industry-experience requirements vary among hospitality programs, a majority adhere to a skills-oriented format. The guides for these programs include the following:

- Allowing the students to participate in training programs with a professional in the students' major area of study, to enhance their skills and as preparation for management responsibilities.
- Gathering hospitality knowledge from the industry and applying it in the classroom.
- Gaining valuable experience in a field of interest to the student.
- Making the student more competitive in securing a position with a hospitality operation upon graduation.
- Comparing and contrasting theoretical hospitality principles with day-to-day industry practice.

The employer would hire the students under identical conditions to those afforded regular employees. Industry-experience courses should not be used to provide a pool of free labor for hospitality operations. Students should be compensated for their services, so their work experience is more realistic and credible.

Unlike cooperative education, industry-experience courses do not require the students to work extended periods of time, particularly if they are registered for full-time study. But students might want to take on outside employment to defray the cost of a college education. An industry-experience requirement as part of a hospitality-program curriculum should help alleviate some of the students' financial anxieties. In any case, students must establish their own balance between courses taken and hours worked in an outside job.

HOURS WORKED AND CREDIT EARNED

We asked our respondents to tell us how many hours of industry experience their program requires (excluding cooperative education).

Exhibit 1 Hospitality Program Work Requirements and Academic
Credits Earned

GREATEST NUMBER OF REQUIRED HOURS		
Programs	Hours	Credits
Program A	1,800	9
Program B	1,600	0
Program C	1,250	15
Program D	1,200	3
Program E	800	15
SMALLEST NUMBER OF REQUIRED HOURS		
Programs	Hours	Credits
Program V	0	2
Program W	4	4
Program X	30	3
Program Y	40	1
Program Z	80	0

We compared that time requirement to the number of academic credits earned in the practicum. The results for the programs with the
largest and smallest work requirements are shown in Exhibit 1. Four-
year hospitality-education programs typically require students to complete 400 to 800 hours for a Bachelor's degree, depending on what
value each program places on industry experience.

As Exhibit 1 shows, the requirement of hours worked in industry
ranged widely—from a work requirement of 1,800 hours down to no
fixed requirement at all. Ironically, the program requiring the biggest
outside time commitment did not give the greatest amount of credit
for that work. The median number of work hours required was 535
and the median academic credit given for the work requirement was
3.5 credit-hours.

Some of our respondents indicated an uncertainty as to the proper
allocation of academic credit at their institutions, because non-faculty
members are overseeing students' activities outside the classroom. One
administrator commented, for example, "What we can't see, we can't
control or supervise. Therefore, little or no course credit should be
received." But most of the respondents agreed that outside experience
could only be a benefit to students.

SUPERVISION

Faculty members are stretched relatively thin over the 100-plus four-year hospitality programs in operation throughout the U.S., and inequities exist with respect to faculty allocations. A faculty member's academic burden might not allow the person to take on the added responsibility of supervising students' practicums. Many colleges and universities have granted release time for these faculty members to free them from some of their academic duties. Industry experience is difficult to supervise if the coordinator or director cannot or does not make on-site visitations to monitor the student's performance.

We received a wide variety of responses to the question of how industry experience was supervised. Sixty-four percent of responding programs retained a separate status for the administrator of the industry-experience program. The amount of time these coordinators spent per semester ranged from 12 down to two contact hours per week. For non-faculty industry-experience administrators, the range of contact hours per week was between a high of 25 and a low of ten.

The survey revealed the financial constraints placed on the administration of industry experience. One respondent commented, "The person designated for the position is tied into the budget, and allowances for on-site visitations of more than 100 miles from campus are reviewed on an isolated basis." A majority of the respondents indicated that some parts of the year required more supervision, and others less. One director indicated that he was paid less during the summer and worked the most during the winter months.

SECURING EMPLOYMENT

The hospitality programs we surveyed used a variety of methods to arrange student employment. About half of the programs allowed students to select their employer from a list of sanctioned companies. Another 20 percent gave the program coordinator the responsibility of placing the students in hospitality operations, thereby ensuring that the student ends up with an approved operation. The placement office was seldom used to find students employment—approximately one in ten programs exercised this option. The remainder reported using a combination of methods.

REPORTING REQUIREMENTS

Before awarding academic credit, most programs required students to submit documentation or substantiation in written or oral form to verify completion of the work experience requirement. Since practicums usually involve no formal class meetings or examinations, most of our respondents required that the student submit a log of work activities prior to the end of the semester. The grade or credit earned was dependent on the extent to which the report met program criteria.

For example, at the University of New Haven, we require our students to submit a 30-page report on their work experience, together with a typed daily log. The log is to include the following information about each day on the job:

- Date and hours worked (a timecard photocopy is required),
- Job-related responsibilities,
- Special problems encountered, and
- General comments, remarks, or observations.

Both the log and the report must be submitted to the industry-experience coordinator on or before the last day of classes for the semester. Nearly 60 percent of the surveyed programs required a written report, while one-quarter required an oral presentation. Only three percent requested both oral and written reports. Thirteen percent required no report at all.

POTENTIAL CHANGES

According to our survey, most hospitality-program administrators at the four-year level are satisfied with their current industry-experience format. Just over 80 percent of respondents anticipated no changes in their classes. Those who did expect modifications generally projected an increase in the number of hours students would be required to work. Few project a change in the academic credit hours awarded. As one program director commented, "It's easier to increase hours than to argue with curriculum committees about altering the credit received."

To summarize our survey results:

(1) A significant percentage of four-year hospitality programs require students to complete at least 535 working hours, for which the students earn an average of 3.5 academic credits.
(2) A large majority of hospitality programs require a written report from their students, rather than an oral report.
(3) Nearly two-thirds of hospitality programs provide for separate coordination or direction of the industry-experience course by retaining an individal who works exclusively with

the program. Nevertheless, most programs leave it to the student to secure his or her own employment.

(4) A vast majority of the hospitality-program administrators surveyed are satisfied with their current industry-experience courses.

The measure of a hospitality-education program is certainly not restricted to an industry-experience requirement. Academic integrity, faculty resources, and quality of facilities constitute the main measure of a program's effectiveness. It is imperative, however, that we continue to monitor the demands the industry places on our industry-experience requirements. We would like to see more industry input in the determination of how many hours the student should work in these programs and in the number of academic credits these programs are worth. Such cooperation would make industry-experience programs even more valuable to the students and to the industry.

17
HOSPITALITY INTERNSHIPS:
AN INDUSTRY VIEW

James F. Downey and
Linsley T. DeVeau

Industry respondents to the same survey of academicians (see immediately preceding article) opted for more stringent requirements for interns. Respondents also objected to institutional biases toward certain and against other career tracks and called for closer supervision of interns by faculty.

Hospitality recruiters had the opportunity to express their views on hospitality programs and current hospitality internship requirements when the University of New Haven conducted this follow-up to our original study on internships. Our first study [*See preceding article, ed.*], published in the August 1987 issue of *The Quarterly*, summarized the structure and requirements of hospitality internships in four-year hospitality programs and presented hospitality educators' views on what constituted an adequate internship program. To complete our analysis of hospitality internships, we sent recruiters a survey much like the one previously sent to educators to find out what they think an internship should be. In this article, we will report on the results of the second survey.

THE EDUCATORS' VIEW

To review, our first survey showed that most four-year hospitality programs require students to complete 500–550 hours of internship. Students earn an average of 3.5 academic credits for 500–550 hours of employment. A majority of the program administrators surveyed said that the only documentation of the experience required of students was a written report. Nearly two-thirds of the schools employed a director or administrator for their hospitality-internship program but required the students to secure their own employment.

A majority of the respondents stated that they were satisfied with their current program with regard to internship hours required and credit awarded, type of documentation required, program administration, and student-employment coordination.

VIEW FROM THE FIELD

We sent surveys to the 50 largest lodging and food-service corporations that provide management-training programs for entry-level managers and received 21 responses. The respondents represented a variety of hospitality recruiters, including managers of college relations, directors of human resources, management-selection coordinators, and personnel representatives.

MORE EXPERIENCE

We asked the recruiters whether four-year programs were requiring too few contact hours in their curriculum. Six out of ten recruiters agreed that programs do not require enough internship hours. Nearly two-thirds indicated that a range or 1,500 to 2,500 hours should be required to complete the internship component of a hospitality program. Although a substantial percentage of the respondents thought students should spend more hours working in the field, two-thirds agreed that the three academic credits customarily awarded for internships was adequate for 500 to 1,500 hours of internship.

BETTER COORDINATION

Fifteen out of the 21 recruiters agreed that a director or coordinator should be hired to oversee the internship program, and more than half agreed that the program director's job should be a full-time position. When asked how students' placements should be arranged, over two-thirds of the recruiters disagreed with the educators' preference that the students find their own jobs. These respondents felt that placements should be arranged through the institution's placement office or by the internship coordinator.

MORE DOCUMENTATION

The hospitality recruiters were not satisfied with the customary way student-internship experiences are documented. While most educators felt that a written report was adequate, the recruiters preferred a two-tier report with both written and oral components. Some respondents cited the need for public-speaking skills in the hospitality industry and pointed out that an oral internship report would provide students with an opportunity to develop those skills.

THE UNDECIDED

The respondents who chose the response "undecided" with respect to internship hours and student placement said that they were hesitant to recommend specific requirements because of the difficulty some students experience in finding appropriate placements. These recruiters observed that jobs in the industry are most plentiful in the summer, but internships generally are scheduled during the academic year when faculty members are available to oversee the students' work experiences. In addition, they pointed out that it is difficult for students to find jobs that coordinate with their academic schedule. Some respondents also noted that students can't always find a placement in their area of specialty due to geographic considerations—lack of transportation or sheer physical distance from a suitable site.

MIXED REACTIONS

The hospitality recruiters were generous with their comments about four-year programs, internship requirements, and their recruiting experiences at institutions that offer four-year programs. Only one respondent said that the current programs and recruiting opportunities are excellent. Another recruiter observed that programs and recruiting experiences have improved greatly over the last decade, and a third respondent indicated that his firm's recruiters were generally satisfied with the institutions they deal with. The remaining comments were less positive.

SELLING THE SPATULA

Many of the recruiters from the food-service segment indicated that four-year programs are not supplying their recruitment needs. Some respondents felt that hospitality educators are not representing their operations in a positive light. A recruiter from the fast-food segment said, "In my experience, most programs need to do a better job of telling about or showing the opportunities in the restaurant segment of the hospitality industry, especially in the fast-food segment."

A representative from the institutional food-service segment expressed the same concern. "Overall, our division doesn't seem to be as glamorous to students as other divisions, so we rarely recruit at universities."

A third respondent said, "I find that most HRI graduates only want to work in hotels. Educators should emphasize all opportunities within the hospitality industry." Another food-service recruiter agreed and noted that his firm has more success with placement centers.

A respondent from the rooms-only hotel segment was also unsatisfied with students' perceptions of careers in rooms-only and felt that hospitality educators should make students more aware of career opportunities in that segment.

FALSE EXPECTATIONS

Many respondents, particularly those representing the food-service segment, commented that students graduating from four-year programs don't have realistic expectations about work in the industry. A fast-food recruiter said, "Hospitality curriculums don't teach students what to expect if they are looking for a career in quick service." Another recruiter remarked that students are ill-prepared, both physically and mentally, for the rigors of the industry. This same respondent noted that students' salary expectations are too high, given the hands-on nature of food-service careers. One recruiter noted that four-year program graduates expected to start higher on the career ladder than was appropriate. The recruiter from the rooms-only hotel segment was satisfied with both the academic preparation and the work experiences of new recruits but observed that many students graduating from four-year programs have unrealistic expectations about starting positions, salary, hours and working conditions.

NO HOSPITALITY

One respondent who had little success recruiting from four-year programs laid the blame on schools that allowed few recruitment visits and presentations from his segment. This respondent felt that recruitment rates would climb if recruiters were allowed to make presentations starting in the students' sophomore year to "plant seeds for future reference."

THUMBS UP FOR HANDS ON

Food-service recruiters were emphatic about the importance of work experience. Their comments included: "Some type of supervisory field experience should be a requirement. The classroom is not reflective of real life in a restaurant", "We have found that students graduating from schools that require restaurant experience as part of their curriculum are better prepared for entering the workplace"; "We look for industry experience, and we place equal emphasis on this experience and course work"; "Students' degrees don't entitle them to much if they can't perform on the job, produce profits, and retain employees. Those who succeed in our business do it with per-

Exhibit 1 Hospitality Educator and Corporate Recruiter Internship Program Comparison

Internship Criterion	Hospitality Educators	Corporate Recruiters
Required hours	Majority report 500-550 hours.	Prefer 1,500-2,500 hours is adequate.
Credit earned	Three credits for 500-550 hours worked is satisfactorily	Prefer three credits for 500-1,500 hours worked
Internship placement	Majority believe student should seek his or her own employment.	Prefer that the internship coordinator and placement office assist student in seeking employment.
Type of report required	Vast percentage indicate a written report is sufficient.	Indicate a combination of written and oral policies should apply to report requirements.
Program coordinator	Most believe a part-time individual should be retained.	Prefer that a full-time individual be hired.

Source: University of New Haven School of Hotel, Restaurant and Tourism Administration.

sonality, business acumen, and a service mentality—with or without a degree."

FINDING THE BALANCE

The combined survey results show that there is substantial disagreement between hospitality educators and industry recruiters regarding the content, structure, and administration of internship programs. Exhibit I summarizes and compares the two groups' responses. If four-year programs are to achieve their goal of preparing students for hospitality-management careers, program administrators must listen to recruiters from companies offering management-trainee position and respond to these-industry demands.

We suggest that hospitality-program administrators evaluate and monitor their industry and academic ties to achieve an adequate balance. As a first step, programs should require students to work more hours to right the imbalance between study and experience. When internship programs meet industry expectations, the students will be the primary beneficiaries.

18
A SURVEY ON HUMAN RESOURCE DEVELOPMENT INTERNSHIPS

Patricia L. Patton and Doreen F. Dial

Personnel professionals' responses to a survey strongly affirm the value of experiential learning in professional training. The study further reveals that even professionals who have never done an internship place heavy weight on its value.

Being an intern is a little like getting your feet wet before going off the high dive; you know you want to go swimming but you'd like to test the water before taking the big plunge. It makes sense for a person interested in a professional field to see what it's all about before diving headfirst into a new career. Part-time or temporary internships are a viable training method that give both students and professionals making a mid-life career change the opportunity to explore new ventures.

Before the mid-seventies, traditional paths of entry into human resource development positions were primarily non-academic. People entered from diverse fields such as sales, production, personnel, teaching, and administration. Success in the HRD field varied as much as entry-level competencies and organizational survival techniques, says Robert Bove in a 1984 *Training & Development Journal* article, "HRD Yesterday." Yet in today's highly competitive marketplace, most people hoping to enter this specialized job area need some relevant education or experience to open the door.

VALUED TRAINING

Internships are a valid part of job education systems and a requirement in many certificate and degree programs. They are a form of on-the-job training in which people gain supervised experience and practical knowledge that is relevant to a specific field. An internship offers a chance to learn about the roles and functions of practitioners in an organization. Appropriate learning and training experiences give interns a feel for the dynamics of a real organization, as well as feedback on their work without the threat of a full performance appraisal, say Blalac and Wallington in a 1985 *Training & Development Journal* article, "From Backpack to Briefcase." Internships are also good ways to boost a person's self-confidence and marketability.

Organizations themselves can benefit greatly from internship programs. Although interns may work at a slower pace than practicing professionals, they are valued because they are eager to learn, cost little or nothing, and keep the professional training staff on its toes with their inquisitive nature and fresh ideas. They are also a valuable resource for future hiring. As the academic and business communities recognize the mutual benefit of "Learn-while-you-work" experiences, more and more employers are saying "yes!" to internships.

Internship programs in HRD are quite new, and literature on their rate of success in meeting the learning and training needs of interns and the profession is scarce. In an attempt to target local HRD activity and pinpoint potential internship sites for future San Diego State University students, we conducted a survey of 125 local HRD professionals. Our purpose was to find out what practitioners think about internships and to present a realistic picture of what career aspirants can expect from such experiences. The results reveal some interesting perceptions.

METHOD

SUBJECTS

We chose 125 members of ASTD's San Diego Chapter as a sample group for the survey. The participants were selected from the 1986 Membership Directory based on their professional titles. To be eligible for selection, individuals had to be

- employed by an educational institution;
- a member of a human resources team;
- involved in various personnel functions;
- or an HRD consultant.

The survey group comprised 45 men and 80 women, all of whom either were employed currently in the HRD field or had been recently, Six professionals were chosen to help conduct structured interviews of participants—three were university faculty involved in HRD training, and three were HRD practitioners.

MATERIALS

To gather information from the chapter participants, we developed a survey questionnaire modeled after those used in similar studies, such as the ASTD Competency Study. The Social Science Research Laboratory at San Diego State agreed to provide consultation, computing assistance, and analysis of the survey. The questionnaire asked for demographic information, number of years' experience in HRD, and status of employment. Fifteen questions addressed specific concerns that the literature suggests are pertinent when considering internship placements in HRD settings (see Figure 1, which also includes the survey's basic results). A cover letter accompanied each survey and briefly explained who we, the researchers, were and why the survey was being conducted. The questionnaire also was used as a format for conducting the structured interviews.

PROCEDURE

The questionnaire first asked for demographic information. Then it listed specific questions concerning internships, asking people to indicate which answers(s) would best represent their opinion, experience, or knowledge about internships in the HRD profession. The survey included open-ended, closed-ended, and forced-choice questions. All answers were anonymous. A self-addressed, stamped envelope prompted a quick return of each survey, with a one-week turnaround requested.

During the structured interview sessions, each professional was asked a set of questions concerning HRD and internships. Here again, interviewees were asked to respond based on their opinions, knowledge, education, and experience in the field.

SURVEY RESPONDENTS

Results from the survey respondents represented a return rate of 37 percent. The respondent group comprised 25 men and 18 women; three of the respondents did not indicate gender. Their ages ranged between 25 and 56, and all but one were residents of California.

The number of years of experience in the HRD field varied as follows: 15 professionals had been in the field more than 10 years, and 11 between two and five years. Three had less than two years of experience, and two respondents had none at all. Currently, 41 of these professionals are employed in the HRD field, and five are employed in other fields.

Across all male and female age groups, more than 17 percent indicated they were placed as interns through an educational program. Nine percent indicated they were placed through an organization;

four percent found internships through their own efforts. The interns indicated their areas of interest as follows:

- management training—11 percent;
- career development—4 percent;
- human resource planning—2 percent;
- non-profit organizations—2 percent;
- other areas, such as teaching, technical training, vocational rehabilitation, and survey research—11 percent.

Figure 1—Survey questions related to HRD internship programs

1. Have your ever served an internship in the HRD field?
   (26%) yes   (74%) no
2. If yes, what was the length of your internship?
   (2%) Up to 6 weeks   (4%) 4 to 5 months
   (2%) 6 weeks to 2 months   (4%) 6 months
   (9%) 2 to 3 months   (7%) more than 6 months
   (2%) 3 to 4 months   Please specify _____
3. During that time were you a student or professional?
   (17%) student   (7%) professional   (7%) both
4. If you were a student, did you receive credits?
   (83%) yes   (17%) no
5. How many hours per week did you intern?
   (2%) does not apply   (11%) 15 to 20 hours
   (9%) 5 to 10 hours   (0%) 20 to 25 hours
   (4%) 10 to 15 hours   (4%) more than 25 hours
                                          Please specify _____
6. Was the internship:
   (11%) paid
   (17%) not paid
   (72%) not applicable
7. Were you placed through:
   (17%) an educational program
   (9%) an organization
   (4%) other. . . .
       Please specify: _____
8. What was your area of interest?
   (0%) not applicable   (2%) consultation
   (4%) career development   (0%) organization/program

(11%) management training   design
(2%) non-profit organizations   (2%) human resource planning
                         (11%) other. . . .
                         Please specify _____

9. Based on your experience and knowledge, do you believe that companies/organizations provide interns with appropriate amounts of learning and training experiences?

    (28%) yes   (22%) no   (26%) don't know

10. Were you ever offered full-time employment by the organization upon completion of your internship with them?

    (13%) yes   (13%) no   (33%) not applicable

11. What is your opinion of internship programs? (you may check more than one item.)

    (30%) they meet the training and experiential needs of the intern

    (7%) they do not meet the training and experiential needs of the intern

    (41%) they are beneficial to the company/organization

    (63%) they are beneficial to the needs of the intern and the organization

    (13%)the amount of practical, hands-on experiences is sufficient

12. Do you think internships should be a requirement for individuals enrolled in certificate or degreed programs in HRD/T&D?

    (67%) yes   (11%) no

13. Currently, is there an in-place internship program in your company or organization?

    (39%) yes   (39%) no

14. Would you consider entering an internship program at some time (or, again) in your career?

    (28%) yes   (30%) no   (11%) don't know

SURVEY RESULTS

Twenty-six percent of the respondents had internship experience in the HRD field. The average length of an internship was reported to be two to three months. During the internship period, more than 17 percent of the respondents were students enrolled in an educational program. Seven percent were practicing professionals, and another seven percent worked in the field while attending school. Nearly 80 percent of the student respondents indicated they received academic credit upon completing their internship; 17 percent did not receive credit.

The number of hours served per week as an intern varied. Eleven percent indicated they served 15 to 20 hours per week, while nine percent indicated they served five to 10 hours per week. Only 11 percent of the respondents reported they had a paid internship; more than 17 percent reported they did not receive remuneration. Asked whether they were ever offered fulltime employment with the organization after their internship, 13 percent were, and 13 percent were not.

To indicate their opinion of internship programs in general, respondents were asked if an internship should be required for people in certificate or degree programs in HRD; 67 percent indicated it should.

More than 39 percent of the respondents indicated there is an internship program currently in place where they work. Across all male and female age groups, 28 percent indicated they would consider entering an internship program at some time (or again) in their career; 30 percent indicated they would not; and 11 percent indicated they weren't sure. Based on the respondents' experience and knowledge, more than 28 percent believed that companies or organizations sponsoring internships provide interns with appropriate amounts of learning and training experiences. Twenty-two percent said they did not believe companies do provide enough experience, and 26 percent did not know.

INTERVIEW RESULTS

The information gathered from the six structured interviews does not allow for statistical analysis. The interviews did reveal, however, congruence of the survey questionnaire respondent group and the interview group.

Based on these interviews, student interns tend to have a theoretical orientation to occupational fields. Yet internships help them translate that orientation into a more practical approach. A majority of interviewees said that internship programs help to meet the training, academic and experiential needs of both the intern and the organization. There is much to be gained by each party, interviewees said.

For organizations, interns generate fresh ideas that can stimulate professionals and may be the impetus for new or revised programs and projects. While some organizations offer paid internships at lower salary ranges than for professionals, others benefit from the temporary help they receive at no cost.

Many of the survey interviewees enrolled in an education program during their internship said they were not paid. Even without a pay-check, however, they said they still benefitted from the direct, learn-while-you-work experience while, at the same time, fulfilling their educational requirements. Almost all HRD programs either require that students do at least one internship or at least provide the option of doing so. Most programs also give academic credit to students . . . exposure provided during any internship will always vary from one organization to another. On the question of whether companies or organizations provide interns with appropriate amounts of learn-ing and training experiences, opinion was divided almost equally among HRD professionals. Several respondents indicated that com-panies should provide even more practical, hands-on opportunities. More than a quarter said that a two-to-three months internship was enough time to integrate personal or academic experiences with or-ganizational ones.

Of the few respondents who were practicing professionals during their internship, most came into the organization to work on a specific project (as often happens with consultants). Those who were both students and professionals often were hoping to upgrade their edu-cational background or to expand their areas of expertise. For those professionals making a mid-life career change or transferring to an-other HRD specialty area, an internship served as a convenient ve-hicle.

Most respondents were encouraged to know that half of the survey respondents were offered full-time employment upon completing their internships. Also, most respondents seemed generally satisfied with their experiences, implying that internships met many of their needs and offered opportunities to clarify career choices and learn about the field without having to make a total work commitment to it.

Interns should never assume that all of their training needs will be met simply because they are participants in such a program. Interns have a responsibility to themselves to ask questions, make suggestions, and demonstrate an interest in the organization they are serving. Self-initiative is very important, as is taking time to become acquainted with other employees, accepting and learning from constructive crit-icism, and trying to make the most of the learning opportunity. The responsibility for making an internship a worthwhile training expe-rience lies with both the intern and the organization.

19
THE INSTRUCTIONAL PRACTICES OF GRADUATE LEVEL PUBLIC ADMINISTRATION INTERNSHIP PROGRAMS

Mary L. Auth

Internships at the graduate level apparently tend to supplement experiential learning with a heavier dose of other academic and scholarly activities. A survey of 96 public administration programs at universities uncovers details of their management, requirements and practices. Among the most significant findings: most internships include more than one academic component; more than half require three or more campus-based learning assignments; and the most favored collateral requirement is the analytical research paper.

Public administration educators have often viewed internships as one potentially effective way to provide a link between classroom learning and real-life practice. Because of this belief, public administration programs have included internship components in their curricula at an ever-increasing rate.[1] Internships, then, are an accepted curricular strategy in public administration education, a strategy shared with most other professional fields.[2] The rationale for including them is to provide an opportunity for transition from the university to the work environment, an opportunity "to bridge the gap between the academic and professional worlds."[3]

Even though internships are a commonly accepted curricular strategy, a review of the literature about internships reveals a variety of approaches to internship education. The specific goals, content, and instructional processes of internship programs differ greatly from school to school.[4] There are many reasons for this diversity, including differences in financial resources/support, structural arrangements, sizes of programs, and kinds of students. Because of these and other factors, diversity in internship content and processes is inevitable and not necessarily detrimental. However, there is also evidence of diversity in the quality of internship experiences as determined by faculty student, and agency evaluations and this evidence has led to an increasing concern about planning and administering internship programs more effectively.[5]

That there is a need for "qualitative improvements" in many internship programs is recognized.[6] Suggestions about how to make such "qualitative improvements," however vary greatly. This is logical since internships are an "elaborate mosaic" of complex relationships and interrelationships, all of which must be planned, coordinated, and managed effectively in order to ensure over-all success.[7]

INTERNSHIP PROGRAMS

The internship experience has been conceptualized as a tri-dimensional relationship between the intern, the university, and the placement agency, each participant with its own set of responsibilities, expectations, and roles.[8] D. S. Chauhan discusses the various "contact points" in this triangular relationship, noting three "operational dimensions" of interrelationships: (1) between the university and the student intern; (2) between the student-intern and the placement agency; and (3) between the university and the placement agency.[9] Each of these "operational dimensions," although part of the whole that comprises the internship experience, has its own set of possibilities and dilemmas.

Scholars and educators who are interested in improving internship education have directed their attention to various aspects of the internship "mosaic," some addressing the tri-dimensional relationship as a whole, others the various sub-relationships that are part of the whole. One of the most important sub-relationships in the triangle involves the first contact point—the relationship between the university representative and the student—especially as that relationship relates to the educational structuring of internship learning.

The purpose of this paper is to discuss some of the instructional aspects of internship education and to report the results of a recent survey about the instructional practices of existing graduate level internship programs. The paper includes the following sections: 1) a discussion of the role of educational structuring in internship education; 2) a description of academic components and learning activities frequently mentioned in the literature; 3) a discussion of the survey methodology; 4) a report and analysis of the survey findings; 5) a description of the types of written materials being used; 6) a summary of survey results; and 7) some concluding remarks about the need for further research about and evaluation of the instructional practices of internship programs.

THE EDUCATIONAL STRUCTURING OF INTERNSHIPS

Primary responsibility for planning, implementing, and evaluating the academic relevance and learning outcome of an internship program rests with the university, usually represented by an internship program director and/or a faculty mentor.[10] That this responsibility lies in the first operational dimension—intern to university—is logically valid because of several factors. First, it cannot be assumed that agency supervisors are in any position to provide the theoretical and academic elements of learning although they are an obvious source of practical learning. Second, even in the "teaching" of practical elements, placement agency supervision is known to be uneven and, sometimes, ineffective.[11] Third, the university representative is ultimately responsible for evaluating the educational quality and learning outcomes of the internship and assigning grades to interns.

This responsibility provides an appropriate rationale for inclusion of campus-based academic components in internship programs. The academic components can be conceptualized as the instructional approaches needed to direct the internship learning experiencing in academically relevant ways. These components can be defined as the specific academic/scholarly practices and assignments that are separate and distinct from the work-related assignments of the agency. They are related to the formal instruction of "educational structuring" of internship components.[12] Educational structuring through academic components, then, is a mechanism for controlling the content and process of learning, ensuring academic relevance, and evaluating learning outcomes.

Literature and research about educational structuring and the effectiveness of specific academic components and requirements has been relatively limited. In 1979, Thomas Murphy pointed out that even though " . . . the educational value of internships has been demonstrated in a broad variety of programs . . . there are still many pitfalls awaiting interns and many programs still need to improve their academic component."[13] Since that time, recognition of the importance of academic components has been growing, especially among educator-practitioners who direct internship programs on a daily basis. A recent collection of articles about public affairs internships includes a section on "Making The Internship An Academic Experience" and recommends some specific instructional methods for ensuring academic relevance.[14] A recent survey by Edward Twardy on graduate level internship programs of NASPAA-member schools revealed that 93.7 percent of all responders had some required academic learning activities for interns and "many responses included written comments about recent or pending changes in the academic require-ments . . . all of these comments concerned adding requirements to program."[15]

The role of on-campus academic components and activities in facilitating and structuring internship learning needs to be more sys-tematically explored. The question becomes what instructional pro-cedures, processes, and practices facilitate internship learning most effectively? That possibilities for improving learning effectiveness, through well-planned instructional interventions, is a well-accepted concept in the educational literature. The possibilities and limitations to these interventions in internship learning environments are worth investigating.

ACADEMIC COMPONENTS AND LEARNING ACTIVITIES

The literature about public administration education and intern-ships often includes discussion of various academic components and learning activities/assignments that are believed to be effective in guiding internship learning. The most frequently mentioned campus based academic components are pre-internship orientations, intern-ship seminars/workshops, regularly scheduled meetings between intern and faculty mentor or internship director, and post-internship seminars/meetings. The most frequently mentioned campus-based assignments are journals/diaries, learning contracts, research papers, and valuative and self-assessment essays.

Although most of the academic components and learning activities mentioned above are self-explanatory, others need further definition and comment. The following discussion will focus on some of the characteristics of and issues about internship seminars, learning con-tracts and journals that have been identified in the literature.

Internship seminars or workshops are frequently recommended by both theorists and faculty involved with internship program direction. Graves considers an integrated seminar one of the "essential com-ponents" of internship education.[16] Murphy suggests that the inclu-sion of such seminars is on the increase and indicates that "most programs have become more formal in terms of the use of the in-ternship seminar." He believes that this trend "should lead to an en-hancement of the quality of internships."[17] Descriptions of and prescriptions for these seminars, however, differ in terms of curricu-lar and instructional emphases. As Frantzich points out, "providing an integrating seminar for interns with widely diverging backgrounds is no mean task."[18] He recommends a curricular approach that iden-tifies substantive topics that focus on internship experiences and an instructional approach that uses discussion and simulations in a flexible format.

Learning contracts are another instructional device that are well-represented in the education and public administration education literature. Kozma, Belle, and Williams point out that learning contracts are particularly applicable to independent study and experiential learning situations where direct guidance and instruction are limited.[19] The key characteristic of such contracts is the identification of learning goals and objectives that are agreed upon by the learner and the instructor. In internship environments, this agreement would ideally include the intern and both his/her "instructors"—that is, the campus mentor and the on-site supervisor.

Journals or diaries are also much praised in the public administration internship literature. Frantzich believes that "the daily journal is an absolute necessity for an intern."[20] Graves discusses the journal as a "instrument of learning" that "allow[s] the intern to assess his/her role in the placement and reflect on the internship experience."[21] Both of these authors recommend a set format for this assignment in order to ensure that analysis and self-assessment occur.

Although the above mentioned components and assignments are mentioned frequently in the literature, more information is needed about their actual use and effectiveness in practice. In order to gather information about the instructional aspects of internship education, a survey of *i* _rnship directors/faculty involved in graduate level internship programs at NASPAA-member schools was conducted. The survey focused on identifying the number and kinds of on-campus instructional activities being used by existing programs and on gathering descriptions and evaluations of commonly used academic components and assignments.

SURVEY METHODOLOGY

A nationwide questionnaire survey of NASPAA-member schools with graduate internship requirements was used to gather information from internship directors/faculty about internship instructional practices and to solicit perceptions of respondents regarding the usefulness of specific academic components/learning assignments.

In order to ensure that the survey questionnaire would reach the most appropriate population and the most qualified persons, two steps were taken: 1) the population was limited to those programs that had self-reported having internship requirements in the 1986 NASPAA Directory; and 2) a pre-survey letter was sent to the NASPAA representatives of the universities described above requesting that they identify the person on their campus who was most knowledgeable about graduate internships. This mailing, sent in August, 1987, included a self-addressed, stamped postcard for easy response and had an original response rate of 105 (75 percent). In September, 1987, a follow-up mailing resulted in the receipt of an additional 23 responses, making an overall response rate of 126 (90 percent).

In November, 1987, a self-administered questionnaire was mailed to the 126 persons identified in the pre-survey phase. This first mailing resulted in the receipt of 59 questionnaires, a 46.8 percent response rate. Two follow-up attempts in December, 1987 and January, 1988, increased that number to 96, making an overall response rate of 76.2 percent. These response rates match or exceed patterns of return found in the methodological literature on mail surveys and indicate a high degree of representatives in the sample.[22]

RESEARCH RESULTS

Survey respondents represented 96 public administration programs of varying size located throughout the United States. The survey was designed to gather information from these respondents about the instructional practices of their internship programs. The data not only provide descriptive information about the kinds of activities and assignments that are used and valued but also provide an indication of the amount of education structuring in existing internship programs. The following section summarizes some of the main findings of the survey.

The respondents indicated what academic components were part of their program. These responses were first tabulated in terms of the number of times each was mentioned and then ranked in order of frequency. Table 1 shows the tabulation and ranking of the responses.

As Table 1 reflects, regular meetings with a faculty advisor and pre-internship orientations are the most frequently included components; however, post-internship meetings and internship seminars/workshops are also commonly used.

The number of components that a program includes is also useful information. Although the included components may differ in terms of comprehensiveness, the number of components a program has does suggest, to some degree, the amount of structuring being applied to the internship experience.

The data reveal that a significant number of programs include more than one academic component in their program. The frequency distribution, displayed in Table 2, indicates the average number of academic components per program.

These data clearly indicate that internship programs are relying on

Table 1 Academic Components

Academic Component	Citations	Programs
Regular meetings with faculty advisor	62	64.6
Pre-internship orientation	60	62.5
Post-internship meeting	50	52.1
Internship Seminar/workshop	39	40.6
Other Components*	16	20.8
None	3	3.1
		(n = 96)

* Other components mentioned by respondents included meetings with the internship coordinator or on-site supervisor, peer group meetings, site visits, and evaluation components such as written evaluations by either the intern or the on-site supervisor.

Table 2 Number of Academic Components Per Program

Number of Academic Components	# of Programs	% of Programs
0	4	4.2
1	17	17.7
2	31	32.3
3	31	32.3
4	11	11.4
5	2	2.1
	96	100%

a multiplicity and combination of components rather than just one to structure the internship experience. The great majority of programs (78.1 percent) include two or more academic components in their programs and almost half of the programs (45.8 percent) reported that three or more components were included. Only four programs (4.2 percent) reported no academic component. This suggests that educational structuring through on-campus components is an important consideration to those trying to direct internship learning.

The data regarding the number and kinds of learning activities or assignments required of interns also reveals a concern for structuring. A tabulation and frequency ranking of the number of mentions of specific activities/assignments is shown in Table 3.

The data clearly indicate that, although an analytical research paper is the most common assignment, other activities and assignments are also frequently required. Besides the activities and assignments iden-

Table 3 Learning Activities/Assignments

Activity/Assignment	# of Citations	% of Programs
Research Paper/Analytical	61	63.5
Journal/Diary/Log	41	42.8
Valuative Essay	40	41.7
Research Paper/Descriptive	38	39.6
Learning Contract	36	37.5
Self-Assessment Essay	20	20.8
Other	31	32.3
None	1	1.0
		(n = 96)

Table 4 Number of Activities/Assignments Per Program

Assignments	# of Programs	% of Programs
0	1	1.0
1	22	22.9
2	16	16.7
3	31	32.3
4	17	17.7
5	4	4.2
6	4	4.2
7	1	1.0
	96	100%

* These figures should not be interpreted as individual and separate activities/assignments. In some cases, one assignment may include two or more of the different categories.

tified in the questionnaire, respondents indicated that other assignments being used included a variety of written assignments, including resumes, technical writing and legal research papers, oral reports and examinations, reading assignments, portfolios, and work-site research projects.

Again, the number of assignments/activities per program is an informative indication of the perceived value of structured learning activities in internship education, so a frequency distribution was tabulated. Table 4, shows the results of this tabulation.

As Table 4 shows, more than half (59.4 percent) of the programs reported the inclusion of three or more campus-based learning ac-

Table 5 Perceived Value of Academic Learning Assignments

Priority	Learning Assignment	Mean Value Rating*
1	Analytical Paper	4.34
2	Descriptive Paper	3.64
3	Valuative Essay	3.18
4	Journal	2.93
5	Self-assessment Essay	2.87
6	Learning Contract	2.84

* Mean value rating was calculated by summing individual rating scores and dividing by the number of citations in each category.

tivities. It is also important to note that only one program reported no learning assignments or activities required by the academic program. These numbers, of course, refer only to campus-based learning activities and do not assess the quantity or quality of the experiential learning activities that take place in the placement agency.

Another question was posed to determine the perceptions of the respondents about the value of certain academic activities frequently mentioned in the literature. The respondents were asked to rate these activities on a scale of one (low value) to five (high value). Table 5 represents a ranking of the perceived value of individual learning assignments based on the mean value rating given to each.

The analytical research paper was clearly considered to be the most valuable campus-based learning assignment, although the descriptive research paper and the valuative essay also rated above the mid-range mean value of three. It is important to note, however, that the clear superiority of the analytical research paper may indicate a preference of academics for more traditional assignments rather than either the preference of students or the effectiveness of such papers in terms of increasing desired learning outcomes.

What is of particular interest in these data is that journals, learning contracts, and self-assessment essays all received an average rating of below three, which indicates that the respondents, as a whole, perceived their value to be less than would be suggested in the literature. It was assumed that the journal, in particular, would be given a higher rating because of the frequency with which it is recommended in the literature. Further analysis was, therefore, done in order to see how much agreement existed on these ratings. A frequency and relative frequency analysis showed the following: (See Table 6)

These relative frequency distributions suggest that these activities are valued differently by different respondents but that each of these

Table 6 Relative Frequency of Value Ratings

	Journal	Learning Contract	Self-Assessment Essay
Value Rating	# of Responses	% of Responses	% of Responses
0	1.2	2.6	2.9
1	22.9	26.0	17.1
2	18.1	10.4	18.6
3	21.7	23.4	21.4
4	12.0	20.8	31.4
5	24.1	16.9	8.6
	100%	100%	100%
	(n=83)	(n=77)	(n=70)

activities/assignments is perceived to be very valuable by some respondents. In fact, each of these activities was considered valuable by the majority of respondents. Journals were given an average value rating of three or above by 57.8 percent of the respondents, learning contracts were given an average value of three or above by 61.1 percent of the respondents, and self-assessment essays were rated at three or above by 61.4 percent of the respondents. This observation is confirmed by the fact that, when asked in an open-ended question to identify activities or assignments that they had found especially useful in promoting learning in internships, the respondents recommended the journal/log/diary almost as frequently as the analytical research paper.

In summary, existing internship programs rely on a variety and multiplicity of academic components and learning assignments to structure the internship experience. In particular, regular meetings with faculty advisors, pre-internship orientations, and post-internship meetings are each included by a majority of programs and analytical research papers are required by more that three-fifths of the programs. Differences between programs do exist, however, in terms of both the number and kinds of academic components and learning assignments included in the program.

WRITTEN MATERIALS

The number and kinds of written materials that an educational program provides to the student/intern or the placement supervisor are another indication of the amount of educational structuring as-

Table 7 Comprehensive Written Materials

(Based on materials received from 31 programs)

Type	# of Materials
Internship handbooks/guides/guidelines	15
Internship seminar/course syllabi	8
Placement supervisor handbooks	3

sociated with that program. In order to asses the kinds of materials being used, the respondents were asked to include any written materials used by the internship program. The following discussion summarizes the content of these materials.

Thirty-one schools (32.3 percent of the respondents) sent written materials about their internship programs. These materials ranged from a one-page "Learning Agreement" to an eighteen-page, bound "Internship Guide." Table 7 summarizes the materials received.

Other more specific materials, that were either part of the more comprehensive packages or were sent separately, covered a variety of topics. Table 8 lists the different types of materials that were received.

The number and kinds of materials indicate that internship directors and faculty advisors are, in many cases, attempting to structure the internship experience through the written medium. Although these materials differ in terms of their comprehensive and their intended audience, each represents a step toward defining and directing internship learning and requirements. Of particular interest are the handbooks for placement supervisors. Since the uneven quality of on-site supervision is considered to be a major obstacle to effective internship learning, such handbooks represent an attempt to address this problem rather than ignore it.

SUMMARY OF SURVEY RESULTS

In 1988, a nationwide survey of NSAPAA-member schools with graduate level internship requirements was conducted in order to gather empirical data about the instructional practices of existing internship programs. The survey results in the receipt of 96 questionnaires from internship directors/faculty located throughout the United States, representing a response rate of 76.2 percent. The survey focused on identifying and assessing the number and kinds of on-campus mechanisms being used to structure the internship learning process.

The results show that public administration internship programs are using a variety of academic components and learning activities to guide the on-site internship experience and ensure that internships are educationally relevant. Although programs differ in terms of the number and kinds of academic components and assignments they include, all of them rely on some kind of on-campus educational structuring to supplement the experiential learning that takes places in the placement agency.

The survey revealed that:

1) Programs rely most frequently on meetings with faculty advisors, pre-internship orientations, and analytical research papers;
2) More than half of the programs surveyed include regular meetings with faculty advisors, pre-internship orientations, and post-internship meetings as academic components;
3) The great majority of programs include two or more academic components and almost half of the programs include three or more;
4) More than three-fifths of the programs require an analytical research paper assignment and approximately two-fifths require journals and/or valuative essays;
5) More than half of the programs require three or more campus-based learning assignments;
6) Analytical research papers, descriptive research papers, and valuative essays were perceived to be the most effective campus-based learning assignments, although journals, self-assessments essays, and learning contracts were also highly valued by some respondents;
7) Many programs attempt to further structure internship learning through the development and dissemination of written resource materials such as internship handbooks and placement supervisor handbooks.

CONCLUSION

Although there is wide agreement among public administration educators that internships *can* be educationally valuable learning experiences for students, there is also a growing awareness that internships *are not automatically* valuable. Because of this awareness, there has been increasing interest in identifying factors associated with effective internship learning and in finding appropriate campus-based activities and assignments to structure internship experiences in educationally relevant ways.

Since internships are an accepted curricular component in public

Table 8   Specific Written Materials

(Based on materials received from 31 programs)

Type	# of Materials
Guidelines for internship papers, reports, projects	18
Statements of purpose	18
Agency supervisors' evaluation forms	15
Internship placement agreement forms	11
Evaluation forms for interns to complete	9
Learning agreement/contract forms/learning objectives	9
Guidelines for learning logs or journals	7
Career development/skills information	8
Guidelines for portfolio	3
Information/guidelines about experiential learning process	1

administration education, it is essential to better understand how universities can ensure that internship experiences have educational as well as practical relevance. Possibilities for improving internship learning effectiveness through well-planned instructional interventions exist but such planning depends on the identification of appropriate and effective instructional strategies. The survey reported here attests to the fact that existing programs are actively involved in the educational structuring of internships. Such involvement underscores the need for more specific valuative research about individual instructional practices and for the development of more systematic approaches to internship instruction.

REFERENCES

1. National Association of Schools of Public Affairs and Administration (NASPAA). "NASPAA Guidelines for Public Service Internships." *Southern Review of Public Administration* 3 (September 1979): 189–195; NASPAA. *Programs in Public Affairs and Administration/1986 Directory*, Washington D.C., 1986; Twardy, Edward, "Survey on Graduate Level Internship Programs and Policies." *NASPAA Publication*, (June 1986):1–8.

2. Darvis, Peter. *Professional Education*, Croom Helm Ltd., London, 1983.

3. Murphy, Thomas P. *Government Management Internships and Executive Development: Education for Change*, D. C. feath and Company, Lexington, Massachusetts, 1973, p. 3; Chauhan, D. S. "Managing Academic-Administrative Internships: A Perspective on Goals, Processes and Constraints." *Midwest Review of Public Administration* 2 (September 1977):199.

4. Murphy, Thomas P. *Government Management Internships and Executive Development: Education for Change*, D. C. Heath and Company, Lexington, Massachusetts, 1973; Murphy, Thomas P., (ed.). "Public Service Internships: The Continuing Evolution—A Symposium." *Southern Review of Public Administration* 3 (September 1979):123–126; NASPAA. "NASPAA Guidelines for Public Service Internships." *Southern Review of Public Administration* 3 (September 1979):189–195; Twardy, Edward. "Survey on Graduate Level Internship Programs and Policies." *NASPAA Publication*, (June 1986):1–8.
5. Chauham, D. S. "Managing Academic-Administrative Internships: A Perspective on Goals, Processes and Constraints." *Midwest Review of Public Administration* 2 (September 1977):197–212; Henry, Nicholas. "Are Internships Worthwhile?" *Public Administration Review* 39 (May/June 1979); 245–247; NASPAA "NASPAA Guidelines for Public Service Internships." *Southern Review of Public Administration* 3 (September 1979):189–195; Balutis, Alan P. and Honan, Joseph C., (eds.) *Public Affairs Internships: Theory and Practice*, Schenkman Publishing Company, Inc., Cambridge, Massachusetts, 1984; Twardy, Edward. "Professional Internships Need Professional Management." Unpublished, 1986.
6. Murphy, Thomas P., (ed.). "Public Service Internships: The Continuing Evolution—A Symposium." *Southern Review of Public Administration* 3 (September 1979):123–126.
7. Murphy, Thomas P. *Government Management Internships and Executive Development: Education for Change*, D. C. Heath and Company, Lexington, Massachusetts, 1973.
8. Hennessy, Bernard C. *Political Internships: Theory, Practice, Evaluation*, The Pennsylvania State University, University Park, Pennsylvania, 1970; Murphy, Thomas P. *Government Management Internships and Executive Development: Education for Change*, D. C. Heath and Company, Lexington, Massachusetts, 1973; Chauhan, D. S. "Managing Academic-Administrative Internships: A Perspective on Goals, Processes and Constraints." *Midwest Review of Public Administration* 2 (September 1977):197–212; Profughi, Victor and Warren, Edward. "The Internship Triangle," in Balutis, Alan P. and Honan, Joseph C., (eds.). *Public Affairs Internships: Theory and Practice*, Schenkman Publishing Company, Inc., Cambridge, Massachusetts, 1984.
9. Chauhan, D. S. "Managing Academic-Administrative Internships: A Perspective on Goals, Processes and Constraints." *Midwest Review of Public Administration* 2 (September 1977):204.
10. Hennessy, Bernard C. *Political Internships: Theory, Practice, Evaluation*, The Pennsylvania State University, University Park, Pennsylvania, 1970.
11. Chauhan, D. S. "Managing Academic-Administrative Internships: A Perspective on Goals, Processes and Constraints." *Midwest Review of Public Administration* 2 (September 1977):197–212; Koehler, Cortus T. "The Responsibilities of Internship Supervisors." *Southern Review of Public Administration* 3 (September 1979):137–145.
12. Hennessey, Bernard C. *Political Internships: Theory, Practice, Evaluation*, The Pennsylvania State University, University Park, Pennsylvania, 1970.

13. Murphy, Thomas P., (ed.). "Public Service Internships: The Continuing Evolution—A Symposium." *Southern Review of Public Administration* 3 (September 1979):126.
14. Balutis, Alan P. and Honan, Joseph C., (eds.,). *Public Affairs Internships: Theory and Practice*, Schenkman Publishing Company, Inc., Cambridge, Massachusetts, 1984.
15. Twardy, Edward. "Survey on Graduate Level Internship Programs and Policies." *NASPAA Publication*, (June 1986):4.
16. Graves, Helen. "Academic Component of Political Internships: The Political Journal" in Balutis, Alan P. and Honan, Joseph C., (ed.). *Public Affairs Internships: Theory and Practiceai*, Schenkman Publishing Company, Inc., Cambridge, Massachusetts, 1984, p. 61.
17. Murphy, Thomas P. "Foreward" in Balutis, Alan P. and Honan, Joseph C., (eds). *Public Affairs Internships: Theory and Practice*, Schenkman Publishing Company, Inc., Cambridge, Massachusetts, 1984, p. xi.
18. Frantzich, Stephen B. "Strengthening the Academic Validity of Political Science Internships: Some Possible Options" in Balutis, Alan P. and Honan, Joseph C., (eds.) *Public Affairs Internships: Theory and Practice*, Schenkman Publishing Company, Inc., Cambridge, Massachusetts, 1984, p. 59.
19. Kozma, Robert B., Belle, Lawrence W. and Williams, George W. *Instructional Techniques in Higher Education*, Educational Technology Publications, Inc., Englewood Cliffs, New Jersey, 1978, p. 367.
20. Frantzich, Stephen E. "Strengthening the Academic Validity of Political Science Internships: Some Possible Options" in Balutis, Alan P. and Honan, Joseph C., (eds.) *Public Affairs Internships: Theory and Practice*, Schenkman Publishing Company, Inc., Cambridge, Massachusetts, 1984, p. 54.
21. Graves, Helen. "Academic Component of Political Internships: The Political Journal" in Balutis, Alan P. and Honan, Joseph C., (eds.) *Public Affairs Internships: Theory and Practice*, Schenkman Publishing Company, Inc., Cambridge, Massachusetts, 1984, p. 61.
22. Babbie, Earl, *The Practice of Social Research* (Fourth Edition), Wadsworth Publishing Company, Belmont, California, 1986, pp. 220–221.

20
EXPLORING THE RELATIONSHIPS BETWEEN INTERN JOB PERFORMANCE, QUALITY OF EDUCATION EXPERIENCE, AND CAREER PLACEMENT

Gerald T. Gabris and Kenneth Mitchell

A careful five-year tracking of interns in a state administered internship program covering four universities yielded valuable correlations between personal (experience-related) factors and the job placement and satisfaction of former interns. Significant findings: good performance in an internship positively affects career placement; interns thrive in broad organizational roles rather than in narrow special projects; and developing good interpersonal skills characterized all successful internships. Recommendation: more stress should be placed on educating intern supervisors.

The requisite of an internship is viewed as an integral component for most pre-career graduate public administration programs. Robert Golembiewski (1979:330) suggests that internships are probably the most valuable educational experience offered to MPA [Graduate Public Administration] students by their academic programs. In one educational survey of MPA alumni from several public administration programs in the Southeast, over 91 percent of the respondents thought their internships provided valuable educational benefits (Ashmore, Lynch, and Threldkeld, 1981:226). Another writer on internships suggests they can provide a vehicle for blending the theoretical perspective acquired in courses with real world experience (Murphy, 1973:5). The salience of internships to public administration programs is reinforced by the fact that NASPAA, while not specifically requiring internships, strongly recommends they be made available for programs seeking NASPAA rostering.[1] Currently, of the 210-member NASPAA programs, 76 percent provide some type of internship.[2] It would appear that internships are here to stay.

Given the ubiquitousness of internships, the question can be raised concerning what general assumptions undergird these programs? One assumption is that internships serve an educational function. Theory is one thing; working in a real world public agency is another. According to one study, PA/A programs probably need to expose their students to even more field work and on-the-job training (Thai, 1985). Only by observing, experiencing, and interacting with people in public organizations can students compare abstract learning with the realities of organizational life.

A second educational function is that internships expose students to raw problems and data that are simply not available in a classroom setting. Interns are frequently assigned to specific policy projects which provide both the host agency and the student with valuable information. Often, interns are invited to staff meetings and briefing sessions to observe how problems and issues are confronted on a day-to-day basis. Less frequently interns may even be invited to engage in the agency decision-making process, perhaps based on the project that the intern been assigned to. Through such experiences, students learn how difficult problems are to solve and how problem resolution often requires substantial amounts of intra-organizational cooperation and teamwork. Some internships also systematically rotate students in and out of functionally diverse departments in order to cultivate a more holistic perspective on how the organization works. While this experiential educational function is highly qualitative and difficult to measure, it is viewed as extremely valuable to the nurturing process of future public employees.

A third assumption is that internships enhance the interpersonal relations skills of public administration graduate students. To be a successful career employee, an individual must learn to get along well with people in sometimes tense and stressful circumstances. Internships help teach relatively naive persons how to understand and cope with the nuances, needs, and behaviors of other people in organizational settings. In this respect, internships help socialize students into the values, norms, and cultural systems they may encounter while working for a public organization, and can plug students into professional career networks which may prove very helpful in seeking a job.

Finally, and perhaps most important, is the assumption that students who perform well during an internship may receive job offers from the agencies they have interned with. Career placement is at the heart of most pre-career internship programs. Internships provide a low-risk and low-cost opportunity for public agencies to evaluate the strengths and weaknesses of potential employees before they hire them. Ultimately, the purpose of pre-career public administration programs is to train and subsequently place people in public sector jobs. The internship is often viewed as the primary means to this end. Presumably, interns who score high on their performance evaluations, and who perceive their internships as a quality educational experience, should be prime candidates for public sector employment.

As important as internships are to most public administration programs, there is relatively little empirical research regarding the bread and butter assumptions associated with the internship concept. There have been few attempts to evaluate the effectiveness of internship programs to ascertain whether they are accomplishing intended objectives. In a recent article, a similar case is made, suggesting that there have been too few efforts to assess the effectiveness of internship programs in relation to the traditional assumptions used to justify and require them of students (Pugh, 1985).

Given the paucity of empirical research surrounding the whole internship issue, a major purpose of this article is to explore whether internship job performance is related to placement. Secondly, is internship job satisfaction related to higher internship job performance? It may be reasonable to assume that highly satisfied interns are more motivated and perform better on the job. Enhanced job performance may lead to an increase in job offers. Further, are variables such as grade point average, sex, race, age, and prior work experience correlated with intern performance, intern job satisfaction, and career placement? This article will endeavor to answer these questions based on data collected over a five-year period on over 130 former interns who participated in the Mississippi Public Management Internship Program (MPMIP).

WHAT DOES THE LITERATURE TELL US?

One of the more comprehensive attempts to consider the entire internship issue can be found in a symposium which appeared in the *Public Administration Review*.[3] In the aftermath of the 1978 Civil Service Reform Act, there was considerable optimism toward using internships as a mechanism for selecting highly qualified public employees. This was most evident in the establishment of the Presidential Management Intern Program (PMIP) which has as its explicit purpose the selecting and attracting to federal service men and women of exceptional management potential (Campbell and Strakosch, 1979).

Generally, most internship programs are not as selective as the PMIP. Indeed, there is considerable variation in the quality, function, and target groups associated with internships from one public administration program to another. For example, the PMIP is a well-funded program which only selects persons who have completed their graduate coursework. It represents a type of on-the-job training effort where a high percentage of interns go on to receive job offers. Most internship programs operated at the state and local levels are funded on a shoe-string budget and most place interns in internships before they have graduated. One effort to categorize and classify state-based internship programs (of which the MPMIP is one example) is attempted in an article by Arthur Finkle and Warren Barclay (1979). According to these authors, internships can be classified into three basic types. The first is called the "centralized-controller" model. In this case, intern selection, placement, and funding are controlled by a centralized office. These types of programs are usually the most formal and institutionalized.

A second type is referred to as the "facilitative-advocate" model. Here an intern agency serves only as an intermediary between graduate programs and host agencies and does not control the funding of an intern.

The third and final type is called the "controller-advocate" model, which is simply a composite of the first two types. The MPMIP is most similar to the "centralized-controller" model outlined above. The significance of this fact is that almost all intern records, evaluation forms, files, and data are standardized, have been collected over a period of time, and are all located in a centralized office. This greatly facilitates their comparative value which may not be present in less formal and decentralized intern programs.

In the *PAR* symposium, only two of the articles dealt directly with an empirical analysis of internships. The first of these investigated perception of satisfaction and dissatisfaction with the intern experience (McCaffery, 1979). In this analysis it was found that about 73 percent of the surveyed interns were satisfied with their internship experiences. The highest satisfaction stemmed from the feeling of a growing professional awareness and the work environment itself. Interestingly, the actual job did not evoke high levels of satisfaction, with the greatest levels of dissatisfaction associated with the perceived lack of effective supervision while on the job. McCaffery concludes that internships, while promoting a sense of professional growth, do not substantially enhance an intern's managerial or technical skills as much as many interns would like.

In an assessment of his own personal internship experience, Frank Sherwood (1973) makes a similar observation:

> My own internship experience many years ago was frustrating. I was angry throughout the experience, and it was perhaps because of those feelings that I didn't go into the federal service. We were shoved around and given unimportant things to do. There was a systematic putdown, that is, from what I can tell, still going on.

Sherwood's rather negative assessment strikes a raw nerve echoed in the findings of McCaffery. Interns, while appreciating the opportunities for professional growth that internships can offer, are often dissatisfied with the actual work they are given to do.

One of the more extensive surveys conducted on internships is that reported by Nicholas Henry (1979). The Henry survey included 588 respondents from nine different MPA programs. Of this group, 234 had been interns and the remaining number, while employed in the public sector, had never interned. As one might expect, Henry found that former interns considered their experiences as practical and, based on their experience, former interns took less time in finding their first job than did non-interns. However, finding a job did not mean automatic access to managerial responsibility. After five years of working experience, more non-interns than former interns were supervising two or more employees, although former interns were more likely to be supervising larger numbers of people (100 or more). Perhaps one of the more striking of Henry's findings was that former interns were less satisfied with their governmental careers than non-interns and that former interns were more likely to leave the public sector for jobs elsewhere.

Based on what literature and research is available, several generalizations might be made. First, there is considerable variation in the types of intern programs, ranging from highly centralized and formal to those which are merely facilitative and informal. Second, most students are satisfied with their internships in that they afford opportunities for professional growth, but tend to find their actual work responsibilities somewhat trivial. Third, internships are viewed as practical experience which appears at least in the findings of one study, to enhance job marketability and placement success. However, once a job is offered, former interns compete on a generally equal level with non-interns for supervisory roles. Surprisingly, former interns also appear to exhibit a higher level of job dissatisfaction when compared to non-interns and appear more likely to quit their jobs in the public sector. These patterns provide some clues as to what might be expected in an analysis of the MPMIP.

MISSISSIPPI PUBLIC MANAGEMENT INTERN PROGRAM

The MPMIP, which was inaugurated in the fall of 1980, most closely fits the centralized-controller model described by Finkle and Barclay (1979). The MPMIP is established in state law and is handed by the State College Board on a year to year line item basis. All four universities in the state offering graduate degrees in public administration or criminal justice may nominate up to 12 intern candidates per year. The MPMIP has a policy-making board which is responsible for setting program policy, interviewing all intern candidates, and monitoring compliance to program policy. On a day-to-day basis, the program is managed by a MPMIP Coordinator responsible for all intern placement, funding, paperwork, troubleshooting, and program evaluation.

MPMIP interns normally are placed for a one semester period of time. The program provides each student with a standard stipend and serves as the intermediary between the student and the agency.[4] In this program, students are only placed in state agencies with the great majority, 95 percent, choosing to intern in the state capital. During the past four years, 143 students have been placed in intern positions and 137 have fully completed an intern assignment. It is this group of 137 former interns who will serve as the data base for this study.

RESEARCH CONSIDERATIONS

All students nominated to the MPMIP must satisfy several eligibility requirements. They must have an overall graduate grade point average of 3.0 on a 4.0 scale. They must have completed at least nine credit hours of graduate work and have completed at least one course in quantitative analysis. Finally, they must submit a thorough intern application form, a resume, and undergo an oral interview with the intern policy board before they can be placed in a state agency. About 75 percent of all intern candidates meet these requirements.

Once a student is nominated to the program, a file is started for each candidate containing application materials, transcripts, resumes, and information about the candidate's race, sex, and previous work experience. One of the authors of this article has served as MPMIP Coordinator for the past three years and has had complete access to all intern files since the program's inception.

In addition to personal information, several other important documents are entered into each intern's file. At the conclusion of each student's internship, his or her supervisor is required to complete a standardized evaluation instrument assessing the intern's overall job performance. This performance appraisal consists of ten general areas dealing with an intern's ability to get along with people, learning ability, goal accomplishment, and type of work output. Each of these indicators provides the evaluator with a four-point, Likert scale choice. In order to ascertain each intern's overall performance, the authors created an "Intern Performance Index," by summing the scores for each behavioral item. Thus, intern performance can range from a low of 10 to a high of 40 possible points. The intern evaluation form also includes data relating to the number of contacts supervisors have with their interns on a weekly basis, type of work responsibilities, and general assessment of the intern's work.

All MPMIP interns are also asked to engage in a self-assessment of their intern experiences at the conclusion of their internships—a type of exit interview. The post-internship questionnaire asks students to assess the comparative as well as experiential educational value of the internship work assignments, the effectiveness of intern supervision, the challenge of the internship, and new knowledge acquired. A total of 9 attitudinal indicators measured by a six-point Likert scale is asked of each intern. Other information, such as work objectives, number of supervisor contacts, and general assessment of the internship, is part of the instrument. By summing the 9 attitudinal items, the authors created an "Intern Job Satisfaction Index," ranging from a possible low of 9 to a high of 54 possible points.

The value of this data is that it has been closely monitored over the past four years and is stable over time. The alumni of the program have all been subjected to the same types of internship requirements, conditions, selections, selection procedures, salaries, and standardized evaluation instruments. Thus, the data derived from the MPMIP program should provide an excellent basis for testing several basic assumptions regarding internships in general. About the only constraint posed by the MPMIP data is that former interns have not been surveyed after an extended period of time to see if hindsight provides a better perspective on internship value. Moreover, statistics And records are only kept up to a point a student receives a job offer. No data have been systematically collected on the starting salary, quality of job offer or the like.

STRUCTURE OF THE ANALYSIS

Based on the data in each intern's file, the authors will focus on two basic dependent variables. The first is simply whether the intern did "receive a job offer" at the conclusion of his or her internship. The second dependent variable will be the "intern satisfaction" index. Here the question is whether a student is satisfied with his or her overall educational experience.

Several types of independent variables will be utilized. One will be the overall "job performance" index. Do interns who score high have a better chance at the job market and manifest higher satisfaction levels associated with the internship? The authors will also correlate each specific index item with job placement success and intern satisfaction. This will provide some clues as to what specific aspects of job performance and intern satisfaction are correlated with job place-

Table 1 Demographic Characteristics of MPMIP Interns

		%	N
SEX OF INTERN	Male	44	60
	Female	56	77
RACE OF INTERN	Black	59	82
	White	41	55
RECEIVED JOB OFFER	Yes	47	64
	No	53	73
MEAN AGE OF INTERN	25 yrs.		
MEAN PERFORMANCE SCORE	33.6 (Of Possible 40)		
MEAN SATISFACTION SCORE	43.7 (Of Possible 54)		
	TOTAL N = 137		

ment. Finally, the authors will correlate the intern's age, sex, race, grade point average, and prior work experience with the dependent variables. Presumably, students with higher grade point averages should score higher on job performance and may have better chances at career placement. Through this type of analysis, it should be possible to identify those attitudinal and personal characteristics which are most likely to predict career placement and intern job satisfaction.

FINDINGS

Table 1 presents the demographic characteristics for those students who have completed an MPMIP intern program as well as their mean job performance and job satisfaction scores. Of the students who have gone through the program, 47 percent have received job offers from state agencies. This seems to suggest that participation in the program probably increases one's chances for job placement in that almost one out of two former interns receives a job offer. Females and blacks constitute the majority demographic groups participating in the program. The fact that the program is more female may be partially explained on the grounds that the MPA programs in Mississippi have been attracting more females, and Mississippi has a higher proportion of blacks to whites in the general population (36 percent) when compared to other states. Jackson State University, for example, is almost 100 percent black in terms of its student population. Even though MPMIP students appear to have good job opportunities in state government, the question still remains concerning which factors

Table 2   Zero Order Correlations Between Intern Performance Variables, Job Placement, and Overall Intern Satisfaction

SUPERVISOR EVALUATION INDICATORS	RECEIVED JOB OFFER	SATISFACTION INDEX	PERFORMANCE INDEX
OVERALL PERFORMANCE SCORE (Index)	.21*	.24*	1.0
Are You Willing to Work with Intern Again	.19*	.12	.37*
Did Intern Contribute to Agency	.08	.07	.45*
Intern Gets Along Well With People	.17*	.27*	.76*
Quality of Intern's Work	.20*	.19*	.80*
Intern's Learning Ability	.24*	.18*	.86*
Intern's Initiative	.18*	.18*	.84*
Intern Accomplished Work Objectives	.19*	.21*	.79*
Intern Now Understands Gov't. Better	.19*	.10	.65*
Intern Would Make a Good Employee	.19*	.18*	.73*
I Can Now Supervise Intern's Better	.04	-.01	.44*

* Indicates a P value of .05 or less. Total N = 137.

associated with an internship lead to higher probabilities of career placement success. Table 2 will provide some answers to this question.

The zero order correlations reported in Table 2 show that how well an intern performs for an agency, from the viewpoint of his/her supervisor, does correlate significantly with job placement success. Overall performance score is also predictive of overall satisfaction. Thus, internships do appear to differentiate between types of graduate students who are more likely to develop professional administrative careers. These correlations, however, while statistically significant, are not exceedingly strong relationships. Of all the sub-indicators which make up the job performance index, the intern's learning ability followed by quality of work appear to be the most potent factors predicting placement success. Also of some note is the fact that how well an intern appears to get along with people is the best predictor of overall satisfaction. This would seem to make some sense. Interns who are evaluated highly on getting along with people are probably enjoying their internship at a higher level than those who are less gregarious. This suggests that positive interpersonal skills, in addition to technical knowledge, operates as a primary factor enhancing job success and job performance.

Turning to Table 3, it is clear that overall satisfaction is correlated with job placement success. However, overall intern satisfaction is a weaker predictor of job placement than is job performance. Also,

Table 3 Zero Order Correlations Between Intern Satisfaction Variables, Job Performance, and Job Placement Success

INTERN'S SELF EVALUATION INDICATORS	RECEIVED JOB OFFER	SATISFACTION INDEX	PERFORMANCE INDEX
OVERALL JOB SATISFACTION SCORE (Index)	.18*	1.0	.24*
Internship Was Effective Work Experience	.07	.59*	.10
Work Was Important - Substantive	.22*	.66*	.14
Supervisor Was Effective in Designing Work Projects	.10	.65*	.22*
Percentage of Work Research Oriented	-.16*	.11	-.03
Percentage of Work Management Oriented-Participated in the Decision Process	.12	.40*	.11
Perceived Internship as Challenging	.18*	.72*	.23*
Work Assignments Flexible	.17*	.66*	.18*
Would Like to Work for the Agency	.02	.51*	.09

* Indicates a P value of .05 or less. N = 137.

fewer of the sub-indicators of intern satisfaction correlate significantly with placement success. Interns who perceive their work as more substantive, and who view their internship as more challenging and flexible, have a higher success rate in landing a job. This stands to reason. Individuals who are highly motivated by the perceived educational value of their internships are more likely to perform better.

Another observation which can be gleaned from Table 3 concerns the strategic role supervisors play in determining whether or not an internship is a positive experience. Interns who are given narrow policy related work assignments manifest a very low correlation with overall job satisfaction. These same persons also reflect a negative correlation with successful career placement. On the other hand, supervisors who devise interesting and challenging work projects and nurture projects which are more management oriented (involving the intern in decision making processes), are significantly correlated to overall satisfaction scores. Moreover, whether an intern perceives the work as substantive and also feels that his/her supervisor was effective, correlates significantly with job placement success and overall job performance. In other words, supervisors can really make or break an internship experience and do play a critical role in assisting the intern toward a successful professional career.

While overall performance and satisfaction are correlated with job placement success, the issue still remains as to what other personal characteristics of an intern, such as grade point average, sex, race, age, and prior work experience play in career placement and job

Table 4 Zero Order Correlations Between Subject Personal Characteristics, Career Placement Success, Intern Satisfaction, and Overall Performance

PERSONAL CHARACTERISTICS	RECEIVED JOB OFFER	SATISFACTION INDEX	PERFORMANCE INDEX
Sex of Intern (Male to Female)	-.09	-.01	.08
Race of Intern (Black to White)	.25*	-.02	.19*
Age of Intern	.01	.25	.01
Graduate Gradepoint Average	.16*	.02	.30*
Undergraduate Gradepoint Average	.16*	.10	.27*
Previous Scholarship Received	.23*	.14	.03
Prior Public Sector Work Experience	.03	.17*	-.14
Prior Private Sector Work Experience	.18*	.21*	.13
Received Job Offer with Agency Interned With	.61*	.30*	.14

* Indicates a p value of .05 or less. Total N = 137.

satisfaction. The degree to which these variables impact on career marketability, job satisfaction, and job performance are reported in Table 4.

One of the first things to note on Table 4 is that grade point average, the old standby predictor for just about everything, is not strongly correlated with job placement success. Where there is a significant correlation between grade point average and career placement, the relationships are weaker than those of overall job performance and job satisfaction. Grade point average is uncorrelated with overall satisfaction, but does seem to have some bearing on job performance scores. Thus, it would seem that students who are technically superior do receive some advantage in their supervisory ratings based on this fact.

The sex of an intern has virtually no bearing on placement success, overall satisfaction, or overall performance scores. Race, however, does play some role in job placement. Whites are more likely to receive job offers at a higher rate than blacks, even though blacks constitute a majority of the MPMIP's alumni. Race is uncorrelated with intern satisfaction, although it is related to overall performance score.

Age of the intern has very little to do with placement or overall performance, but is significantly correlated to overall job satisfaction. This may indicate that more mature and experienced interns experience more ready acceptance by agency employees. Because they have more experience, agency supervisors may give older interns more substantive work assignments and responsibility. Age, however, does not seem to be a particular advantage once the student is on the job market.

Another interesting finding is that, while prior work experience does have some impact on successful career placement, a lot depends on the "type" of prior experience. Prior public sector work experience, for example, is unrelated to job success and is actually negatively correlated with overall job performance score. Surprisingly, interns with substantial "private" sector work experience exhibit a statistically higher probability of placement success, and also manifest higher levels of overall satisfaction with the internship experience. One possible reason for this pattern may be that obtaining a job in the private sector is a more competitive and self-initiated adventure. This competitiveness may carry over to an intern's attempts to locate and secure a job in the public sector once he or she graduates and finishes an internship.

Finally, students who do receive job offers upon completion of an MPMIP internship are most likely to receive one from the agency they interned with initially. This appears to justify the assumption that, if you perform well in an internship and cultivate good interpersonal skills, you do in fact increase your chances of receiving a job offer. Interns who received job offers from their original intern agencies exhibit rather high job satisfaction levels—suggesting the presence of intense motivation and enthusiasm for the experience.

The findings of this study suggest that several variables interact together in determining career placement success and educational value with respect to internships. Overall job performance and job satisfaction both play a partial role. The degree to which a student enjoys his or her intern experience hinges upon several factors. One of the most important is interpersonal skill. Those interns who are able to get along well with people find the internship experience more rewarding and tend to receive higher performance scores. Supervisors are looking for people who will fit within the organization's culture in a positive context. Academically bright interns, even though they may possess superior technical knowledge, may not be adept at interpersonal relations. This diminishes their job opportunities. Also, students who are fortunate enough to have effective and dedicated supervisors—who are willing to involve the intern in agency decision processes and provide the intern with challenging and interesting work assignments usually find their interns to be more motivated and productive.

The upshot of the above discussion is that internships serve as important "catalysts" for career placement. If the proper mix of ingredients is present, academically average graduate students may find an internship just the vehicle to develop the interpersonal and motivational skills necessary to land a job. In other words, internships provide opportunity situations for students to develop "qualitative" non-academic skills and talents which may be as equally important in securing a public sector job as are academic credentials. Without internships, many academically average students would probably experience more difficulty in landing their first job.

By implication, internships help equalize job competition between graduate students by enabling them to demonstrate and develop different kinds of skills of interest to public agencies. As one faculty colleague once remarked, "Internships enable average students with solid interpersonal skills to market themselves to public agencies." Their type of skills cannot be taught in a classroom yet are fundamental for effective management. Apparently, public agencies and public managers do place a premium on qualitative skills with the internship often serving as the probationary period utilized to determine the extent to which these skills are present in a given intern's behavioral repertoire. Thus, no single factor associated with an internship is likely to lead to successful career placement.

CONCLUSION AND OBSERVATIONS

The reasons for including internships as a basic requirement in most pre-career public administration graduate programs appear to hold up to empirical scrutiny. Interns who are evaluated as high performers increase their odds for career placement success. Thus, intern performance is one factor influencing successful career placement.

Internships also serve an important educational function. Here, however, the relationship is more subtle and complex. Pure academic achievement is not necessarily linked to internship educational satisfaction and is only weakly linked to career placement. The quality of an internship as an educational tool appears to be more contingent upon the type of work and type of supervision a student receives. Narrow research projects which isolate the intern from the mainstream of agency operations can usually decrease motivation and career placement opportunities.

On the other hand, supervisors who permit their interns to participate within the decision-making processes of the organization, and who work to develop interesting and challenging assignments for their interns, are more likely to find their interns satisfied with the educational benefits of the experience. The higher level of motivation and job satisfaction is correlated to higher job performance and higher levels of placement success. Thus, the supervisor plays a crucial role in determining the educational value of an internship for the intern.

Internships also appear to stress the development of interpersonal relations skills. Those interns who are perceived as getting along well with people are recipients of higher evaluations and are also more successful in receiving job offers. Moreover, interns who are able to cultivate their interpersonal skills also find their internships more rewarding and satisfying in an overall context.

If race is excluded, most personal characteristics, such as sex, and prior work experience, exert only marginal impacts on career placement and internship satisfaction. Yet, prior private sector work experience is significantly correlated with placement success.

Older interns are more satisfied with their experiences than younger interns, in part perhaps, because older interns may be given more challenging work assignments. Grade point average, while correlating with performance score, has little to do with intern job satisfaction.

Based on these findings, several recommendations regarding internship programs in general might be made. First, since the role of the supervisor is so vital to the educational and placement success of the intern, more emphasis should be placed on educating and training supervisors on how they can work more effectively with interns. Although the authors have not seen any research on this topic, it is very doubtful whether many intern programs attempt to work closely with intern supervisors. All too often interns are placed and then forgotten until the termination of the internship. Based on personal experiences, most interns are reluctant to complain about poor supervision or poor work assignment. Most decide to bite the bullet and make the most of it. NASPAA, while suggesting that intern programs should submit to self-evaluation, provides no guidelines on what "roles" intern supervisors should play within the intern process. It is the feeling of these authors that more guidance is needed concerning the role of the supervisor.

A second recommendation is that programs should probably emphasize, especially in special circumstances, broad exposure to agency policy and operations rather than narrow projects. Narrow projects tend to isolate the intern from mainstream organizational operations and are often non-sustaining. The intern in such situations feels detached and pushed aside with generally predictable results of low job satisfaction and job performance. Further, broad projects and exposure to agency operations almost forces an intern to develop his or her interpersonal skills. Students must learn how to get along with people and harmonize with the dominant agency culture.

One way to ensure that work assignments are substantive is to develop detailed and explicit work assignments between the intern and his or her agency supervisor. Again, NASPAA may wish to develop a standardized work agreement form for public administration intern programs. Both interns and agency supervisors would have to agree in advance, in the context of a quasi-contract, what types of projects, objectives, and expectations should be linked to any given intern assignment. When possible, interns should be rotated between different agency departments and subdivisions. Program directors should subsequently monitor compliance to these agreements during and not just after an internship.

Finally, there is a need to develop more comprehensive and valid evaluation procedures for all types of intern programs. The MPMIP does utilize two evaluation forms, but does not evaluate program effectiveness from the standpoint of former interns who have been working in the public sector for some time. Intern programs should engage in more self-evaluation on a frequent basis. One way this might be done is to create a "management information system" (MIS) for each intern program which routinely documents intern data into a centralized computer file. The MPMIP is currently moving in this direction, and the result is up-to-date and highly systematic comparable data on how the program is performing. Data from program evaluations may tell us what types of intern programs work the best in regard to educational value, job satisfaction, and career placement success.

Perhaps what this all leads to is the following observation. We assume they are working. Yet, as the authors have pointed out, internship programs work effectively only if certain factors are present. Since internships are so important to the success of our public administration programs and even more to the students who are required to undergo an internship, it would seem as though they deserve closer and much more frequent scrutiny. Otherwise, we may educate an entire generation of public administrators who, as Frank Sherwood (1973) suggests, find their internships trivial and dissatisfying, thus inculcating a built-in disenchantment toward professional careers in the public service.

NOTES

1. See the National Association of Schools of Public Affairs and Administration (1978). "NASPAA Public Service Internship Guidelines." Washington, D.C.:NASPAA

2. See the National Association of Schools of Public Affairs and Administration (1984). 1984 Directory: *Programs in Public Affairs and Administration.* Washington, D.C:NASPAA.

3. See Henry, Nicholas (1979). "Internships in Public Administration." *Public Administration Review* 39 (May/June):231–232.

4. The stipend for students in the MPMIP is $750 per month for up to six
consecutive months. Interns can intern more than once and are allowed
up to a total of 12 months in the program. About 50 percent of all interns
intern more than once.

REFERENCES

Ashmore, Tim, Sherry Lynch and Susan Treldkeld (1981). "P. A. Program
in the Southeast: An Alumni and Student Perspective." *Southern Review
of Public Administration* 5 (Summer): 211–229.

Campbell, Allan and Lynn Strakosch (1979). "The Presidential Management
Intern Program: A New Approach to Selecting and Developing Ameri-
ca's Future Public Managers." *Public Administration Review* 39 (May/
June):232–236.

Finkle, Arthur and Warren Barclay (1979)."State Government Internships."
Public Administration Review 39 (May/June):236–239).

Golembiewski, Robert T. (1979). "The Near Future of Graduate Public Administration Programs in the U.S. Some Program Minima, Their Common Violation, and Some Priority Palliatives," *Southern Review of Public
Administration* 3 (December):330–331.

Henry, Nicholas (1979). "Are Internships Worthwhile." *Public Administration
Review* 39 (May/June):245–248.

McCaffrey, Jerry (1979). "Perception of Satisfaction-Dissatisfaction in the Internship Experience." *Public Administration Review* 39 (May/June):241–
245.

Murphy, Thomas (1973). *Government Management, Internships, and Executive
Development.* Lexington, Mass.: Lexington Books.

Pugh, Darrell L. (1985). "Evaluation for Public Administration Internship
Programs: An Alternative." *Proceedings: Eighth National Conference on
Teaching Public Administration.* St. Louis, Missouri.

Sherwood, Frank (1973). Quoted in Murphy (1973:238).

Thai, Khi V. (1985). "Does NASPAA Peer Review Improve the Quality of
PA/A Education?" *Public Administration Quarterly* 8 (Winter):422–461.

21
UNDERGRADUATE INTERNSHIPS: AN EMPIRICAL REVIEW

Gerard S. Gryski, Gerald W. Johnson and Laurence J. O'Toole, Jr.

Results of a survey of 78 undergraduate political science depart-ments is used to test the anecdotal assumptions of "think" or "theory" articles that dominate much of the literature on experien-tial learning. A quantifiable picture of undergraduate internships and practices emerges; the only constants in a sea of variables seem to be institutional size and the type of academic calendar followed.

Internships which expose students of politics and public affairs to practical work experience are now nearly ubiquitous aspects of uni-versity curricula.[1] While it is difficult to pinpoint the origins of general public service internships in the United States, the nation's first po-litical internship was not initiated until Wellesley College inaugurated an experimental program during World War II. (Hennessey, 1970:6) Today such programs are a staple of departments of political science, public administration, and public affairs. Many states and numerous local governments administer legislative, administrative, and other intern programs. The National Society for Internships and Exper-iential Education (formerly the National Center for Public Service Internships) provides technical assistance and liaison between gov-ernments and universities; the American Political Science Association has cooperated in the establishment and operation of several pro-grams; and the National Association of Schools of Public Affairs and Administration strongly encourages internship programs in its stan-dards for MPA programs. (NASPAA, 1978a, 1978b)

RESEARCH ON INTERNSHIP PROGRAMS

In spite of their popularity, surprisingly little scholarly attention has been directed to the subject of public service internships. Pub-lished material generally falls into one or more of a few categories: "think pieces" on the utility of internships, the problems they may encounter, and the most appropriate manner of structuring them (usually these are based on the authors' experiences; evaluations of the impact of the internship experience on the interns themselves; and/or descriptions of the operations of some internship programs.)

The "think pieces" on internships are indeed interesting. They document at least two points worth noting: [first], those most closely associated with the administration of these programs at universities are convinced of their value and [second], the presumed benefits of the programs are multiple and impressive. These are said to include numerous positive impacts on the interns themselves learning about politics and administration, akin to the Weberian notion of *verstehen*; role socialization; development of interpersonal, political, and research skills; sensitization to ethical concerns; increase in political or public service commitment and sense of efficacy; and even creation of career opportunities and provision of financial assistance.

In addition, universities and those who sponsor interns also are claimed to be beneficiaries. A university may improve its educational programs and test "its curricula through feedback" (McCaffrey, 1979:242); may enliven classroom instruction through the process of interns relating their field experiences to the subjects under discussion; may develop valuable contacts in government and political life; and may disseminate information about the strength of its programs to those in its environment.

Agencies and political figures might benefit from skilled but inexpensive intern assistance and the students may sometimes serve as agents of change as they bring some of the latest information and innovation from the academic world into the field. Summaries of some of these presumed benefits can be found, for example, in Brereton (1979), Dye and Stephens (1978), Graves (1980), Hedlund (1973), Hennessy (1970), McCaffrey (1979), Massachusetts Internship Office (1974), and Murphy (1973).

Some cautionary and prescriptive analyses about potential pitfalls in the operation of internship programs are contained in Alexander (1977), Murphy (1973), Profughi and Warren (1976), Williams (1976), and Wise (1965).

For all the apparent or presumed benefits of such programs, the empirical studies that have been done to evaluate the impact of internships on the participants have produced mixed results. Whereas qualitative or impressionistic evaluations have often been very positive (see, *e.g.*, Brereton, 1979; Cohen, 1973; Graves, 1980; Hirshfield and Adler, 1973; Koehler, 1980; Massachusetts Internship Office, 1974), some more systematic and quantitative analyses find mixed or negative results. Studies include Balutis (1977) which found little evidence of impact in the case of a legislative internship program; Hennessy (1970) which identified only limited differences between matched samples of interns and other politically-interested students in a couple of separate studies; and Henry (1979) which sampled MPA graduates from nine schools and found that those with prior internship experience seemed to have less supervisory responsibility and lower confidence and trust in their agency than those without such experience (see also the exchange of letters between Henry, 1980 and Guyot, 1980 on this subject). Some systematic studies which have found that internships do exert positive effects include Dye and Stephens (1978) which tested for the quality of individuals' ethical reasoning and Eyber and Halteman (1981:27) which sought evidence that internships "will increase political skill and sophistication."

What is lacking is systematic comparative evidence on the operation of internship programs on a nationwide basis. There has been no attempt to report and analyze such data for similarities and differences among universities with respect to the academic and administrative aspects of internship programs. Individual internship participants, program directors or institutions may have developed strongly-held viewpoints about what sort of program works best or is most congenial in a particular context. Yet, the evaluation reports cited earlier suggest that these viewpoints have not produced any coherent perspective or approach. While at some point it may be possible to draw some empirically-grounded conclusions about how one might best operate an internship program to produce certain results, the first step in this direction, which is the object of this article, is to survey the academic terrain to discover what the range of variation actually is and, in a preliminary fashion, to identify what relationships exist among the academic and administrative components of these programs.

Internship programs serve an array of academic and professional objectives and these will vary by institution and student. The purpose here is not to evaluate these objectives. Rather, the researchers here believe that they can present some descriptive data dealing with a range of options on the basis of which individual institutions can decide what is appropriate to their particular situation based upon the experience of similar schools and similar situations. Based on the literature examined, their own observations, and consultations with colleagues, the researchers have identified what they believe to be several of the main dimensions of internship program operations: structural aspects of internship programs; curricular issues; grading practices; and the role of the internship director.

RESEARCH DESIGN

A mail questionnaire was sent during the summer of 1983 to the undergraduate political science departments of the two largest public institutions of higher education in each state (operationalized in terms of total undergraduate enrollment). The original mailing and two follow-ups later that year generated 78 out of a possible 99 responses (Wyoming has only one eligible school). From these responses the researchers obtained data on the basic structure of internship programs in these departments including academic options and requirements, program designs, grading practices, administrative alternatives, and other significant features of internship programs.

The population surveyed was departments of political science rather than, say, programs in public administration or schools of public affairs, although a number of the responding departments offer undergraduate public administration or degrees. Yet, although many internships were technically classified as being Political Science internships, in actuality most were in an executive setting and involved administrative responsibilities—*e.g.*, executive agencies, hospitals and not-for-profit organizations, research institutes, etc. Most of the institutions surveyed are NASPAA members and almost all of the undergraduate public administration programs at these institutions are administered by the departments included in this sample, cf. NASPAA, 1982).

FINDINGS

Table 1 provides descriptive data on the responding departments and the universities which house them. To determine whether or not there is some common dimension underlying these distributions, several variables were cross-tabulated against each other. Institutional size (student enrollment) and academic calendar (quarter or semester), in particular, appear to have some impact on the requirements, organization, and administration of public service internship programs. While no clearly differentiated models of internship programs emerged from the data, there appear to be some patterns related to how internship positions are secured, uniformity of policy, role of the internship coordinator, internship requirements, and internship evaluation.

In summary, both institutional size and academic calendar provide constraints or supports which shape internship program characteristics. For example, larger institutions are more apt than smaller ones to require intern research or theory and practice reports as contrasted with journals or experience reports. Further, quarter calendar schools use forms and telephone reports rather than formal reports for intern evaluation more often than do semester schools. These two general sets of relationships, involving institutional size and academic calendar, are discussed subsequently in this article. Interestingly, the expectation of relationships among organizational and administrative

Table 1 Departmental/Institutional Characteristics

REGION		UNDERGRADUATE ENROLLMENT	
Northeast	18	Under 10,000	20
Midwest	10	10,000-19,999	49
South	11	20,000-29,999	18
West	22	30,000 and above	14
TERM LENGTH		DEPARTMENT MAJORS	
Quarter	18	Under 150	20
Semester	81	150-299	33
		300-449	17
		450 and above	30
DEPARTMENT FACULTY		FACULTY/MAJOR RATIO	
Under 10	30	Under 10 to 1	15
10-19	26	10-19 to 1	41
20-29	30	20-29 to 1	33
30 and above	15	30 to 1 and above	11

variables and faculty/major ratio and related variables was not supported by the data. At best, the data confirm a diversity of program structures and administration modified somewhat primarily by the variables of institutional size and academic calendar.

STRUCTURAL ASPECTS OF INTERNSHIP PROGRAMS

One is easily impressed by the variety of internship opportunities available to students. The researchers identified some 19 different types, ranging from federal, state, and local agencies to non-profit research organizations and "public interest" interest groups. Any single institution, of course, is likely to offer only a few internship options. State government is the most popular source of internships; 22 percent of the schools reported that two-thirds or more of their internships were with that level of government compared with 7 percent at the local level and 6 percent at the federal level. None of the respondents stated that private sector internships fell into that high-use category, although 43 percent noted that as many as one-third of their positions were in the non-governmental sector.

Institutional size is somewhat related to locus of internship posi-

Table 2 Annual Enrollment in Internship Programs

NUMBER OF STUDENTS	PERCENT OF DEPARTMENTS
1-14	43
15-29	34
30-44	8
45 and above	15

tions. The larger the institution, the more diverse is the locus of positions; that is, none of the larger schools reported having 100 percent of their internship positions at either the local, state or federal levels as did some smaller institutions. At the state level, while five of the smaller institutions reported having no state internship positions, none of the larger schools reported having no state-level positions.

Conversely, some 33 percent of the larger schools have two-thirds or more of their positions at the state level. While private sector internship positions are generally limited, the larger the institution the more private sector placements, *i.e.*, 80 percent of the institutions with less than 10,000 enrollment had no private sector placements compared to 46 percent for institutions with over 20,000 enrollment.

With respect to academic calendar and source of internship position, semester institutions have higher numbers of placements at the federal level than do quarter systems, 36 percent to 8 percent respectively with a third or more federal level placements. Interestingly, private placements are more often used in the West than in any other region.

Virtually all (98 percent) of the programs in which political science students participate are administered by the political science department. Auspices occasionally are shared with the university (5 percent) or with the state for state legislative programs. While most departments sanction a variety of specific internship opportunities, the tendency is to house a diverse collection of internship positions in a single internship program or course (52 percent).

The vast majority of schools (83 percent) offers internships every term including summer. Eleven percent of the programs are offered only once a year, which is often the case with state legislative programs. Enrollment in the programs generally is rather modest (Table 2). In almost every case (98 percent) internships run the entire academic term, just like any other course. With respect to the amount of academic credit awarded for internships, there appear to be two modal categories. In the first (43 percent), students work full-time in their internships and receive a full term's academic credit for that participation (perhaps in conjunction with a readings requirement or course). In the second approach (42 percent), the internship counts as one (or occasionally two) course(s). The department requires a certain number of weekly hours (usually 8–11) to be devoted to the internship for academic credit to be awarded.

One can only speculate as to the reasons why departments opt for one or the other approach, although one element surely would have to reflect a judgment as to the centrality of the internship experience to the student's overall course of study. Academic calendar provides at least one clue to credit variance. Fifty-seven percent of the quarter systems offer term credit compared to only 15 percent of the semester systems. Semester systems are more inclined to offer only one course credit, 33 to 7 percent.

Financial compensation, through the agency or organization accepting the intern, is available generally. Although 21 percent of the schools reported that none of their interns was paid, an even larger number (30 percent) said that over two-thirds of their interns received some compensation. Smaller institutions more often than larger ones have a higher percentage of interns receiving compensation, 44 percent to 10 percent with two-thirds or more receiving compensation.

None of the responding departments reported that completion of an internship was a requirement of its political science major. A small number of departments, offering concentration in public administration and/or criminal justice, did have such a requirement for those majors but those concentrations other than political science form a special class to be discussed later. Nine schools (12 percent) do not have any internship programs at all for their undergraduates. In most cases these are departments which have fairly large MPA programs and apparently decisions have been made to invest available resources to generate and administer internships into the graduate programs. For example, the data show that there is an inverse relationship between the existence of an MPA program and the requirement for an internship experience in undergraduate public administration programs. Only 12 percent of the undergraduate public administration programs in schools with the MPA program require an internship compared with 60 percent in non-MPA granting institutions. One could conclude that NASPAA standards encouraging internships at the MPA level contribute to concentration of internship resources at that level.

When asked whether the policies and procedures for different internship programs in the same department could be characterized by uniformity or considerable variation, 69 percent reported the former. However, within the group the larger institutions tend to utilize uniform policies more often.

With the exception of the readings course, which is usually offered as a companion course to the actual internship, relatively little effort is made to integrate the internship with other departmental course offerings or programs. Only 25 percent of the respondents indicated any such effort and even in those cases it was usually restricted to having a particular course serve as a prerequisite to the internship. There is a tendency, as might be expected, for smaller schools to coordinate the internship with other courses. Only 7 percent of the schools offer a post-internship course, the purpose of which is to reexamine the internship experience in the context of the literature. All of these schools are smaller schools.

Some type of reading component is often a requirement for completion of the internship, either a companion reading course or a reading component as part of the internship itself. Fifty-nine percent of the schools employ one or the other option and 69 percent of this number require the readings component. The overwhelming majority of departments offering a readings component attempts to integrate it with the actual internship experience (72 percent), a situation in marked contrast to other attempts at integration noted above. Again, larger schools more often offer and require a readings course than do smaller schools, 67 to 40 percent and 56 to 30 percent, respectively.

With only one exception, every department requires some form of written work from its interns. There are several options of which the modal approach is the completion of an internship paper or a journal. Other options worthy of particular note are the completion of a research or a major "theory and practice" paper in which the student examines theories and tests hypotheses from the academic literature in light of the internship experience. It is of interest to note here that institutional size appears to be strongly related to type of internship requirements. The larger, research-oriented institutions more often require research or theory and practice papers, 40 to 10 percent, respectively, to zero percent for institutions with less than 10,000 enrollment. The smaller institutions rely more heavily on the traditional internship duties report or journal.

GRADING PRACTICES

Fifty-four percent of the departments assign letter grades to their interns while 19 percent grade on a pass/fail basis (7 percent have some combination of the two). The grade distribution is fairly narrow, with 63 percent of the departments reporting that all students received essentially the same grade (owing in part to the significant number of departments that grade on a pass/fail basis). While the majority of all institutions has a narrow grade distribution, semester calendar schools have a broader distribution than do quarter calendar schools, 44 to 15 percent.

Departments generally exercise the major responsibility for awarding grades. When asked to specify the percentage of the interns' grade that is determined by the agency supervisor, almost half of the respondents said none while only 12 percent indicated that the agency was responsible for two-thirds or more of the entire grade. The larger the institution, the less the agency role is in determining internship grades. Eighty-nine percent of the larger institutions allow less than a third of the grade to be determined by the agency. None of the larger schools allow the agency to determine over a third of the grade compared to 44 percent in this category for schools under 10,000 enrollment. Only 17 percent of the departments reported that the agency supervisors were asked to suggest a specific grade (the rest provided a general evaluation). Considerable variation exists with respect to the department policy regarding the medium by which the agency evaluates the intern. While a plurality of the departments requires a brief letter, other means employed include, in decreasing order of usage, detailed written reports, telephone evaluations, and standard forms. Only one department did not ask for any agency evaluation at all.

All of the schools with less than 10,000 enrollment use letters and reports compared to 50 percent for the larger schools. The larger the school, the more diverse is the reporting method including 20 percent by telephone and 20 percent who use a form. Academic calendar also specifies this relationship. As might be expected, quarter systems, probably due to time constraints, more often rely on the use of the telephone and standard forms. The aim of these grading practices clearly indicates that the academic departments consider internships academic work and that they rather than the agency people are in the best position to ascribe various academic gradations to that work— even though in practice the gradations have a narrow distribution. However, both institutional size and academic calendar tend to specify the method used.

THE INTERNSHIP COORDINATOR

The success of a department's internship programs is heavily dependent upon the role of the internship coordinator. The integrity of the internship programs requires the specification of at least some uniform policies and practices, especially since internship programs often are run essentially autonomously from the rest of the department's programs. The survey was designed to elicit information on three aspects of the coordinator's status—centralization of authority, responsibilities, and compensation.

CENTRALIZATION

The larger the school, the more likely the internship program is to have a single or general coordinator, 90 percent to 50 percent. Most departments (70 percent) appear to have chosen the centralization option. One might assume that this structure has the potential to locate responsibility and insure uniformity across programs. However, the data show no relationship between centralization and policy uniformity.

RESPONSIBILITIES

The internship coordinator serves as a general administrator responsible for developing and directing the program. Two additional responsibilities are discussed below.

First, the coordinator either has or shares responsibility for the identification of internship positions. Respondents were asked to estimate the percentage of internships found by the coordinator, the students themselves, and from unsolicited requests by agencies for interns. Surprisingly, this responsibility is almost equally shared by students and the coordinator: 37 percent of the departments reported that over two-thirds of their internship positions were generated by the internship coordinator; another 37 percent said that over two-thirds of their internships were generated by students. Interestingly, in this case, the larger the school, the less likely is the coordinator to play a role in finding internship positions. Fifty percent of the largest schools reported that the coordinator generated no internship positions compared to zero percent for the smallest schools. These data run counter to the researchers' experience and warrant further review. Internships coming from unsolicited sources are a small percentage of the entire pool, with only one department reporting more than one-third of the slots coming from this source. The percentage of internship positions generated from unsolicited sources is much higher in the smallest institutions, 66 percent to 25 percent.

While the responses appear to be internally consistent, the actual process of securing internship positions may be more complex than suggested by the data; that is, coordinator or departmental responsibilities might well include the establishment and maintenance of an internship position roster or a set of relationships with sponsors within which individual interns secure positions. In such cases, one would conclude that students and departments perform complementary roles in internship position securement.

Second, conferences with students are an integral part of the internship and are usually arranged on an individual basis or as general meetings for all enrolled interns. Between these two alternatives, departments usually opt for the individual conference format with the majority of the departments scheduling conferences from one to five times a term. Institutional size, in part, governs the distribution; that is, 60 percent of the schools with over 30,000 enrollment hold either bi-weekly or weekly conferences compared to 20 percent in this category for schools with less than 10,000 students. General intern meetings are more infrequent. Thirty-seven percent of the schools do not schedule such meetings and those that do confer on a varied schedule.

COMPENSATION

Compensation for internship responsibilities can be direct or indirect. Indirect means by which coordinator compensation occurs usually take the form of staff support and resources. Fifteen percent of the departments report that some travel allowance or reimbursement is provided while a much smaller percentage provide extra secretarial help or a graduate assistant. The overwhelming majority (78 percent), however, provides no additional staff support. Larger institutions more often provide staff support for the coordinator than do smaller schools. Twenty percent of the coordinators at the largest schools receive support from an undergraduate coordinator or from graduate assistants while none of the smaller schools receive support in these forms. Smaller institutions, where they do provide support, most often do so in the form of a travel allowance.

Table 3 lists the more direct ways in which departments have elected to compensate their internship coordinators. Clearly the predominant response among the respondents is to give one course credit to the internship coordinator.

SPECIAL PROGRAMS

Most departments house whatever variety of internship opportunities they have within one general internship program or course. Even among those departments that offer more than one major (e.g., international relations, law and society, urban studies, area studies, etc.), the norm is for the students to take internships under the general internship program, if they take them at all.

There are two notable exceptions to this rule—special internship

Table 3 Coordinator Compensation

COMPENSATION	PERCENT OF DEPARTMENTS
Chair serves as coordinator; no direct compensation	2
Director of undergraduate studies serves as coordinator	9
Advanced graduate student serves as coordinator	9
Coordinator receives one course credit	44
Formula (assigned faculty sponsors)	3
Part of teaching load for individual faculty	21
Other	4

programs designed exclusively for public administration or criminal justice majors. Several schools offering these concentrations have their students participate in the general internship program but a number have designed separate programs tailored to the specific needs of students in these two majors. Internships may have special significance for these majors since they may bear a close relationship to the students' subsequent careers. In addition to the "on the job" experience, the internship serves as an orientation to assist the student in deciding on career choices. Of course there is always the possibility that an internship with a particular agency will lead to a career opportunity upon graduation. The researchers did not attempt an exhaustive analysis of these special programs, in part because they share several characteristics and emphases with the general political science programs discussed above. Instead they focused on the differences found in these special programs.

Of the departments surveyed, 14 offer an undergraduate public administration major but less than one-third of these require an internship. Only one of these offers a required post-internship course. Readings courses receive less prominence in these internships—only one department makes it a requirement. In general, and with the limited data available, the best the researchers can conclude is that, when compared to political science, the emphasis in public administration shifts at least slightly to the practical and away from the academic value of internships, though of course the two are not mutually exclusive.

Criminal justice internships follow a similar "applied or career-oriented" pattern. Of the 12 departments that have a criminal justice major, some three-quarters offer an internship program and seven of the 12 require participation in it. As might be expected, local government internship programs are most prominent; each program has at least 40 percent of its positions with that level of government. One program has a post-internship course and it is a requirement. As in the case with public administration, readings courses receive less emphasis than in political science internships; less than half the departments offer one and only one requires it.

Evaluation and grading practices differ significantly for criminal justice internships. They have a fairly broad distribution of final grades and agency supervisors usually have more input in grading decisions. The agencies generally are more thorough in their evaluations, with most departments receiving detailed written reports from agency supervisors.

Students in criminal justice programs are slightly more likely to experience closer supervision from the faculty coordinator in terms of individual consultations and group meetings. Part of this is attributable to the fact that some criminal justice internships are explicitly designed and described as "career orientation."

CONCLUSIONS

Although it is not possible to subsume the internship programs offered at these institutions under a few clearly-drawn empirical models, at least one pattern is unmistakable. While the literature on internship programs, referenced earlier, contains a fairly straightforward set of normative guidelines suggesting the most appropriate ways of handling such programs, these are largely honored in the breach. If it is indeed true, for instance, that programs are likely to work well when they are administered intensively, clearly recognized in the university's reward structure, and provided with substantial resources, when consultations between program coordinator and students are frequent (*e.g.*, weekly or more often), and when the coordinator visits regularly with interns' sponsors (see, *e.g.*, Haines, 1970:20–21; Hedlund, 1973:22–25;), then the institutions represented in this study are not benefiting from such configurations. Of course, the oft-mentioned recommendations for handling such programs may be erroneous. It is impossible to tell if this is so since the normative injunctions remain substantially untested.

The most general and obvious conclusion that can be drawn from this study is that diversity in the organization and administration of undergraduate internship programs is the norm. However, some patterns do emerge when programs are reviewed with respect to certain select variables, especially institutional size and academic calendar.

Each of these appears to provide constraints or opportunities which tend to modify the programs.

The larger institutions are generally more centrally organized, better supported, allow less agency control, have a research and theory emphasis not found in smaller institutions and have more diversity in internship placements and evaluation methods. On the other hand, smaller schools integrate the program more into other programs. Type of academic calendar also tends to influence internship program organization and administration. Time constraints evidently induce quarter schools to evaluate interns through different methods, to provide them term credit, and to assign grades with narrower distribution than do semester schools.

Finally, there appears to be a generalized impact on undergraduate internship programs located in institutions that offer the MPA. These conclusions must be offered with caution since a multivariate analysis would be required to separate out the impact of institutional size, academic calendar, and other variables. However, some patterns appear to be valid. MPA schools tend more often to leave internship position securement up to students, have a single internship coordinator, generally centralize internship administration, provide more staff support, depend less on agency control, supervise interns more closely, and are more applied, at least in terms of the use of journal and experience report requirements rather than research or theory papers.

While the data from this survey do not lend themselves to normative conclusions, the researchers suspect that internship models exist which would provide standards of internship program effectiveness. Such models would depend first of all on the objectives of the internship programs and these might validly vary from general education to career development. However, within stated objectives it can be logically concluded that program structure and administration would ultimately influence program effectiveness. At present there appears to be a variety of program configurations that have evolved due to serendipitous, historical, and recourse factors. Probably what has happened is that traditional departmental structures and procedures have been applied to the internship arena without any clear reasons for doing so. What is needed and warranted, given the incomplete and contradictory conclusions available in the literature concerning the role, structure, and value of internships, is an intensive qualitative analysis of what configurations or parts thereof do, in fact, contribute to high quality and productive internship experiences. This study has, at best, identified current configurations and processes. What remains to be done is to determine which of these optimally contribute to the achievement of internship program objectives.

NOTES

1. An earlier version of this article was delivered at the annual meetings of the American Society for Public Administration, Denver, April 10, 1984. The authors acknowledge with gratitude the assistance provided by John Heilman in the data management of this article.

REFERENCES

Alexander, James I. (192 "Institutional Design of Public Service Internships: Conceptual Academic and Structural Problems." *Teaching Political Science* 9 (Spring):127–133.

Balutis, Alan P. (1977). "Participation through Politics: An Evaluation of the New York State Assembly Intern Program." *Teaching Political Science* 4 (April):319–328.

Brereton, Thomas F. (1979). *Design and Implementation of an Effective Internship in Urban Public Affairs*. San Antonio: Department of Urban Studies, Trinity University.

Cohen, L. S. (1973). "Evaluation of State Legislative Internship." *Public Service Internship News* (November/December):5–8.

Dye, G. G. and J. B. Stephens (1978). "Learning Ethics through Public Service Internships-Evaluation of an Experimental Program." *Liberal Education* 64 (October):341–356.

Eyler, Janet and Beth Halteman (1981). "The Impact of a Legislative Internship on Students' Political Skillfulness and Sophistication." *Teaching Political Science* 9 (Fall):27–34.

Graves, Helen M. (1980). "Comparative Political Internships: Assuring Academic Validity." *Teaching Political Science* 7 (January):219–230.

Guyot, J. F. (1980). "Giving Internships the Benefit of the Doubt." *Public Administration Review* 40 (March/April):201.

Hedlund, R. D. (1973). "Reflections on Political Internships," *PS* 6 (Winter):19–25.

Hennessy, Bernard D. (1970). *Political Internships: Theory, Practice, Evaluation*. University Park: Pennsylvania State University Studies, No. 28.

Henry, Nicholas (1979). "Are Internships Worthwhile?" *Public Administration Review* 39 (May/June):245–247.

———(1980). Response to Letter. *Public Administration Review* 40 (March/April):203.

Hirschfield, R. S. and N. M. Adler (1973). "Internships in Politics: The CUNY Experience." *PS* 6 (Winter):13–18.

Koehler, Cortus T. (1977). "Directing and Supervising the Intern." *Public Management* (January):2–6.

———(1980). "The Intern and the Internship: From Beginning to End." *Teaching Political Science* 7 (April):329–335.

McCaffrey, Jerry T. (1979). "Perceptions of Satisfaction and Dissatisfaction in the Internship Experience." *Public Administration Review* 39 (May/June):241–244.

Massachusetts Internship Office (1974). *Internships in Public Policy: Students in Public Service.* Boston: Massachusetts Internship Office.

Murphy, T. P. (ed.) (1973). *Government Management Internships and Executive Development.* Lexington, Mass.: D. C. Heath.

National Association of Schools of Public Affairs and Administration (1978a). "NASPAA Guidelines and Standards for Masters Degree Public Service Internships." Washington, D.C.: NASPAA.

————1978b). "NASPAA Public Service Internship Guidelines." Washington, D.C.: NASPAA.

————(1982). *Directory of Programs in Public Affairs and Administration.* Washington, D.C.:NASPAA.

Profughi, Victor and Edward Warren (1976). "Role Relationships in Internship Program Management: The Vital Job of the Academic Adviser in the Placement Process." *Teaching Political Science* 5 (January):199–207.

Williams, Thomas J. (1976). "The Faculty Advisor's Role in Intern Supervision." *Teaching Political Science* 4 (October):101–110.

Wise, Sidney (1965). "The Administration of an Internship Program." Unpublished paper presented at a conference on internships sponsored by the American Political Science Association and the Ford Foundation, Las Croabas, Puerto Rico (April).

22
MAKING AN INTERNSHIP WORK

Jason Berger

A clear guide is provided to companies (in this case, public relations) wanting to set up an internship program, including a handy outline for constructing an internship job description. Advice is offered on some of the management and human relations implications of adding a college intern to a professional organization.

Most public relations degree programs either require or strongly encourage an internship. Having bright, energetic and ambitious young college students on your staff can help you fill critical productivity needs. In addition, sponsoring an internship demonstrates your organization's commitment to improving the quality of public relations.

We are witnessing this development first-hand in the Department of Communication at Duquesne University of Pittsburgh. Just a few years ago, student applications outnumbered available positions. Now, the reverse is true. Requests for internships are outpacing interested student applicants by more than ten to one.

What makes this trend even more significant is that many of our sponsoring organizations are just not calling and saying: "We need an intern." Their staffs are spending a great deal of time and resources developing policies and procedures that will produce a program beneficial to all the parties.

The following suggestions will help you initiate an internship or improve your current one.

VERIFY THE NEED

The first step is to decide whether your organization has enough educationally sound and professionally regarded work for an intern. An internship is a contract or reciprocal agreement between your organization and the college. You are required to provide a proper learning atmosphere for the student. The student, in exchange, will be expected to perform entry-level work.

If appropriate work is not available, and you still hire an intern, expect the brighter students to complain. Very soon, expect the school to terminate the program. This action will not speak well for your image within the public relations community.

Along with professional-level work, your organization also needs supervisors with the instructional skill to work with the intern. A successful intern supervisor should be a natural teacher who enjoys and has the time and patience to help young people grow professionally. The supervisor should also be willing to take risks as the intern begins to assume responsibilities that can affect the bottom line. He or she must also put in the extra time required to help develop the intern's creative, strategic, interpersonal and editorial skills.

After deciding that you have the work and the right supervisor for the intern, the next step is to produce a job description which should be submitted to the college for the student to review.

"The job description can help advertise the internship among competing candidates" said Charles Weber, director of public relations, Peoples Natural Gas Company, Pittsburgh. "It sets the standards that the student, school and organization must live by. It becomes a management and evaluation tool during and at the completion of the semester."

Weber's job description is an excellent model worth copying. It is organized in the following sections:

Key results. Describes the educational value of the program. The job description opens with the following statement: "The public relations staff receives quality assistance in the execution of its programs and Peoples Gas gains recognition in the academic and corporate community for its willingness and efforts to support the development of young adults for the work force."

Basis for accountability. Describes all the student's responsibilities.

Organization. Describes the reporting structure of the internship.

Nature of position. Describes in general terms the mission of the organization's communications department and what the student should be expected to learn from the internship.

Relationships. Deals with the different internal and external "publics" the student will interface with on a daily basis.

Knowledge, education and skills required. Besides insisting on work toward a communications degree, this section states the student must have excellent personal computer, writing, verbal and time-management skills.

Predominant tasks. Outlines day-to-day activities such as writing stories for internal publications.

It is clear that Peoples Gas is serious about its internship program. Writing a job description in a similar manner will make it clear to both the student applicants and their college that your program is legitimate and will be both educationally and professionally sound.

At our university we run half-time and full-time internships during 15-week semesters. A half-time internship consists of an 18-hour week. The intern receives three credits. A full-time intern earns six credits for working a 36-hour week in a "simulated work environment."

Different schools have different grading policies for internships. Duquesne's policy is a letter grade (A to F) which is decided jointly by the sponsor and the faculty director. Other schools give a Pass/Fail grade. (*Editor's note: PRSA and the Public Relations Student Society of America (PRSSA) sponsor Public Relations Internships to Develop Expertise. Guidelines for PRIDE internships, including grading, compensation and eligibility information, are available from the PRSSA Director, Educational Affairs, at PRSA Headquarters*).

Once the internship begins, have the faculty advisor brief you and the supervisor about the grading criteria. Make sure that you reiterate to the intern that there is a grade at the end of the program and that you will participate in the decision.

SET COMPENSATION POLICY

With semester-length internships, compensation also comes into play. Compensation is tricky, particularly in such rough economic times. At Duquesne we encourage, but do not insist on, some form of compensation. It can be either an hourly rate ranging upward from minimum wage, which some of the Fortune 500 corporations based in Pittsburgh pay, or the more popular stipend. The stipend normally covers transportation, lunch and incidental costs.

In determining your compensation policy, remember that many students, particularly commuters, will have to resign or curtail their part-time job activities to accept an internship. They are eager to make the sacrifices. Offering a stipend will be a sign from you that you are willing to meet them at least halfway in support.

In addition, many students will have to justify an unpaid internship to their parents. This can be difficult as college tuition escalates and financial aid is cut. We have lost a few interns the past two semesters because their parents insisted they hold part-time jobs. Offering a stipend, or some form of minimum compensation, will help potential interns persuade their parents of the value of the program.

SPONSORING AN INTERN

It is a mistake for you to call your local college and simply say: "Send me an intern." And then, if the applicant is a "nice kid," make the offer to the first one that applies.

Your search for an intern should be similar to recruiting entry-level professional employees. This way you send out a message that you want the "best," and encourage students to compete for the position.

We present Duquesne students with binders of available positions along with the job descriptions. They apply for positions as if they have graduated. We inform students that they will compete for interviews and their evaluation will be based on how well they interview, and their writing samples.

Once the program begins, problems can surface quickly. It has been our experience that the intern's most common complaints are about working under pressure and having to juggle too many tasks.

Remember, they are students and quite young. Most students internalize pressure and will be reluctant to discuss priorities and the pressures of responsibility. Many will treat each assignment as a homework assignment or, worse yet, a test. But, as I've learned quite quickly in a year as Duquesne's intern coordinator, when asked about pressure, the students will talk.

As your program unfolds, it will be your responsibility to encourage your intern to open up, to articulate the positive aspects of the internship as well as the problems of being pressured. You can then help the intern develop sound time-management and anti-stress skills.

If you plan to delegate occasional secretarial work, expect some students to complain. The rule we have at Duquesne is a simple one. We tell students if the secretarial work is shared by everyone in the work area—tasks such as photocopying, answering the phone when the receptionist is away, typing on the computer and mailing one's own correspondence—they don't have a legitimate complaint. But if he or she is the only "employee" performing secretarial work, then the sponsor is violating the agreement they made with the college.

Basic public relations skills, such as researching and preparing media lists, writing simple business correspondence, doing mail merges on a PC and assembling press kits, are entry-level skills students should have learned prior to the internship.

Another problem that can surface is sexual harassment of the intern. When confronting sexual harassment, it is important for the students to fend for themselves *first*. Many interns have reported that they solved the problem themselves, a sign of emotional maturity. But unfortunately, this is not always the case. We encourage our students to immediately seek help from us and the sponsor at the firm in the strictest confidence to solve the problem. If the problem is the supervisor, we move quickly to either complain to that person's manager, or pull the student out of the program. We then place the student in another internship.

SUPERVISION IS KEY

No business or organization is too small for an internship as long as the student is supervised by an experienced public relations professional. Small "Mom and Pop" firms can provide excellent experience for an intern. For an internship to work, the principals of the firm must be available to supervise and teach. If they are not, the internship will be a waste of time.

V. INTERNSHIP CASES

23
INTERNSHIPS ARE KEY TO DIRECT MARKETING PROGRAM

Richard A. Hamilton

A pioneering academic program in Direct Marketing at the University of Missouri-Kansas City requires an internship course of all undergraduates. Interns meet with professors regularly, keep diaries, make project reports in their class. It is important for the interns to be paid so that they feel and think like employees/professionals—not like students.

Over the past several years direct marketing sales have grown at a pace estimated to be 50 percent faster than retail store sales.

In addition, the same business factors that make direct marketing so attractive to retailers—measurability, accountability, retrieval of information to form customer databases—have increased the use of direct marketing by the industrial and nonprofit sectors to generate sales leads, include smaller customers in catalogues, increase memberships, and raise contributions.

Because this continued growth is expected to continue well into the future, and no degree program existed at an accredited school of business administration, the University of Missouri at Kansas City (UMKC) decided to begin such a credit program two years ago [1983] at the bachelor's and master's levels.

The founding of UMKC's Center for Direct Marketing Education and Research was made possible through $570,000 grant from the Direct Marketing Educational Foundation.

Many other universities have begun to offer courses in direct marketing to help fill the employment gap that direct marketing organizations have faced for years, and which is being exacerbated by the tremendous growth in direct marketing activities. As those programs move toward complete majors or degree programs, we at UMKC stress the importance of requiring an internship course along with them, particularly for undergraduates.

Our course prerequisite requires completing all other direct marketing courses in the curriculum, maintaining a 2.5 grade point average in them and an overall 2.5 grade average.

The student must complete 250 hours of on-site intern experience between 10 and 20 weeks. Specific work schedules are decided by the students and sponsoring organizations; students may schedule around other classes, and organizations may be available to help interns as needed.

Perhaps the most time-consuming portion of the course is acquiring sponsors, screening them, and matching students with available internships.

Although UMKC's undergraduate program is still small enough (25 internships during the 1985 spring semester) so that acquiring sponsors is still passive, an information and lead—generating brochure has been developed for use if and when the number of students becomes large enough to warrant using it.

However, the quality of current and past interns will have a direct impact on current and future internship sponsors. Positive internship experiences will somewhat automatically generate repeat sponsors. Unfortunately, negative experiences probably will eliminate a potential sponsor forever.

The operational aspects of the internships include biweekly professor-student meetings, diaries, class projects, seminar presentations, and personal responsibilities. Meetings in small groups are held to update the professor on the interns' learning experiences, to monitor the meaningfulness and academic credibility of their internships, to verify that the predetermined programs are being followed, to help students with any difficulties they have encountered, and to share the varied learning experiences among students.

Interns also must keep work diaries. For each eight-hour period of internship experience students must record how the time was spent, what they learned, and other pertinent observations, particularly those dealing with differences or similarities between direct marketing in academia and on the job.

Each entry must not exceed one handwritten 8 1/2″ × 11″ page. Diaries are to be maintained on a current basis and must be submitted to the professor for the previous two-week period at the biweekly professor-student meeting. Supervisors verify the information in the diaries by signing them.

Interns must submit written academic reports on experiences for which they had primary responsibility. The nature, scope, and subject of the project are agreed upon by the sponsor and the professor.

Students are required to present their class projects at seminars attended by their supervisors and classmates. Presenting class projects before their own supervisors, other students, and other direct marketing professionals has yielded very high-quality presentations.

Students are paid hourly wages for their internship duties by their sponsoring organizations, usually $4 to $5 an hour. There are two reasons for paying them:

- The compensation is to impress upon them that they are traversing the academic world into the "real world." As such, they understand that their compensation is not a scholarship, a gift, or aid, but reimbursement for their duties as employees.
- Although we understand the employer is not reimbursed by UMKC or by the student for the time spent in providing the learning experiences, we feel that paying a wage, even if it's minimal, adds a further commitment to the sponsoring organization to make the internship meaningful for the students.

My suggestions for a direct marketing curriculum that includes an internship requirement will, I hope, help other institutions start a similar program to make the overall direct marketing program more meaningful.

24
AN INTERNATIONAL INTERNSHIP PROGRAM AT NEW HAMPSHIRE COLLEGE

Dorothy S. Rogers

New Hampshire College reached across the seas to set up international internships for its Retailing Program in Europe. Soon students from other colleges were attracted to the program followed by European sales executives congregating in New Hampshire for a seminar. Even a small private college can make an important contribution with a little innovative thinking and action applied to the often hum-drum world of internship management and development.

In the summer of 1975, New Hampshire College, Manchester, New Hampshire, sponsored its fourth International Internship in Retailing Program. This highly successful overseas cooperative education program has been planned and coordinated since its inception by this author.

As in the previous years, the 1975 program gave American college students an opportunity to spend six weeks studying and working in foreign retail firms with placement from Scandinavia to the Far East.

The purpose of such work-study experience is two-fold. First, to broaden the educational background of future business people by exposure to business techniques in countries economically associated with the United States. Second, it enables the American interns to actually become part of another culture by working and living in a foreign environment.

The program was initiated in 1972 through the assistance of the National Retail Merchants Association. At the annual convention of the National Retail Merchants Association contacts were made with store directors from France and Denmark. They were most enthusiastic about the idea of participating in a student work/study project, and as a result of that meeting and months of correspondence, five New Hampshire College students became interns in the pilot program in June. They were placed in stores in Copenhagen, Denmark and

Paris, Orleans, and Rouen, France, studying European retailing techniques and utilizing business principles learned at New Hampshire College.

This first effort was a success. Each intern had a marvelous experience and returned to class with a new sophistication and a better understanding of how to apply textbook principles to real-world situations. As for the participating firms, they were even more enthusiastic at the conclusion of the program than they had been at the beginning and were anxious to renew the project the following summer.

Throughout the fall of 1972 work continued on development of the program for 1973 and, in the summer of 1973, the program continued. Additional European retail firms offered internship positions and for a second year New Hampshire College students were able to add further dimension to their lives.

Interest in this "Work and Play in Europe for College Credit" program increased and requests came in from colleges throughout the United States asking to have their students included in this unique New Hampshire College European apprenticeship. As a result, students from colleges in Florida, Minnesota, and Massachusetts were accepted in the 1974 program. The expanded program included two new retail firms in France, one in Denmark, and one in Belgium. The international open-door policy which started in 1972, bestowing immeasurable benefits on students, management, and consumers alike continued to grow. New Hampshire College and a number of leading European retailers were making a positive contribution in the area of international relations.

The next step was to make this a world program, not just a European experience, and when contacts were made for 1975, stores in Asia, Australia, South America and the Caribbean were invited to participate. The response was most gratifying and the 1975 program saw students from all corners of the United States leave for all corners of the world.

Both in 1973 and 1974, while American students were being sent to work as interns in Europe, European retailing firms reciprocated by sending their junior executives to a seminar in retail management which was conducted for three weeks during July at New Hampshire College. With this, the exchange was complete. Cooperation between an educational institution and a select number of international retailers was furthering the careers of young Americans and young Europeans giving each group the opportunity to combine theory and practice in a culture different from their own. The basic principle of cooperative education was being extended throughout the world.

Once accepted as interns, the American students spend six weeks living in a foreign country and working in a world-famous retailing establishment. Time is spent both meeting the customer and working behind the scenes in organizations, marketing, merchandise control, and promotion. Management puts the intern through an intensive "training period" which calls for application of classroom theory to international business. Training includes central market visits, attendance at fashion showings with the stores' buyers, and the opportunity to sit in on department meetings and store-wide executive meetings. As plans for the next season unfold, the student is given the chance to offer suggestions and ask questions pertaining to merchandising and promotion practices. One French retailer (a chain of 155 stores with headquarters in Paris) included a trip by private jet to four outstanding stores in its group located in different provinces within the country. The students gained an invaluable experience by observing, first hand, the wide variety of customer types served by this one firm and could relate the merchandising of each store to the particular needs of each trading area. What better way to develop an understanding of the cultural differences within one European country! The intern learns that even in one culture, differences become as important a factor in selecting goods for resale as they are in a cultural "melting pot" like the United States. Prior to observing this, students assume, when studying world marketing procedures, that each country can be treated as a single market segment. After this experience that incorrect observation becomes a major point to consider and is discussed at length in their final reports. Also, back in the classroom the following fall, each participant makes a major contribution to the learning process of his or her peers who were not fortunate enough to have had the first-hand exposure.

In Rouen, France, a New Hampshire College student was asked to gather records to be used as "background music" for an "American Sale." He conscientiously went about selecting current rock-and-roll and country-western music, only to be told, "No, no American music! Marches like in your Fourth of July parades!"—Another lesson was learned that day by both parties. The student found out that the provincial French idea of typical American music was much different than ideas encountered in Paris, and the promotion manager learned about the kind of American music considered "typical" by a "typical" American.

In Denmark, the government controls sale advertising and, as a result, all retail stores advertise sales only at specified times during the year. Coming from highly competitive marketing society, this technique comes as a "cultural shock" to the student. The policy is studied along with its effects on both Danish retailing and the Danish consumer. The student's report then contains an in-depth analysis of the contrasting system, another victory for cooperative education.

In Hong Kong, the store president himself prepares the training program to be followed during the internship, and allows a week at its conclusion for the student to write an analysis of the program. This report then becomes a planning tool and he gains by receiving an objective view of his operation, seen through the eyes of an American college student.

While all this is taking place overseas, back in the United States more cooperative education, international style, as a young French assistant store manager is shown inventory and sales figures by the president of an American Catalogue-Warehouse-Showroom. Amazement shows on his face and is apparent in his voice as this young European marvels at the openness of the American businessman.

As the seminar in retail management progresses, the foreign participants are fascinated by American theory and practice. During the course of three weeks they are given classroom instruction in retailing principles by leading United States retail educators and executives. They spend time in the New York market visiting Seventh Avenue showrooms, international textile firms, and an international buying office. This is followed by actual in-store observation where each has the opportunity to view, "in the field" the practical side of retailing under the guidance of a line manager. Finally, a "brainstorming session" ties it all together. Information is exchanged and concepts are analyzed. Heated discussions take place concerning the application of theory to practice and comparisons are made of the American retail scene to that of each participant's country.

Both in the New Hampshire College classroom, where the program begins and ends, and in the actual world of the American merchant, education is the goal. It is the combination of these two worlds, a cooperative effort, that leads to total education for those who are fortunate enough to be participants in this unique exchange program which is built on the cooperative education philosophy.

New Hampshire College is a career-oriented institution of higher learning and, as such, has always believed in a marriage between reality and theory. It was this inherent philosophy that provided the basis for our cooperative education program that has successfully exposed students to American industry since 1969. Now, as the study of international business becomes more important on American campuses, New Hampshire College is extending this philosophy to encompass world industry.

Starting with retailing, the student sees international business from both the consumer and management points of view. In this way, two objectives are accomplished: 1) an understanding develops concerning the need to study each cultural segment as a basis in market planning, and 2) there is exposure to management and management strategies as practiced in each culture. Armed with this knowledge, true learning is more likely to occur, and coupled with the theory of the classroom, a better prepared candidate is ready for the world of international business.

As for the foreign business people who attend the New Hampshire College sponsored seminars, they are exposed to both theory and practice and also benefit from the basic philosophy of the college. As a result, they return to their jobs better able to relate to American culture and the American economy.

25
INTERNAL AUDITING INTERNSHIP

Dennis L. Kimmell and
Sharon L. Kimmell

Some departments in companies that are heavily involved in internships miss out on the advantages of participation, such as recruiting good graduates and building an awareness of their aspect of the profession among students. This nuts-and-bolts discussion of the value of such a program includes exhibits showing timetables and suggested duties for interns in internal auditing departments.

Accounting internship programs, initially conceived to provide students with an opportunity to obtain invaluable accounting experience, offer numerous benefits to internal audit departments which participate.

Involvement in these programs enhances the participant's reputation and visibility within the college and the regional community, improves prospects of attracting top accounting students as employees, alleviates temporary personnel shortages during year-end procedures, and provides staff for special research projects.

Public accounting firms have been avid supporters of internship programs, but, historically, internal audit departments have not participated to the same extent. This limited participation may be attributable to a self perpetuating cycle in which companies do not participate due to a lack of knowledge, and yet never acquire an understanding of the benefits of student internships due to a lack of participation.

The result of such uninformed decision making is an immeasurable loss to students, universities, and internal audit departments. All groups stand to benefit significantly from the internship experience.

THE BASICS

An internship is a university/accounting department-sponsored program. It provides students, usually juniors but sometimes seniors, with a one-time opportunity to gain practical experience and receive academic credit on either a letter grade or pass/fail basis. The internship experience lasts anywhere from 10 weeks to six months although 10 to 12 weeks is the norm.

Typically, the program takes place the first part of the spring semester (January to mid-March) or during the winter quarter. Some schools do offer summer internships; however, these tend to have fewer participants than winter programs.

To help ensure that the experiences are productive and positive, students desiring placement in an internship position must meet a set of program standards. Most schools require a minimum cumulative grade point average for all course work completed (*e.g.*, 2.75) and a slightly higher minimum grade point average in their accounting or perhaps business course work (*e.g.*, 3.00). Additionally, most schools require the completion of a certain group of accounting courses (*e.g.*, the principles and intermediate series). Some schools set a minimum grade that must be attained in those required courses (*e.g.*, no grade lower than B-). Students are often required to obtain letters of recommendation from a designated number of instructors and/or previous employers. Such letters are placed in the student's internship file and are made available to interviewing firms.

Many schools allow firms to state additional requirements or restrictions that students must meet such as:

- Specifying higher grade point averages than those required by the program.
- Requiring completion of additional accounting courses (*e.g.*, auditing, to enhance internal audit skills or courses that pertain to an internal audit special project).
- Requiring a willingness on the part of students to engage in significant travel.
- Specifying a longer than normal internship period.

Students may also be required to temporarily relocate or undertake a significant daily commute, which makes the internship viable for almost any internal audit department, regardless of its location.

Allowing a company to specify additional requirements optimizes the interview process (*i.e.*, interviewers do not waste time with unacceptable students) and eases the assignment process whereby companies and students are matched by mutual preference ratings.

SELECTION PROCESS

The actual selection of interns is usually accomplished by having the individual students select and sign up for interviews with the participating employers. Some schools require students to interview with every firm for which they meet the requirements. Others allow students to select those employers with whom the would like to interview. The interviewing process extends over several weeks.

At the end of this period, typically one of two procedures is followed. Some schools allow student/firm matches to be determined on a *laissez faire* basis. Offers are directly communicated to individual students who decide whether or not to accept the offer. This approach can result in a number of unmatched employers and students. In addition, it has the potential for creating a bidding war among participating companies.

Other schools make the internship assignments by matching firms with students. Under this alternative, employers are required to rank each student interviewed using a scale that indicates the student's degree of acceptability. The same requirement is made of students— they must rank the employer. This approach usually results in the placement of all or most students, but can give internship directors a few sleepless nights since they must perform the matching. (Exhibit 1 shows a typical form for the rating process.)

COMPENSATION

Although many students would regard the opportunity to obtain relevant work experience as adequate compensation, most are not financially able to miss an entire school term while earning no income. The compensation level is a function of the school and its location and traditionally falls between 60 and 75 percent of the starting salary for new, inexperienced staff auditors. Generally, students are compensated at time and one-half for overtime, and some schools require different levels of compensation based on the intern's level of preparation.

Programs in which matches are made on a *laissez faire* basis usually set no compensation requirements or may establish some minimum level of compensation. The university granted matching programs usually require each employer to pay a predetermined level of compensation. This stipulation eliminates a biased selection or rating of firms by students based on compensation and reduces the potential for conflict among students and also among companies. In the author's experience, no firm has ever declined participation in the internship program because compensation levels were unreasonably high. (See Exhibit 2 for a timetable of major steps in a semester-oriented program.)

DIRECT BENEFITS TO INTERNAL AUDIT

The most significant benefit to the internal audit department is the acquisition of additional human resources to help perform year-end

Exhibit 1 Instructions for Completing This Form

On the schedule below is a list of the students participating in the SPRING Semester 1988 Internship Program in Accounting.

PLEASE RATE EACH STUDENT AS TO ACCEPTABILITY USING THE FOLLOW CODE:

    5   We would really like to have this student intern with our firm.
    4   We will accept this student as an intern if none of our first choices are available.
    3   We would accept this student as an intern reluctantly.
    2   We will not accept this student as an intern.
    1   We did not interview this student.

You may have several students in each rank. Within each rank would you please mark your first preference with a "1," your second preference with a "2," etc. This will help make the assignment process more effective. Your anonymity is assured.

PLEASE COMPLETE AND RETURN ONE COPY OF THIS FORM BY OCTOBER 9, 19__, TO: DIRECTOR-ACCOUNTING INTERNSHIP PROGRAM - UNIVERSITY OF XXX.

We will accept no more than ____ of the students listed on this form as interns during the SPRING Semester 19__.

Firm Name _____

RANKING FORM

STUDENT NAMES	ACCEPTABILITY				
	5	4	3	2	1
Student 1					
Student 2					
Student 3					
Student 4					
Student 5					
Comments:					

procedures. The internal audit department can obtain qualified personnel at a very reasonable cost without having to permanently increase staff size. The intern can assist the external auditors or can be used to free up department personnel for jobs requiring more experience and knowledge. In either case, the department is better able to accomplish its performance goals while managing related costs by using the intern (a lower-priced resource) effectively.

Interns are also frequently assigned to special projects. Projects, which would be possibly vetoed because their completion requires a

Exhibit 2 Timetable of Events

ACTIVITY/EVENT	SPRING	SUMMER
Invitation to employers to participate	Mid-July	Early March
Deadline for application from interested students	Late July	Mid March
Student/firm interviews	September	April
Notification of student/firm assignments	Mid-October	Mutual decision
Internship experience commences	January	Mid-May
Completion of internship	Mid-March	Late August
Employer evaluation of intern	Late March	Late August
Research paper due	Late April	Late August

permanent increase in staff, become viable with the availability of temporary, skilled, low-cost personnel. A list of typical activities assignable to the internal audit intern is provided in Exhibit 3. This list is by no means exhaustive and internship assignments are only limited by the imagination of the internal audit manager and staff.

Managing the personnel function in internal audit is also enhanced by internships. Audit managers have the opportunity to evaluate a "potential" permanent employee without the commitments associated with hiring someone for a full-time, permanent position. Thus, the internal audit internship can serve as a trial run, improving employment decisions made within the department.

By increasing student and faculty awareness of employment opportunities in internal auditing, internship participation enhances a department's probability of attracting top accounting students immediately upon graduation.

This increased awareness works two ways. First, the internship interview process requires the presence of an internal audit department representative on campus. This presence provides an opportunity to enlighten some of a school's top accounting students and its faculty about career opportunities in the internal auditing field and in the represented department. Second, interns usually return to campus eager to share their experiences with other students. As a result, many students, who might otherwise not have considered an internal auditing position, reevaluate their career goals.

INDIRECT BENEFITS

Participation in an internship program enhances a company's and the profession's visibility and stature within the university community.

Exhibit 3 Student Intern Job Assignments in Internal Auditing

Internal Control Work Systems documentation Analytical review procedures Source document review (invoices, purchase orders, production tickets) for   compliance with systems documentation Orientation to EDP auditing
Account Balance Work Bank reconciliation review Accounts receivable confirmations Inventory purchases vouching Fixed asset additions vouching; review of depreciation calculations Intercompany account reconciliation review Accounts payable vouching Prepaid expenses Long-term debt Construction-in-progress Expense account vouching
Physical Inventory Observations/Reconciliations Test Counts Cutoff information Inventory tag control
Developing Personal Computer Applications
Research Accounting/Tax Topics
Improve Workpaper Organization
Special Projects Evaluation of the changing relationship between internal and external auditors Using microcomputer/expert systems in accounting/auditing Evaluating alternatives to reducing rising costs of health care Assisting external auditors

If management believes that the company has benefitted from participation in the internship, then greater recognition for the internal audit effort is likely to result. Also, if the image of the internal auditing profession is enhanced, which is a likely outcome of increased contact with students and faculty, the image and importance of each internal audit department is positively affected.

CONCLUSION

Internal auditing has as much career potential and challenge as public accounting, and it is incumbent upon internal auditors to communicate with students and inform them about the profession. The internal auditing internship represents a unique opportunity to communicate with students. A testimony to the benefits of the program is the large portion of repeat participants.

The internal auditing profession has not pursued top accounting students as aggressively as have public accountants. Perhaps this phenomenon is a result of a willingness on the part of internal audit departments to wait until top graduates become disillusioned with public accounting and search out new career options. However, a more likely explanation is simply that internal auditors do not realize the necessity for the aggressive recruitment of students and marketing of their firms. Each internal audit department must determine the extent to which and manner in which it will become involved in campus~related activities. With an awareness of the available options and an understanding of the costs and benefits, we believe the optimal decision will be to participate.

26
AFTER THE SHEEPSKIN . . . WHAT'S NEXT

Kenneth E. Christian and Dennis M. Payne

Applying the lessons of teacher-training internships (student teaching) and medical internships to the security field, one can see the close link between theory and practice. Several examples are given of how interns and academicians have supplied the theory that resulted in dramatic results when applied by professionals working closely with them.

"The private security industry should encourage the development of: certificate, associate of art, or associate of science degree programs designed to meet local industry needs; undergraduate and graduate programs to meet private security needs."

That quotation is taken from the 1976 *Report of the Task Force on Private Security*. Can you imagine applicants for entry-level security positions with associate's and bachelor's degrees? Wishful thinking, you say? Perhaps not. Take a look at what has happened in law enforcement over the past twenty years.

In 1967 a presidential commission recommended a college education for law enforcement officers. At that time Michigan, for example, had only one school of police administration. Now, in Michigan alone, there are more than two dozen two- and four-year programs and several graduate programs.

In the late '60s, there were few college graduates in local law enforcement agencies and fewer chiefs or command personnel with degrees. In fact, a chief with a graduate degree was almost unheard of.

That's not the case today. Lee Brown, who has served as director of public safety in Atlanta and Houston, has a doctorate. Dr. Joseph McNamara is chief of police in San Jose, CA. Georgia has two chiefs of police with doctorates—Dr. George Napper in Atlanta and Dr. David Epstein in Savannah. Others, such as Dave Cooper in Madison, WI, and Bill Hegarty in Grand Rapids, MI, have extensive graduate studies beyond their master's degrees.

There are still others with master's degrees and the bachelor's degree is becoming a common requirement for more chiefs' positions. The educational recommendations for police officers, first proposed by the 1967 Task Force, are on their way to becoming reality.

The private security industry, however, has not made as much progress. Perhaps it is undergoing an experience similar to the one the business management field went through in the early '70s. In 1971, a *Fortune* magazine survey found that businesspeople believed less than half of the business college graduates could apply theory to the real world. Businesses wanted graduates who were productive, and they did not believe a degree necessarily made people more productive. About half of the businesspeople surveyed had switched or planned to switch much of their recruiting to junior college graduates, high school graduates, and returning veterans.

Other findings of the *Fortune* survey may also have a bearing on security programs and employment. Businesspeople had lost confidence in the value of the college degree as a screening device and in the ability of the professors themselves to relate theory to actual experience, which many felt was as important as an MBA.

If any of the *Fortune* survey can be interpreted as an indictment of university programs in general, then educators must answer two questions: What can be done to make the recruitment of college graduates more profitable for the security management field? How can security professionals and educators better prepare the future generation of professionals in this field?

MICHIGAN STATE'S UNDERGRADUATE SECURITY PROGRAM

Students at Michigan State University are required take junior level courses in police, corrections, and legal processes; juvenile delinquency; and security systems. At the senior level, students take courses in loss prevention, theft control, and assets protection. Elective courses are available in risk management, business law, finance, accounting, management, and the regulations of the Occupational Safety and Health Administration.

Security personnel today must be prepared for complicated and diverse work. To be successful, they must know about the concept of vicarious liability, sexual harassment in the workplace, and issues in labor and industrial relations, to mention only a few subjects. A thorough grounding in the underlying philosophy and implementation of the 1964 Civil Rights Act is also a must for today's security managers.

Michigan State University's preprofessional security program does not pretend to turn out trained security officers. Graduates of Michigan's program must enter security training and career development programs before becoming security professionals.

MODELS FOR SECURITY PURPOSES

If the security field wishes to move toward professionalism, its practitioners must go out of their way to nurture the neophytes, as practitioners do in other fields, such as the education profession. Students in the college of education spend time in the university learning about processes and theories. Then the school systems open their doors to orient, train, and even learn from the students during their teaching internships.

Students must meet designated objectives and so must members of the school system. At the conclusion of an internship, the school district may gain a new teacher, the education systems in general may gain a teacher, and occasionally a student leaves the education field, realizing he or she is not cut out for teaching. Whatever the outcome, the on-the-job training and evaluation play a major role in furthering the teaching profession.

Some may argue that the education internship model will not work in security because the two fields are so different. Security personnel must deal with confidential matters and make decisions that can affect people's livelihoods, liberty, and sometimes even their lives.

Perhaps medical internships are a better model. Although medical students fresh out of school may make mistakes, hospitals have developed training programs that slowly increase students' responsibilities and monitor their progress. At the end of successful internships, medical students begin their residencies in specific areas of interest, again in a hospital. Hospitals, as well as medical school, are truly centers of learning for the medical profession.

The nursing profession also has undergone considerable change in the past twenty years. Increased litigation required some nurses to begin studying several issues they had not previously addressed. All nursing schools require their students to spend many hours on the floor, observing and working in a controlled environment. Nurses, then, are also products of both an academic and an experiential education.

The colleges of education and medicine teach theory and process in their preprofessional programs, and a few years later a practicing professional appears. Why can't this process work for the security management profession?

DEVELOPING THEORIES

The role of academia in security management is to look at the field from a distance, research, analyze, develop theory, and suggest change and innovation. The role of security practitioners is to be receptive to suggestions, question the assumptions underlying them, work for improvement in security operations, and take advantage of the services of colleges and universities.

One of the roles of academia is to develop theory. While that may sound far removed from the world of security, it isn't. A university professor developing theory is working parallel to the investigator developing a major case. Both are trying to find out what happened and how it happened.

Both researchers and investigators are involved in empirical or observational enterprises—that is, both must gather and analyze data with which to develop a case. Both employ a variety of techniques, such as interviews, observations, and experiments, to gather the evidence. Both must ultimately depend on logical analysis to meet the test of "beyond a reasonable doubt."

Furthermore, both the research and detective depend on theory to complete their assignments successfully. Theory is not something apart from fact; theory refers to the ordering of facts into some meaningful arrangement. Theory may be defined as set of interrelated principles and definitions that serves conceptually to organize selected aspects of the empirical world.

Thus, fact and theory are interdependent; facts help to initiate theories. The fact that most murder victims have been killed by someone they know has generated several theories about homicide. We would be lost in a world of facts if we did not have at least some theories to sort them out. For example, without the theory or concept of motive, how would an investigator develop a starting point and guiding principles for an investigation? He or she would be like Charlie Chan's number one son—unable to recognize evidence even if he fell over it.

TESTING AND APPLYING THEORY

In the '50s the theory prevailed that patrol was the backbone of the police department. When patrol vehicles were not answering requests for help, they were engaged in preventive patrol, creating an impression of omnipresence. Whether patrol prevented crime was not questioned; it was accepted as fact. Only the merits of one-person versus two-person patrol and motorized versus foot patrol were being debated. Based on an untested theory—and thus, a faulty premise—decisions were made across the country in end foot patrol. One-person patrol cars became vogue.

This theory wasn't questioned until the 1970s, when an experiment was conducted from October 1, 1972, to September 30, 1973, in the Kansas City, MO, police department "to measure the impact routine patrol had on the incidence of crime." Researchers employed a methodology that determined traditional routine preventive patrol had no significant impact either on the level of crime or the public's feeling of security.

The experiment further showed that the noncommitted time of police officers (60 percent in the experiment) could be used for purposes other than routine patrol without any negative impact on public safety. The results suggested police administrators could increase police effectiveness by as much as 150 percent by basing patrol strategies on specific crime prevention and service goals as opposed to routine preventive patrol.

Another example of applying theory to the real world is the burglar alarm project conducted by academicians and students in Cedar Rapids, IA. They observed, gathered facts, analyzed evidence, and developed a theory. The culmination of this joint venture between a community and a university was the installation of low-cost burglar alarms in high-risk locations with the alarms tied into the police department. The results were a decrease in successful burglaries, a decrease in attempted burglaries, a decrease in the value of goods lost in burglaries, and an increase in burglars apprehended at the scene. The theory and design came from students and professors, while law enforcement practitioners implemented the plan—each group did what it does best.

It is probably safe to assume most students get enough book learning. What they need more of is field experience. As the Kansas City and Cedar Rapids projects show, theory can be applied to the real world. Those who are striving for more professionalism in security management are urged to get to know local educational institutions, instructors, and students and work with them to provide a laboratory for the development of professional security personnel. An educational internship in security can give an organization the opportunity to improve the entry-level professional and the industry's future labor force.

27
INTERNS GO BEYOND OJT—
LINK THEORY TO THE WORKPLACE

Beverly James

A communications internship program uses a series of five directed reports that channel students in applying theories learned in the classroom to the experiences and observations gleaned from internships. Outlines for the reports are supplied in detail.

The University of Alaska at Fairbanks has developed an internship program that bridges the gap between theory and practice by requiring students to practice their critical as well as technical skills.

The internship requires a series of reports that focus the students' attention on particular aspects of journalism. Through these structured reports, interns are expected to reflect critically on their media experiences and to discover how these experiences relate to concepts studied in coursework in the humanities and social sciences both inside and outside the Department of Journalism and Broadcasting.

Because of the geographical isolation of Fairbanks and the severity of the weather, most internships are served locally, either in town or on campus. Fortunately, a relatively wide range of options are open: 11 radio stations, 4 television stations, 1 daily and 2 weekly newspapers. Students have been quite resourceful in seeking out other organizations willing to host interns. Thus, in a typical semester last year, we had students working as a UPI correspondent, an editor at a monthly native newsletter, a scriptwriter for the Federal Bureau of Land Management, a researcher for the University of Public Affairs office, as well as the more traditional positions—a copy editor at a daily newspaper, and production interns at radio and TV stations.

Before registering for the course, students must work out a proposal and have it approved by the instructor and the media supervisor. The proposal spells out the goals of the internship, the duties and responsibilities to be undertaken, the information and skills to be acquired and any products that are to be generated. The class is conducted as an independent study, with regular meetings between students and the instructor. In addition, seminars are held at the beginning and end of the semester so interns can share expectations and experiences. The course carries 3 hours of credit and is graded on a pass/fail basis.

Six reports, around four pages in length, are due at two-week intervals. The first two reports are descriptive accounts of the student's duties as well as the structure and operation of the organization. The next four reports are more analytical and attempt to probe such issues as routinization of the news process, indoctrination of workers into an organization, sedimentation of news values, economic and legal constraints on the practice of journalism and social responsibility of the press. Most students are familiar with these concepts, and with a little prodding, they are able to recognize in practice what were previously somewhat sterile classroom concepts. The following guidelines are issued for writing the reports:

Report 1. Describe your activities, duties, and responsibilities. What is the relationship of your position to the overall functioning of the organization? How does your work relate to past academic and/or professional experiences, and how is it expected to fit into any future plans?

Report 2. Discuss the organizational structure and the day-to-day operation of the media outlet. Identify the main positions and departments in the organization. What are the functions of each, and how do they fit together?

Report 3. Analyze the process through which the media outlet gathers, processes and distributes news, information, and entertainment. How does a given event come to be defined as newsworthy? Who makes this decision, and on what basis? How is the newsworker made aware of editorial policies? What are the strengths and weaknesses of the overall operation?

Report 4. Describe in general terms the financial basis of the media outlet. What are the main sources of revenue and the main expenditures? How does the financial structure influence the media product? How are conflicts resolved between the business and editorial offices?

Report 5. Discuss the relationship between the media outlet and the social environment. What groups constitute the audience? What kinds of information are available about the audience and its needs? How does the media organization identify and attempt to carry out its obligations and responsibilities to the public, to the community, and to other institutions?

Report 6. Integrate the findings of your previous reports and evaluate the practicum itself. In general, this report should answer the question, "What has this experience taught you?"

The focus of the reports is necessarily flexible because of the individualized nature of the internship. For example, the UPI correspondent had limited access to her superiors and was physically removed from the organization. Her reports included reviews of portions of Oliver Boyd-Barret's *International News Agencies* and examinations of the . . . financial shakeup at UPI [at the time].

In general, however, the guidelines provide an appropriate map. While some students have been unable to go beyond a superficial analysis of their experiences, a surprising number have made incisive and insightful observations. One cynic insisted that a local newspaper's greatest service to the community is to provide a vehicle for the sale of unwanted junk—the classified ads.

Perhaps the main problem has been our failure to explain our intentions adequately to media supervisors. As equal partners in this undertaking, they have a right as well as a need to understand the nature of the exercises. In gathering information for their reports, students can be quite pointed in their questioning. The response of some supervisors has borne out the adage that the watchdog resents being watched. Other supervisors apparently have only a shallow understanding of the historical and philosophical bases of mass communication and give glib answers that are all of little value to interns. In any event, it is our responsibility to convey to all participants a sense of what we're trying to accomplish through the internship: professional training for the overriding importance of journalism to contemporary society.

28
HOW TO DESIGN A COLLEGE
STUDENT INTERNSHIP PROGRAM
THAT WORKS

Michael D. Ames

California State University's (Fullerton) Management Department and Northrop's Electrical Mechanical Division designed a successful production and operations management internship. Once the joint venture was deemed worthy, a senior faculty and a company manager were assigned to prepare a final proposal. Having a sense of "ownership" in the program, Northrop was willing to fund it. Eventually, two-thirds of the first 36 interns were hired by Northrop. A 14-point plan is presented for establishing effective internships in management, but it is applicable to any discipline.

Experience suggests that there is a recipe for designing successful production and operations management internship programs for college students. The necessary ingredients are outlined briefly in Table 1.

An internship program for operations management students is a college credit program jointly sponsored by an academic institution and a company. The program explains exactly how the sponsoring company's production and operations management system works, and it provides each student with supervised, hands-on exposure to selected elements of the sponsoring company's system.

From the sponsoring company's standpoint internship programs are relatively inexpensive if they are viewed as a recruitment tool. The cost of one mistaken new hire through regular channels can easily fund a six-to-eight-week internship program for ten qualified applicants. Many of the nonstaff resources needed for the program are a natural by-product of operations. Cost of staff time required is at least partially offset by useful work produced by the students, and is probably less than it would take to recruit and interview a similar number of job applicants.

Table 1 Necessary Ingredients for a Successful Production and Operations Management Internship Program

The list below follows a typical program cycle. It is important to note that many ingredients have to be recreated each time a new cycle is begun.

1. **Top Management Commitment.** At least one key manager from the company and one from the university must sponsor the internship program and be willing to reward contributors.

2. **Development of Sales Presentation.** The program must be sold to company and university participants. They must be convinced that the benefits outweigh the required resource commitments.

3. **Early Resource Commitment.** Resource commitments are required well in advance. It takes time to include the program in budgets, to develop agendas to blend program activities with available manager time, and to select and notify the students.

4. **Human Resource Staff Support** Sponsors need to enlist the help of the company's in-house human resource management staff to set up the program and expedite the hiring of qualified students.

5. **Selected Ratio.** Potential student participants must be screened based on their interest; successful completion of operations management classes, closeness to graduation; attitudes; and, lastly, grades. Invite only those passing the screens to participate.

6. **Orientation.** Have knowledgeable managers give both academic supervisors and student interns a thorough, overall orientation to the company's production and operations management system. Do this even if it is intended that interns will specialize in particular areas.

7. **On-site Involvement by Academics.** Faculty must be familiar with the workings of the company. They must help the students analyze and understand their experiences during the course of the internship program.

8. **Manager Involvement.** Involve operations managers in developing the agenda for the internship program, including a formal training agenda and schedule for interns to be placed in their departments.

9. **Critical Analysis of the Internship Experience.** Students need to critically analyze their on-the-job experience to gain the most from it. The student should suggest a solution for each problem noted.

10. **Teaming.** Have the students work in teams and assign them a regular employee as a buddy to insure questions are dealt with thoroughly as they arise.

11. **Rotation.** In addition to group or lecture type orientation, interns should be rotated, at least briefly, through each major department in the organization to observe the real work of day-to-day operations.

12. **Student Incentives.** A variety of student incentives can and should be employed to keep interest level and productivity high. These incentives are, in declining order of importance: (a) letting the intern know that, if they do well, they may be offered a job; (b) encouraging the participating managers to view the interns as a resource rather than a nuisance; (c) scheduling periodic question-and-answer sessions with managers and faculty; (d) making sure interns know that their work products will be shown to key managers; (e) arranging payment of a stipend for the intern which is contingent upon successful program completion; and (f) awarding grades for work done.

13. **Balance Workloads.** Spread the presentation burden. Maintain a balance between one-to-one tutoring and group presentation.

14. **Plan to Repeat.** The time and effort required for initial program setup makes even more sense if it can be amortized over several program cycles.

CASE HISTORY OF A SUCCESSFUL PROGRAM

The Northrop/CSUF Invitational Program in Operations Management (NI/POM) illustrates how an internship program can be implemented successfully between a company and a university. NI/POM has been conducted three times: in Summer 1983, 1984, and 1985. It is co-sponsored by Northrop's Electrical Mechanical Division in Anaheim, California and the Management Department, School of Business Administration and Economics of California State University, Fullerton. NI/POM originated as a shared vision of Northrop's president and a senior faculty member at CSUF. Both saw the need for a linkage between academia and the real world of production operations and agreed to initiate an effort to create one in Orange County, California. Two people, the division's manager of training and a senior faculty member, were charged with preparing a formal proposal for the program. They prepared several drafts highlighting the benefits and weighing them against each of the resource requirements and issues. Several key personnel at the Division and the University were conferred with during proposal preparation, including the legal staff of both organizations, the assistant to the division's vice-president and general manager, the vice-president of operations, and the dean of the business school. This process took several months.

Once initial agreements concerning the nature of the program and the resources to be dedicated to it were reached, the final draft of the program proposal was typed. Viewfoils outlining the proposal were developed and a formal presentation was made by the two drafters to the division's executive committee. A final funding commitment was made three months before the planned starting date of the program.

Here is how the program was structured:

- Twelve CSUF production and operations management graduates/seniors were selected. Alternates were selected each year to insure exactly twelve actually participated.
- They participated full time as interns for 6 1/2 weeks.
- Late May to mid-July.
- At the Division's manufacturing facilities, specifically in each of the six operating departments.
- Each program began with an orientation. In the first year, top management from division staff and each operating department made presentations over a three-day period. In the second and third years, the initial orientation was one day with additional presentations made periodically throughout the remainder of the program. Plant tours were provided early in each orientation. Each year students were paired into six teams which rotated through the six operating departments. In the first year they spent one week in each department and met with two professors for a debriefing each Friday. Late each Friday they met with the Vice President of Operations, the operating managers, and the faculty for review and evaluation of current workweek activities. In the second and third years, the weekly

meetings were retained, but rotations among departments were set up as detailed orientations. Two days were spent in each department. Each intern then picked one department to work in for the remaining month. Each year, a final debriefing and evaluation of the program was held on the last day of the program. Interns made formal presentations to a meeting of participating managers and top university personnel. This session was concluded with a graduation ceremony during which the President of the University awarded certificates of completion to the interns.

- Northrop's Electrical Mechanical Division provided funding for stipends of $100 per week per student. An internship supervision award was also granted to each of the two faculty members. These awards were also nominal and were larger the first year when the time required to set up the program was greater. A significant portion of the funding was earmarked for use by the Management Department at CSUF to enrich and improve the educational process for production and operations management students. A steering committee made up of two Northrop managers and one CSUF faculty member administered disbursement of the funds. All funds were given to the university and placed in a foundation account, then student stipends and other disbursements were made from that account.

NI/POM experimented with two different approaches to the internship, one during the first year and the other during the second and third years. Both were successful as learning experiences, although both interns and managers seemed to prefer the second and third years' experiences. The approach used in the first year put the students more in the role of spectators than participants in the day-to-day work of the department. In the second and third years the students had more time in their chosen department to get involved in real work. The interns enjoyed accomplishing meaningful tasks and the managers got a number of special projects done that their staff would not have had time to get to otherwise.

For example, in the third year of the program interns researched procurement histories, checked the status of purchase orders, processed materials action requests to insure they had valid requirements, tracked down "lost" parts, tracked down "lost" paperwork, redesigned computer reports used to release purchase orders, helped design floor layouts for a new assembly area, processed industrial work requests, executed material adjustments and transfer transactions, obtained proper signatures needed to fix and move problem parts, performed follow-up audits on variances from specifications, set up visibility charts for the 747 floor beam production area which tracked performance, and created standard spreadsheets to facilitate preparation of percentage completion reports for 747 shipsets.

In general, the interns were assigned tasks that required routine interface between departments, or between the company and its suppliers. Interns were constantly on the telephone or making personal contacts across departmental boundaries to work out immediate solutions to little problems. The nature of the problems assigned the interns can best be described as small, but bothersome. The problems were those that someone has to look into, such as rivet edge margins and inspection standards, solvent uses and safety, space requirements to efficiently kit large parts, or time standards and their relation to goals set by shipping deadlines.

Two final observations are worth noting about the structure of NI/POM. First, each year, the departments that gained the most from the interns were the ones that had a formal work agenda planned prior to the interns' arrival. Second, Northrop encouraged NI/POM alumni who were now employees to act as mentors for current interns. This approach greatly facilitated the interns' orientation process, making them able to tackle useful tasks sooner.

Each intern has a handout describing the NI/POM Program Requirements, distributed at the beginning of the Summer program. Students were also given a NI/POM worksheet that they were required to use for their daily diary. Participants were asked to evaluate every aspect of the program and to grade their experiences in four dimensions: clarity, level, interest, and hands-on.

What about the bottom line? Over two-thirds of the 36 interns were offered jobs at Northrop at the end of their internship. All but one of those offered jobs accepted a position with the company. To date, only one of those hired has resigned (not, incidentally, to go to work for a competitor, but to go into the family business). What about performance? Comments by managers about their new subordinates are very complimentary indeed. The manager of quality assurance, for example, feels his new people have "completely changed the direction of the department." NI/POM alumni have already earned a number of promotions. The Vice President of Operations sums it up well: "These young people haven't yet learned it can't be done, so they go ahead and get the job done."

END NOTE: WHAT ELSE CAN BE DONE

Certainly an internship program such as that described in this article is one good way to improve the linkage between production and operations management programs in academia and in industry; it brings the two worlds closer and helps students make more intelligent career decisions. Still more can be done. Internships can provide a springboard for further cooperation efforts.

For example, faculty and managers can work together to keep curriculums up to date and relevant to the practical needs of industry. Once faculty become thoroughly familiar with local industry through internship programs, they can offer classes with more practical usefulness to the manager returning to the classroom for continuing education. Realistic simulations of production problems can be developed in a laboratory setting and results analyzed by both faculty and managers. New, more efficient production management techniques can systematically evolve from such cooperative effort.

29
STUDENTS GET ON-THE-JOB TRAINING BY HELPING COMMERCE DEPARTMENT DISTRICT OFFICES SERVE EXPORTERS

Staff, *Business America*

Commerce Department offices in Connecticut and Oregon used student interns to help American companies improve their international exports. In Connecticut, Quinnipiac College (Hamden) provided the students, 21 of them who worked 18–20 hours a week with different companies. The companies paid a fee to the college's International Business Center. In Oregon, the students had diverse majors and came from several colleges. Participants received an International Business Students Certificate.

CONNECTICUT

A project employing trained student manpower to assist small and medium-sized firms in their export effort was completed recently in Connecticut with remarkable success. The project was unique in that the companies paid for this service, expected to achieve certain predetermined export related goals, and gave the students considerable authority in helping the company achieve those goals. The project thus included both consultancy and implementation by students, and went far beyond market research studies. With the help of these student interns, eight companies made export sales for the first time.

The success of the project is particularly interesting because it was initiated and conducted by a relatively small New England college with a long and consistent commitment to Connecticut exports. Quinnipiac College, located in Hamden, Conn., has offered export marketing programs since 1973; this project involved students who had received rigorous education in export marketing and financing in addition to other international business courses. The College has been active in the Connecticut business community's international trade promotion activities and many of its graduates are employed in Connecticut firms of all sizes engaged in international trade.

The project was conceived and administered by Dr. Vasant Nadkarni, Director of Quinnipiac's International Business Center. It was funded by the U.S. Department of Commerce's Economic Development Administration through the state of Connecticut's Department of Economic Development. The Connecticut District Export Council's Education Committee and Gary Miller, Director of the International Division of the state's Department of Economic Development, helped shape the program to suit the needs of a wide range of Connecticut firms. The execution of the project was the responsibility of the Quinnipiac College International Business Center.

Twenty-one trained students were carefully selected from among upper classmen who had completed courses in export marketing and international business. These students were placed with 21 companies who contracted with the college for the services offered under the project.

Some of these companies had never exported before, others had some prior experience in exports, and still others desired expansion of their already established export operations. Thus, the assignments to the students ranged from setting up export capabilities to enhancement of already existing export programs. In the former group, eight internships produced export sales orders, and in the latter group, one internship assisted the firm in locating an overseas sales office and another assisted the client firm in representing its products in a trade show in Osaka, Japan.

One student landed a $6,000 order from a firm in Venezuela for a small New Haven company that employs 20. The company manufactures chemical specialties, cleaners, and lubricants, and distributes widely in the United States. The company's president believed exporting was beyond the company's scope, but the intern, with the help of Ann Bacher, a Trade Specialist in the Commerce Department's Hartford Office, used research sources the company "never knew existed." The student had to follow up on the order from Venezuela with considerable skill and patience until the shipment was made and payment received for in U.S. dollars. The students had to work closely with the Venezuelan customer in obtaining release of foreign exchange under the highly restrictive Venezuelan government regulations.

Another intern initiated, developed, and instituted an overseas program for a non-manufacturing company which is a major distributor of aluminum products. According to the letter to Quinnipiac from the company's sales manager, the intern "became the person responsible for understanding our company, its capabilities, and for developing ways to penetrate the overseas market. This meant doing all the research, letter presentations, mailings and follow-ups. It resulted in $12,000 in orders, so far, with more than acceptable gross profit, but more importantly (the intern) identified the areas where our effort will be directed for future growth. (He) has put us in the overseas business."

Another student intern demonstrated "superb ability" and "professionalism" in assisting the client company in establishing a sales office in the "selected country." In acknowledging the sales leads obtained by still another student intern, her client company stated: "It is not unusual that considerable time is required for actual business to develop and we anticipate further results from (the student's) efforts."

The above are a few examples of what students with training, guidance, and opportunity can achieve for small and medium-sized companies interested or engaged in exports.

The interns worked 18–20 hours per week for six months with the client companies and took, at the same time, two specially designed courses which reinforced their goal-directed efforts. The companies made everything from the belt buckles to cheese, and their work forces ranged from 200 to 400 employees. Each company paid a fee to Quinnipiac's International Business Center and received in return student services and consultancy with the Center.

In conjunction with the internship phase of the program, two two-day workshops were conducted by the International Business Center in cooperation with Commerce's Hartford Office, for the benefit of company personnel and student interns. The Center topped the project off with a Career Night acquainting students with career opportunities in international trade.

The success of this pilot has generated a growing list of small and medium-sized firms of Connecticut who have approached Quinnipiac's International Business Center for assistance in a range of export-related efforts.

The center expects to repeat the program each year with a new group of student interns and companies. Variations in the design of the program are likely, such as concentration of the internships on selected country markets and organized overseas trips for students and company personnel enabling personal negotiations with overseas clients.

Eric Outwater, Regional Managing Director for Region I and Director of the Hartford Office, in commenting on the remarkable success of this Commerce Department grant, pointed out that "the students didn't just sit at a desk and produce a report, but went one giant step further and actually carried out what their reports suggested—they went out and sold the product."

OREGON

Firsthand experience with the intricacies of world trade—that is the training ground provided for students by the Portland District Office, U.S. and Foreign Commercial Service. Every term since 1979, interns from several Oregon universities and colleges participate in this "real world education."

Two programs offer these opportunities: volunteer internships for Oregon students and a Federal International Trade Administration Co-op Program for graduate students, who are full-time and salaried, as part of a training and rotation plan. Most of the students have traveled internationally. Lloyd R. Porter, District Director, feels that the interns, who come from a base of diverse educational backgrounds, contribute fresh viewpoints and personal skills to the functioning of the District Office.

The internship program benefits the Portland District Office and the Oregon international business community as well as interns themselves. The interns are a great asset in promoting US&FCS goals. After training in a variety of research procedures, interns assist trade specialists on special projects. Projects include designing promotional literature, preparing export statistical and forecast models, updating computer files, facilitating seminars and conferences, and assisting exporters with market research and development plans.

The Oregon international business community profits from the free assistance and support in marketing efforts, along with increased productivity from the Portland District Office. In the long run, interns will enter the job market with skills in export procedures.

Interns unanimously endorse this training. For most, it is an introduction to the international business arena. They appreciate a chance to apply theories learned in school and to participate in cooperation (local/national) programs. Research skills are cultivated. Opportunities exist for a close-up look at Oregon industries and marketers. This in-depth view reveals the workings (and hazards) of the international marketplace: targeting and servicing markets, selecting distributors or agents, financing procedures, the importance and frustrations of export licensing for high-tech firms, and logistics of transportation and distribution. Well-developed marketing plans can go afoul if, for instance, docking facilities at a selected port of entry are inadequate. Huge freight costs arise if raw materials or products must be rerouted to another port and then transported inland. Student interns profit by learning from this vantage point.

These interns present a cornucopia of rich experiences and interests. Karen Wilde, a co-op intern in an interdisciplinary Master's program at the University of Oregon, spent this summer traveling in

Scandinavia, Western Europe, Italy and Greece. She found Europeans very innovative in packaging and efficient in utilization of land. Karen has extensive cross-cultural experience.

Teresa Taylor is completing both a co-op internship and a master's degree in International Studies at the University of Oregon. Teresa is presently finishing her thesis on Japanese direct investment in Oregon. She has a degree in French and English. During the next year in Washington, D.C., her rotational training through the divisions of ITA will cover a broad scope of Commerce Department activities.

A political science major at Portland State University, Tony Andrews, is also seeking an International Business Studies certificate. He is studying German in preparation for an international business career.

Another Portland State intern, Lisa Weaver, will receive a Personnel Management degree and International Business Studies certificate. This summer, she participated in the Oregon State System of Higher Education Language Program, speaking only German for two months in the Austrian Alps, Munich and Kassel, Germany. Afterwards, she traveled throughout Europe for a month. This experience opened new dimensions of the "real world" to her and cultivated an interest in international business.

Yvonne Cornell traveled to the People's Republic of China to study Chinese this summer, after receiving a bachelor's degree in Business Administration and an International Business Studies certificate from Portland State in June. Her University Scholars' thesis explored marketing strategies of three successful Northwest firms doing business in China. Yvonne has assisted in numerous seminars offered by the Portland District Office. Her career goals center on promoting trade and understanding between China and the United States.

In summary, the Portland District Office internship program contributes both to Oregon exporters and the educational and professional enrichment of participating students.

30
AN ASIAN PERSPECTIVE ON SECURITY

Daniel A. Grove

Individual institutions can develop their own industry-specific international internship program, as Penn State University did. Close ties to a Pacific Rim security firm enabled the university to offer unique international internships for students interested in the private sector of police sciences. A practical primer for establishing international internships is given, as well as details of daily operations and the long-distance evaluation instruments—a must for any college or company thinking of the overseas internship plunge.

To serve an administration of justice internship with a private investigative firm is quite unusual. To do an internship in Asia is also out of the ordinary for American college students. But for five Pennsylvania State University (PSU) students, both of these rarities have become reality.

In May 1984, the CTS Group, based in Hong Kong, arranged an intern program with Penn State's Administration of Justice Program. To date, five students have had the opportunity to work in a private security setting in the heart of Asia.

It all began at the 193 ASIS Seminar in Washington, DC, when a group of professors and administrators from Penn State were seeking assistance in developing a corporate security curriculum for their justice administration program. They asked a group of ASIS members of varied experience and backgrounds to serve in an advisory capacity.

Daniel A. Grove, Penn State '54, was attending the Seminar from Hong Kong. He was invited to sit in and, in what in retrospect seemed a jet-lagged moment of weakness, volunteered an internship program with CTS, of which he is a director. Discussions at Penn State and in Hong Kong produced guidelines and the study of potential problems. When the venture was deemed feasible at both ends, it was "all systems go."

On the Penn State side, there was concern over the academic benefits to the students, the possible danger to which they might be exposed, and the many pitfalls and culture shocks presented by living in a foreign country.

CTS is basically a British company, but it has an international character. The managing director and founder, Anthony R. Gurka, first came to Hong Kong in 1963 with the British military police. He stayed on in business and in 1969 set up an investigative firm known as Commercial Trademark Services. The company specialized in investigation and consultation regarding violations of trademark, patent, and copyright matters. In 1975 it opened a liaison office in Taiwan. In 1980, it set up its own office in Taipei, Taiwan.

In July 1982 Grove joined the firm as a director and shareholder from Levi Strauss and Co., where he had been serving as security manager for Asia Pacific. Retired from the FBI in 1979, Grove, who speaks Mandarin Chinese, established the FBI Liaison Office at the American Consulate General in Hong Kong in 1966 and for six years served there. During part of that time, he covered Southeast Asia, Australia, and New Zealand in a liaison capacity.

It was in 1982 that Gurka began to expand the scope and size of Commercial Trademark Services. The change of the company's name to The CTS Group brought a marked expansion in services and the opening of offices in Singapore and in Manila, the Philippines.

The company developed a corporate security support program and made plans to set up in Malaysia and Thailand. A major boost to the expansion came when Neil D. Hamilton joined the group in December 1983. He brought a wealth of experience from the Hong Kong Police, the Hong Kong Independent Commission Against Corruption, and the Hong Kong Security Group, one of Asia's largest security operations, where he was assistant general manager. Most important to CTS, Hamilton brought an excellent knowledge of security systems and hardware. It was not too long before CTS was heavily into consulting with a group of firms manufacturing in Thailand, Malaysia, Singapore, and the Philippines.

All this helps explain the CTS decision—in fact, its desire—to press ahead with the internship program. It was felt the program would help combat the ever present "gum shoe" image besetting almost all private investigative firms. Further, and perhaps most important, it was thought the exposure to the pricing problems and other issues faced by firms like CTS could eventually be of great help in overcoming any distrust existing between private investigator/consultants and those who employ them. Finally, it was agreed the work being done by CTS and the region in which it is being done could offer a fantastic study and work opportunity to Penn State students. Of note, 90 percent of the CTS employees had never heard of Penn State at this time.

CTS and Penn State agreed that the students would be responsible for transportation to and from Hong Kong and for housing, food, and other living expenses. CTS agreed to pay each student an assistant manager's salary, which could cover the housing and food cost. CTS has made every attempt to find suitable, reasonably priced housing—a most difficult task in Hong Kong.

CTS also said it would try, whenever possible, to expose the interns to other overseas work, probably in one of its sub-offices. CTS would pay the transportation costs.

Sean O'Mara, PSU '85, and Kirby Wood, PSU '84, were the Penn State pioneers. They arrived in Hong Kong in late May 1984 and became heavily involved in a research project relating to a highly successful undercover operation that netted the recovery of 2,500 stolen microchips.

O'Mara accompanied Neil Hamilton on a survey and investigative trip to Penang, Malaysia. Wood spent six weeks working in the CTS Taiwan office. Both had heavy exposure to the CTS emphasis on report writing and investigative management techniques.

From late January through April 1985, Melinda Rishkofski and Ed Donovan served as PSU interns with CTS. Again, both were heavily enmeshed in the reporting scene and both had the opportunity to work in other offices. Donovan, whose father is a professor on the PSU Administration of Justice staff, worked in Taiwan. This office has a heavy workload but, happily for young students, it is staffed by a number of young expatriate managers.

Rishkofski went to Manila, where the CTS manager, Baron L. Buck, is a former US Air Force Officer and polygraph examiner. She had the opportunity to observe the considerable problems of bringing relief to clients in that country. She also did extensive research on emerging radical trade unions in the Philippines.

When Donovan and Rishkofski were in Hong Kong, it was a most difficult time for housing. After many disappointments in trying to locate suitable accommodations, the CTS Group decided it would be best to scale back the internship program to the summer season when more rooms are available.

Jon Burgan, PSU '85, recently completed his three-month training program Like those before him, he began with a week's orientation, learning the company's overall structure, functions, and rules by spending a great deal of time with Gurka, Grove, and Hamilton.

Then Steve Payne, the Hong Kong general manager, took over. He trained the intern regarding the daily work routine, administrative procedures, and reporting requirements that an assistant manager at CTS must know.

The Hong Kong office currently has four investigative squads and a total of twenty-four investigators. Each squad is headed by a manager and chief investigator. The interns work with each of these squads for about a month until their skills are sufficient for working in Taiwan.

Assignments of interns are based on the needs of CTS. It would be nice if each could serve in or visit all the CTS facilities, but salaries can't be justified on that basis.

Included in the Hong Kong training is a program of familiarization with American and Hong Kong government agencies. Briefings take place at the American Consulate General. Assistance has come from the regional security office, the Royal Hong Kong Police, and Hong Kong Customs, which is charged with enforcement of trademark, patent, and copyright laws. Burgan spent a night on patrol with the marine police in Hong Kong, observing their watch for illegal immigrants. Efforts are under way to set up similar briefing sessions in sub-offices.

Interns also attend discussions with clients whenever possible, but only with the agreement of the clients. O'Mara and Wood, through the kind cooperation of the Intel Corporation's corporate security department, sat in on the step-by-step planning of a complicated Intel "buysell" undercover operation. This operation produced a major breakthrough in uncovering a theft ring operating between Penang, Malaysia, Singapore, Hong Kong, and Taiwan. They both became very familiar with the people and the terminology involved in the integrated circuit manufacturing industry.

For their efforts, the interns earn thirteen credits: two credits for preparation of daily field logs, three credits each for three papers submitted during the course of the internship, and two credits for the work in CTS.

The field logs are a primary resource used in preparing the practicum papers. The log entries are made daily, averaging two handwritten letter-size pages per day and a total of at least 120 pages by the end of the internship. The logs need not be typed. They are submitted with each paper. The logs are participant observer logs and include details about interesting and unusual events, avoiding extensive reporting on daily routines.

The first paper focuses on social dynamics and the organization with which the intern is associated. It provides a comprehensive description of the agency as it functions in the local community. This paper is ten to twelve typed pages long. It comments on community characteristics, agency history, agency clients, agency personnel, interorganizational relations, and contemporary agency problems. Also due with the first paper is a one-page research progress report. This report defines the research problem and the variables mentioned in the student's research statement. It also describes the research methods the intern plans to use.

The intern's second paper assesses the researcher role; it is also eight to ten pages long. PSU stresses that the intern is primarily a researcher observing the social setting of the internship. Among the points suggested for comment are:

- The research role. Which of the various field researcher roles have you adopted (complete observer, observer-as-participant, participant-as-observer, complete participant)? Was your choice of role dictated by your assignment in the agency, by the requirements of your research project, or by both? Have you encountered any problems in your research role? Does your role allow you to get at the data necessary to conduct your research?
- Establishing entree: Establishing a rapport and gaining acceptance is one of the most difficult problems a field researcher encounters. Were you successful in establishing a good working relationship in the agency? Did you find it necessary to use a variety of approaches, or did one strategy work well in all cases? Are you satisfied that you have established sufficient rapport to get the information you will need and to judge its validity?
- Mapping: When you first arrived at the agency did you find it necessary to orient yourself to time schedules, locations, people, and organizational roles? How did you accomplish this? Are you satisfied that you have command of temporal, spatial, social relations?
- Recording date: Have you had any problems writing up your observations and maintaining adequate field notes? How have you gone about the task of keeping accurate field notes?
- Sampling: Depending of the scope of your research question, you may have encountered difficulties with sampling the population under study. If you did find it necessary to sample cases or to limit the number of interviews you conducted, what sampling method did you use? Did you adopt a quota sample? A snowball sample? Or some other approach?

Field researchers often make the mistake of only talking to "friendly" informants and overlook those who are less likely to represent the majority opinion. What have you done to ensure that all views have been obtained within your organization? What factions exist and how do they agree or disagree about specific issues?

The final research paper reports on the implementation and results of the research project. This paper should be seven to ten pages and should discuss all aspects of the project. Penn State suggests the following format for this paper:

1. *Introduction*: Present the topic of your research. Include operational definitions of all variables.
2. *Data collection*: Provide detailed descriptions of the data collection techniques used. Discuss the implementations of these techniques.
3. *Findings*: Present and discuss your research findings and their social importance. Are these findings in general agreement with expert opinion?
4. *Bias*: All research (yes, even yours) contains bias. From the critical perspective of a neutral third party assess the reliability and validity of your findings. How did you resolve these reliability/validity issues? Be specific in addressing the full gamut of contaminating factors.
5. *Problems*: Discuss any problems you encountered in your research.

The interns receive grades from all the CTS managers responsible for their training. Each manager has a grading sheet from PSU. The average of the grades from the various managers forms the final grade sent in at the end of the training period. During the orientation, the interns are told their ability to interact with the clerical and investigative staff will be weighed heavily, as it is important for people working in Asia to learn to adapt to local customs and manners so they can be effective in the foreign environment.

The students have felt they have had unique opportunities for research in Asia. For example, one paper examined the efforts of the Taiwan government to come to grips with their piracy problem—the counterfeiting of goods. Another focused on unions in the Philippines. The international aspect of CTS work continues to provide a vast area for research. Over time, this will enable Penn State to develop an excellent repository of information for use by its administration of justice students, particularly those interested in a corporate security program. Thus, all students will benefit from the internship program.

31
INTERN PROGRAM YIELDS DIVIDENDS TO STUDENTS, FIRM

John T. McCarrier

The marketing department of a major manufacturer uses informal and formal campus contacts to keep a successful internship program running from year to year. The company utilizes a highly structured program with limited interface with college faculty, to provide motivation and meaningful experiences to interns. The bottom line: clear cut benefits to the company and resume building for the interns that can launch their careers after graduation.

Supplementing the staff of a market research department with part-time students is a very workable systems that pays large dividends to the hiring company and the students.

Five years ago, a hiring freeze collided with our [Toledo Scale, Columbus OH] need for additional staff. Our temporary solution of hiring several students from the marketing department at Ohio State University for part-time work has become a permanent practice.

I am convinced that this program is mutually rewarding; I recommend it wholeheartedly to other market research managers.

A market research department is an excellent place to use student help. Much of the work is organized into discrete projects that can be scheduled with varying levels of effort during the students' term to match available resources.

This contrasts with many departments that must produce consistent results daily.

Working on projects also gives students fast feedback and a feeling of being responsible for an identifiable result. The variety of work we do keeps students constantly challenged and learning.

Students bring a freshness to their jobs that more than compensates for their initial inexperience. Their enthusiasm makes them good telephone interviewers and carries them through routine chores.

Our market research department is located in Toledo Scale's world administration headquarters in Worthington, Ohio. Most major departments, including general manager, finance, field sales, product marketing, data processing, and international operations, are located in the building.

Toledo Scale has manufacturing facilities in the United States and six foreign countries, and distributes products in more than 50 countries through direct sales and distributors.

The market research department interacts with almost all other departments of the company, including field sales, warranty, engineering, order entry, and product marketing. This gives students an overview of the entire company and a chance to see how these functions interact.

Our department serves three major product areas: retail products used primarily in supermarkets, standard industrial products, and scale systems used in manufacturing facilities.

Each intern is given responsibility for one area in addition to doing outline duties and working on projects that involve more than one area. This system gives interns a feeling of belonging to a team, as well as making them more knowledgeable and effective in their assigned product areas.

The first step in starting this type of program, after checking with your employee relations department, is to contact the placement or student employment office at a local college or university.

It is helpful to limit yourself to one source school rather than trying to keep track of exams and holiday schedules at several. Many colleges have internship programs that allow part-time or short-time work in business.

Ohio State University, Columbus, has an active program for placing interns. Its professional practices programs placed more than 620 students last school year.

The rules differ among schools as to what types of work experiences qualify as internships, but this is secondary. Having a work experience is valuable to students whether or not it appears on their transcripts.

We began by drawing from one business fraternity that had contacted us about doing research projects. Our first interns recruited their replacements from the same fraternity during the last quarter of their senior year.

Interns now recruit their replacements from many sources, not just from one professional fraternity. The most common link between new and old students has become taking classes together and often being members on a team doing a class project.

Having interns find their own replacements works well for several reasons; they know they are leaving a legacy behind and will be remembered partly for it; current interns know the demands of the job and can identify other students who can handle them; incoming interns have an added motivation to do well and not make their predecessors' judgment look poor.

On occasion we have had to call the professional practices program at Ohio State to locate candidates if they were not available through our student sources.

Another alternative I have in finding replacements for graduating interns comes from teaching a market research course at Ohio State. This presents an opportunity to recruit from among the best students in the class. They already know me and my approach to market research, and I know their written and verbal presentation skills.

Most new interns join the department during the spring quarter of their junior year, and are trained by the graduating senior who recruited them.

They work full time during the following summer and part time during senior year. This gives them an entire summer to learn the job, which makes their part-time hours during the school year very efficient.

If all interns were on this schedule we would have a complete turnover every June, but this never happens. Inevitably, one of them graduates at the end of a different quarter, so there always is one experienced intern in the department.

When I interview prospective interns, the first thing I look for is chemistry. Does the student have the type of personality I can work with? Because we will have to work closely, especially during training, it is essential that we get along.

The next factor is the ability to work with the clerical people in other departments. This skill is more than just self-confidence.

Anyone with sufficient self-confidence can learn to work with managers, but the ability to work with the people in the trenches is a rarer commodity. Asking for help from clerical employees is a difficult thing for many college students.

Many of our best interns have left other part-time jobs to work for us. Previous experience in an office has not been a good indicator of success, but other part-time work during the school year has been.

Students who plan to go into industrial sales or marketing tend to be excellent interns because they can see how it will help their careers. Those hoping to go into advertising and retailing have worked out less well, because they have difficulty seeing the practical value of what they are learning on the job.

A one year internship seems best because it gives students enough time to become proficient on the job and provide a return on the time invested in their training.

The students are looking ahead to graduation during senior year and can endure the less exciting parts of their work knowing that it will last only one year.

Additionally, finding the needed maturity and marketing background in younger students is difficult. The few times I have hired students more than a year away from graduation generally have not worked well. I tell incoming students to plan going through three phases on the job: confusion, confidence, and boredom. Initially, it can be overwhelming to be put in a corporate headquarters with product managers asking for progress reports on phone surveys, national sales managers questioning the latest region sales potentials, and general manager on the phone asking for the latest financial data on a group of competitors.

The first month on the job is the critical time for new interns. They work closely with an experienced intern and do small projects so they can have some quick success and feel as if they fit in.

The confidence phase develops slowly and can be kept from turning into boredom during the rest of the year by a continuing variety of projects.

Interns come into the program knowing that they will not be considered for full-time employment when they graduate. Although this can lead to the loss of talented people, it forces them to conduct a vigorous job search and not hang on to a slender hope that they will have a job waiting for them.

They are encouraged to apply for jobs elsewhere in the company, not in market research.

Interns are reviewed quarterly and receive raises every three months. This gives them continuing feedback, and the frequent raises are an excellent morale boost. Because interns are not in the program for more than a year, the added cost is automatically limited.

We use a two-part evaluation form. The first half is a set of rating scales on specific characteristics, such as dependability and quality of work. The second is a list of four goals the intern sets, such as learning to use a specific PC software package, managing all aspects of a mail survey, or working with the data processing department to develop a new monthly report.

At the end of the quarter the list is reviewed, and a new one is drawn up for the next quarter. This allows interns to work towards goals that are mutually valuable.

The major problems for the department in having an intern program are the need to train new people every year and the difficulty in doing rush projects just before final exam week, when studying takes priority or during spring break, when interns want to go home or to Fort Lauderdale.

The pace of much of the work in the department is geared to the university's schedule of midterm and final exams, semester breaks, and holidays. Tabulation of a mail survey or a 50-call phone survey may be delayed by these events.

It is simply one aspect of hiring students that must be built into the department's schedule.

The greatest payoff for an intern is learning how a business works by watching and being part of it. Concepts presented in class become much more meaningful after seeing them in action.

Interns also learn to use personal computers to solve real problems and how to write in a businesslike style.

During senior year, job-hunting interns tend to get a lot of second interviews and job offers because they present themselves very well.